LABOR'S LOVE LOST

The Rise and Fall of the
Working-Class Family in
America

Andrew J. Cherlin

Russell Sage Foundation
New York

Library of Congress Cataloging-in-Publication Data

Cherlin, Andrew J., 1948–
    Labor's love lost : the rise and fall of the working-class family in America / Andrew J. Cherlin.
        pages cm
    Includes bibliographical references and index.
    ISBN 978-0-87154-030-0 (pbk. : alk. paper) — ISBN 978-1-61044-844-4 (ebook)
    1. Working class families—United States. I. Title.
HQ536.C439 2014
306.85'08623—dc23   2014024099

Text design by Suzanne Nichols

RUSSELL SAGE FOUNDATION
112 East 64th Street, New York, New York 10065
10 9 8 7 6 5 4 3 2 1

For Susan and Jessica

Contents

List of Figures

About the Author

Andrew J. Cherlin is the Benjamin H. Griswold III Professor of Public Policy in the Department of Sociology at the Johns Hopkins University.

Acknowledgments

THIS BOOK WAS written while I was a visiting scholar at the Russell Sage Foundation in New York City during the academic year 2013–2014. Without the support of this generous fellowship, I would not have been able to write it. I thank the foundation and its helpful staff for supporting my work. Thanks also to visiting scholar Douglas McAdam for his comments. Two reviewers, Paula England and Nancy Folbre, provided excellent detailed critiques of the manuscript that guided my revisions. My wife, Cynthia Osborne, put up with a year of travel back and forth from New York to Baltimore; I thank her for her forbearance.

Chapter 1 | Introduction

AMERICAN SOCIETY HAS now experienced the rise and fall of a distinctive kind of home life: the working-class family. It originated in the early 1800s when the industrialization of the American economy began, and it accelerated later in the century as the growing number of manufacturing jobs attracted millions of migrants from Europe and rural America. It centered on marriage and was, as historians and social scientists like to say, a deeply gendered form of family life. Husbands were expected to take factory jobs and to work full-time—which in the nineteenth century usually meant ten or twelve hours a day, six days a week—throughout adulthood. Wives were expected to focus on the home, managing a meager budget and meeting the day-to-day needs of husbands and children at a time when family sizes were larger and—with no gas, no electricity, no home appliances, no telephone, and often no running water or indoor plumbing—housework was far more arduous than today. Working-class wives also made important contributions to the family income in the nineteenth and early twentieth centuries by earning money at home. They took in boarders—unrelated individuals who paid to live in their home or just to eat meals with them—or did piecework such as assembling hats or shoes. Occasionally, they even worked for wages outside the home. Sons were expected to take jobs at an early age—twelve or fourteen before compulsory school attendance laws raised the age to sixteen—and to turn over their wages to their parents. Daughters were expected to either work for wages or help their mothers at home.[1]

The fortunes of the working-class family crested during the thirty-year period that followed World War II, when incomes rose sharply and prosperity spread more broadly than ever before. The average manufacturing wage more than doubled in purchasing power from 1950 to 1970, allow-

1

ing, for the first time, large numbers of working-class families to attain the middle-class ideal of the male-breadwinner family: husbands doing most of the earning, and wives focusing on homemaking, child-rearing, and emotional support, with perhaps some part-time work mixed in. That period—and particularly the decade of the 1950s, which was at its heart—has held an outsized place in our collective memories of family life. But it was not in any sense a typical period for the American family; rather, it proved to be the historical exception. The post–World War II era, we now can see, constituted the peak years of American capitalism. It was a unique period in which income inequality was at a historic low and industrial workers' wages were high. In the immediate postwar years, the United States, which had emerged from the war victorious and unscathed, was the unchallenged economic power in the world. Rising productivity and dominance in world trade allowed employers to pay male breadwinners historically generous wages while still earning substantial profits. A surge in births—the baby boom—both reflected the optimism of young families and created a heightened demand for goods and services. Generally, a young man could walk out of high school and find a job at a decent wage with the expectation of job security. It is the only period in American history in which the nation's economy was able to support large numbers of working-class families almost solely on the wages of the husbands and the household work of their wives. It is the only time when a young working-class couple could expect to move up to the middle class almost as a matter of course.[2]

To be sure, the male-breadwinner family was a lesser part of the lives of African American families than it was among whites. The cultural ideal of the homemaker who devoted herself exclusively to household work and child care never really applied to African American women. Rather, they had always been expected to work outside the home: first in the fields as slaves, then as sharecroppers indebted to their landlords, then as domestic servants and washerwomen to white households. Moreover, marriage rates had long been lower for African Americans than for whites, and African American men had not been allowed to share fully in the wage gains that accrued to white men; manufacturing and crafts unions for the most part excluded them. Factory owners hired African American men for the least desirable jobs, if at all. This situation began to change after World War II, when the ranks of African American manufacturing workers rose markedly and African American women started to move out of domestic service and into clerical, sales, and service jobs. In 1960 about 45 percent of African American women with children were both married and not working outside the home. That was less than the 79 percent figure for comparable white women, but still a substantial change. And for both African

American and white women, the 1960 percentages for those who were married and not employed were much higher than they would be a generation later.[3]

At midcentury, social observers thought the good times would last indefinitely—that we had reached the end of history and with it, the highest form of family life. Influential sociologists such as Talcott Parsons argued that the male-breadwinner family was well suited to an industrial society: since only the husband had a job, and since occupational success was his goal, the family could easily move from place to place as the husband followed the needs of the labor market. But after the Arab members of the Organization of the Petroleum Exporting Countries initiated an oil embargo in 1973, the economy began a prolonged slump and the postwar boom came to an end. In the 1980s and afterward, many of the manufacturing jobs that had sustained the working-class family moved to overseas factories or were computerized, and as the economy was transformed working-class young adults struggled to sustain the male-breadwinner marriage. Increasing numbers of working-class wives entered the labor force, usually part-time while their children were young and full-time when they were older; unlike some of their middle-class counterparts, they worked more for the money than for personal satisfaction.[4]

Yet even had the economy remained strong, it is likely that the working-class version of the male-breadwinner family would have eventually declined. It faced internal contradictions that the prosperity and optimism of the postwar years hid. For one thing, there was much less for the full-time homemaker to do. Even Parsons recognized that the role of the housewife "has declined in importance to the point where it scarcely approaches a full-time occupation for a vigorous person." Fertility had fallen from the six or seven children that women bore in the early 1800s to the four-child family in the late 1800s, to the three-child family at the peak of the 1950s baby boom. Births fell further after the 1950s as parents realized that the best family strategy was to have fewer children and to invest more time and resources in each of them. Modern utilities and conveniences such as electrically powered washers, dryers, stoves, refrigerators, and vacuum cleaners all became available on a mass scale for the first time and made keeping house more efficient. Granted, a consumer culture invented more work for the housewife—ever-cleaner homes and ever more elaborately prepared meals—but the long-term trend was to diminish the housewife's role.[5]

In addition, the demand for workers in the clerical and service sectors of the economy had begun to increase. Many of these occupations had become feminized during the late nineteenth and early twentieth centuries. From 1850 to 1880, for instance, only 10 percent of people employed as stenographers, typists, secretaries, cashiers, bank tellers, or library attendants were women; by 1930, however, 87 percent were women. More women were obtaining high school and college degrees, which qualified them for the growing number of clerical jobs. The massive but temporary employment of married women during World War II had demonstrated to many women that paid work could be both economically valuable and personally satisfying. Overall, as the tasks of the housewife became less demanding, as the logic of childbearing shifted from quantity to quality, as labor market opportunities grew, and as women's educational levels increased, the restriction of married women to the home led to a particular unease that Betty Friedan famously called "the problem that has no name." In the 1970s, a feminist movement, building on the work of Friedan and others, would develop a sharp critique of the male-breadwinner family.[6]

In a sense, to write about modern life for the American working-class family during the postwar peak is to tell a Dickensian tale of the best of times and the worst of times. The postwar peak was a time of job stability, economic security, and, at a personal level, devotion to home and family. More than nine out of ten young adults in the 1950s married; they did so at younger ages than at any other time in the twentieth century; and they had children quickly after marrying. The divorce rate was unusually stable throughout the 1950s and early 1960s. The industrial laborer took pride in getting up every morning and doing hard, manual work in support of his wife and children. All this was positive—or at least remembered as positive now that the era has passed. But it was also a time of male domination, alienation from work, and restricted horizons for women. Domestic violence was tolerated far more than today; husbands were unlikely to be arrested or prosecuted for beating their wives unless they caused serious injury. In large factories the drudgery of the assembly line was so severe that well-paid automobile workers were sometimes described as prisoners of prosperity. At home, working-class wives struggled with the expectation that they shouldn't work outside the home as well as the reality of tight budgets and unpaid bills. The upside of the working-class family at its height was substantial enough that we should appreciate its accomplishments. Its downside was severe enough that we should not mourn its recent demise. In either case, we are unlikely to see it in such numbers again.[7]

Today there is no doubt that the marriage-based working-class family, whether with one earner or two, is in decline. High school–educated young adults still believe that a young man must have steady earnings in order to be worthy of marriage. (They also think that it helps if a woman does too, but her employment is optional.) Because fewer and fewer men meet this criterion, high school–educated young adults are increasingly postponing marriage altogether. But in a cultural shift from the values prevalent a half-century ago, when living together outside of marriage was shameful, they are instead forming short-term cohabiting relationships. In a further cultural shift, they are having children within these brittle unions—a style of life that would have shocked their grandparents. By the time they are in their late twenties, three-fourths of young mothers who have no bachelor's degree have had at least one child outside of marriage. It is now unusual for non-college-graduates to have all of their children within marriage. A substantial number go on to have children with a second partner, or even a third, creating complex and unstable family lives that are not good for children. The problem of the fall of the working-class family from its midcentury peak, then, is not that the male-breadwinner family has declined—it would eventually have collapsed under its own weight. The problem is that nothing stable has replaced it.[8]

CHARTING THE GROWTH AND DECLINE OF THE WORKING-CLASS FAMILY

To understand the working-class family today we first need to examine its origins and trace its path. The story begins with the start of the industrial revolution in Britain in the late 1700s and in the United States in the early 1800s. One might wonder why it began in Britain and why the United States followed so soon. One reason was the existence of a ready supply of labor for factory work. In what was known as the enclosure movement, large landowners had seized many of the open fields in the British countryside and much of the common grazing land, turning peasants into tenant farmers or hired workers who did not have a deep connection to the land. The hardships endured by these landless workers and smallholders led to a rural-to-urban migration stream that populated the new factories. In addition, Britain's dominance of the oceans provided factory owners with supply lines for raw materials, most notably cotton from the American South, and with markets for their finished products. When the United States later began to industrialize, it solved its labor problem not only by inducing rural people to move to the cities but also by welcoming millions of overseas immigrants. So central did industrial work become, and so stark was the contrast between workers and factory owners in the early stages of industrialization, that observers began to refer to industrial laborers as a class—the *working* class—even though what wives did, and for that matter what farmers and clerks and craftsmen had always done, certainly qualified as work. The historian Eric Hobsbawm dated the first use of the term "working class" in Britain to between 1815 and 1830. In the United States, the creation of a working class began in the early 1800s with the establishment of textile factories in the Northeast, but the greatest expansion occurred after the Civil War.[9]

We can examine the broad historical sweep of the working-class family through a remarkable collection of U.S. Census Bureau records that allows us to chart the demographics of family life since 1880, which is the first time that the Bureau asked directly about marriage. The original handwritten records of the household interviews from the decennial censuses are preserved on microfilm at the National Archives going back to 1850 (with the exception of the 1890 census records, which were destroyed by fire). Demographers at the Minnesota Population Center have drawn random samples of the old manuscript records for each census year until 1930. They created machine-readable files of the forms and merged them with the Census Bureau's own publicly available samples from 1940 to the present. The result is a standardized set of census data files that allows anyone to easily create graphs that display over a century of demographic history.

We can use this extraordinary tool to examine the history of the working-class family—provided, of course, that we define what we mean by this concept. Many definitions are possible; I focus mainly on married-couple families who were raising children and in which the husband was employed in skilled or semiskilled manual work. I restrict my definition to families with children because the well-being of children is the main public concern about family life. Single-parent families were formed, of course, after the death of one of the spouses or, less commonly until the current era, as a result of divorce. But I concentrate on the married-couple family because it was both the numerically dominant unit for raising children from the 1800s through the postwar peak and also the unit around which the ideologies of family life and masculinity developed. I focus on husbands as earners because during that long stretch of time few wives worked for wages outside the home, although their labor inside the home was essential. Since the end of the postwar peak, however, cohabiting-parent and single-parent families have become much more common and, consequently, a marriage-based definition of the working-class or middle-class family is too narrow. So when I consider the recent history of the working-class and middle-class families, I broaden the scope of my inquiry to married and unmarried workers of both genders.[10]

With this definition in hand, let's turn to the database of census records. I first identified all married men between the ages of twenty and forty-nine who were living with a wife and at least one child under eighteen in each census year from 1880 to 2010. I then calculated the percentage who were engaged in manual work in one of three different industries: (1) what the census files call "manufacturing," a broad category that includes the production of durable goods, such as furniture, steel, machinery, ships, railroads, and automobiles, and nondurable goods, such as meat products, baked products, clothes, shoes, and paper; (2) "transportation and utilities," which includes truck, bus, and taxi drivers, railroad porters, and power line workers; and (3) "construction workers," including carpenters, masons, and plumbers. I took the total percentage employed in these three forms of manual work as the best indicator of trends in the size of the working-class family. In other words, I asked the data this question: of all the married men in this age group who, along with their wives, were raising children, what percentage could be classified as "working-class" on the basis of their occupation?[11]

The results are presented in the two charts that constitute figure 1.1. Think of each chart as a three-layer cake, one cake for whites and the other for African Americans. The bottom, dark layer represents transit and utilities employment; the middle, diagonally striped layer is construction employment; and the top, gray layer is manufacturing employment. The height of each layer is proportional to the percentage of all married men with children who are in that industry. These heights can change from decade to decade as new census information replaces the old. The total height of all three layers is the percentage of husbands employed in any of the three industries—my indicator of the prevalence of working-class families.

The story is easy to see. In 1880 the percentage of families that could be classified as working-class on the basis of the husband's job—the total height of the three layers—was about 22 percent for whites and 9 percent for blacks. The most intensive period of industrialization had just begun, and most Americans still lived in rural areas. In fact, 55 percent of white husbands and 83 percent of black husbands were working in agriculture in 1880—a huge layer not shown in the charts. But between 1879 and 1898, manufacturing output doubled, and it had doubled again by 1906, and again by 1917. You can see the percentage employed in manufacturing start to rise after 1880 and then rise further in the 1900s, reaching a peak in 1960 for whites and in 1970 for blacks. In addition, the construction layer gets a bit thicker for whites, and the transportation layer gets a bit thicker for blacks.[12]

At their respective peaks, 43 percent of white husbands and 51 percent of black husbands could be classified as working-class on the basis of being employed in one of these three industries. The rise was mainly due to the expansion of manufacturing, which was the predominant form of skilled or semiskilled manual labor in the early-to-midtwentieth century. At the giant Sparrows Point steelworks established in 1889 just outside of Baltimore, where I live, employment peaked at 30,920 in 1959 and re-

Figure 1.1   Married Men Ages Twenty to Forty-Nine, with Children
Under Age Eighteen, Who Were Employed in
Manufacturing, Construction, or Transportation, by Race,
1880–2010

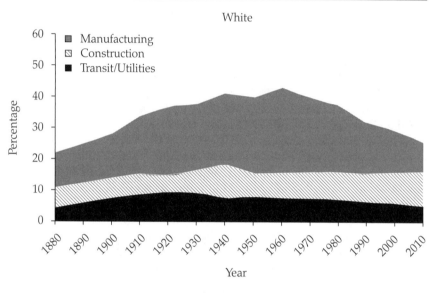

White

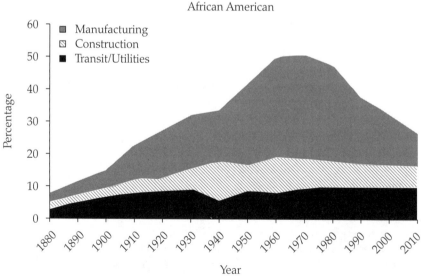

African American

Source: Ruggles et al. (2010).

mained near that level throughout the 1960s. For blacks, the height of the gray layer is much lower than for whites until after World War II, which reflects the restricted opportunities blacks had for manufacturing employment until then. But note that by the 1960s the percentage of black husbands in manufacturing was *higher* than it was for whites (that is, the gray layer is thicker for them than it is for whites). During the peak years, black families were more dependent on manufacturing jobs than were whites.[13]

After the postwar peak, the heights of both cakes plunge, almost entirely because of a decrease in manufacturing employment. Indeed, had construction employment not increased for whites, and had transit and utility employment not increased for blacks, the fall would have been even greater. A profound restructuring of the American economy had begun. Advances in transportation and communication allowed companies to move production to countries where wage levels were much lower. Anyone driving through New England towns can see the red brick buildings that once produced the nation's textiles and shoes standing empty— or perhaps renovated into upscale apartments and boutiques. In North Carolina, one can see the shells of former furniture factories that once produced sofas and dining room sets for American homes. In addition, advances in computer processing allowed factory owners to automate production and to substitute machines for workers. Think of the rows of robots along today's automobile assembly lines. In the steel industry, countries such as Japan and Korea built more efficient plants based on new technologies that allowed them to produce steel at a lower cost. Large ocean-going ships reduced the cost of sending steel to the United States. As a result, it was often cheaper to import steel produced overseas than to buy American-made steel. Employment at Sparrows Point declined precipitously. The plant struggled for decades, and its workforce suffered several rounds of downsizing before Sparrows Point finally closed in 2012, its facilities sold for a pittance for spare parts. For the remaining manufacturing workers, employment was far more precarious than during the postwar peak. Foreign competition and automation, along with the efforts of corporate management and their political allies, had reduced the bargaining power of labor unions, and the percentage of wage and salary workers belonging to unions had declined. It stood at 11.3 percent in 2014. Job losses and job changes became more common because of layoffs and plant closings. The grand bargain of the midtwentieth century between workers and corporations—high wages and stable, long-term employment in return for hard, tedious, and sometimes dangerous work—fell apart.[14]

These developments had their greatest effect on moderately educated young men—those with a high school degree but not a bachelor's degree—who came of age after the mid-1970s. They were the ones who would have taken manufacturing jobs in large numbers had they been born a generation earlier. Occupying the medium-skilled center of the labor market, they watched their opportunities contract as the kinds of manual jobs that high school–educated young men used to take moved overseas or were automated. At the bottom of the labor market, in contrast, the demand for low-skill jobs that could not be exported (such as restaurant and hotel workers) continued to expand, but these jobs paid poorly and had little security. At the top, opportunities for professional, technical, and managerial jobs increased, but they required a bachelor's degree or more. Labor economist David Autor and others have called this phenomenon the "polarization," or "hollowing-out," of the American labor market. Others have written about the "hourglass" economy.[15]

These metaphors can be taken too far: there are some occupations in the middle of the labor market, such as medical technicians, that are growing. But overall it seems undeniable that the kinds of well-paying, secure manual jobs that were available in the 1960s are much less plentiful today. Consequently, high school–educated young men have less opportunity than did the previous generation. The wages of men without bachelor's degrees have fallen since the early 1970s. As the economic foundation of factory work waned, so did the percentage of married-couple families with children that could be classified as working-class on the basis of the husband's employment. By 2010, as figure 1.1 shows, the percentage of white husbands with a working-class occupation had fallen to levels not seen for over a century. The fall was even steeper for African Americans. The figure makes clear that black workers, whose opportunities were restricted for so long, had finally caught up with white workers in the percentage employed in manufacturing by the 1960s, only to see the bottom fall out of the manufacturing sector. In 1974 there were 38,096 black steelworkers in the nation, but by 1988 the number had dropped to 9,958. Overall, then, the figures show that among married couples with children, manufacturing employment for the husband became common in the late nineteenth and early twentieth centuries, peaked at midcentury, and then declined to the present day.[16]

INDUSTRIALIZATION AND THE FAMILY

There is a long debate among intellectuals about whether a true working class ever existed in the United States. Yes, there were millions of workers who earned wages in factories and in other manual occupations. But was there a coherent group that had a common set of experiences and political interests? Large-scale, organized action by workers was less common in the United States than in Europe, except at a few points in time such as the Great Depression. No political organizations comparable to the powerful European labor parties ever emerged. I cannot resolve that great debate; but I argue, along with scholars who came before me, that industrial wage labor produced a distinctive pattern of family life. I am interested in this type of family not just as an economic arrangement but also as a social phenomenon. I'm a sociologist, and this book is primarily a work of sociology. I draw heavily on scholarship in history and economics, but my objective is to tell the story of a singular form of the social institution we call the American family. It is a story of parents and children working together to make ends meet and, for a brief period in the twentieth century, of upward mobility. It is also a story of common conceptions of masculinity and femininity, the social forces that sustained them, and what happened when these social supports weakened. For men, masculinity was connected to physically demanding manual work done in the service of supporting one's family. For women, femininity involved a curious mixture of down-to-earth household labor and rarefied emotional support. At its high point and in the early stage of its decline, before anyone realized how far it would fall, the working-class family became a central part of American culture through vivid metaphors (blue collar), political debates (busing children to integrate school districts), and images in the media (*All in the Family*). It contained internal contradictions that were temporarily surmounted by the prosperity of the postwar peak but soon reemerged and led to its decline.[17]

In fact, the growth of industrial wage labor profoundly affected family life in several ways. First, it moved the primary place of men's work out of the home and separated the work worlds of husbands and wives. Because of the prevailing notions of the proper roles for men and women, married men took the growing number of factory jobs, and married women, though with some exceptions, did not. Instead, married women contributed to the family economy through work done largely in the home. An unmarried young woman might work in a textile mill from an early age, but once she married she was likely to withdraw into the home. Thus, the industrial workplace became largely a world of men. At Sparrows Point, steelworkers did not allow women to enter certain parts of the plant; having a woman appear was considered bad luck—it might portend injuries to the men managing cauldrons of molten metal. The separate work worlds of men and women contrasted with the lives of farming families, whose husbands and wives had worked together. They might have done different tasks—men plowing the fields, women tending the vegetable garden—but their work was interdependent. Among urban craftsmen, the shop was sometimes located next to the home. Factories, however, were centrally located in cities and set, in the early years, next to rivers that provided water power. The husband's journey to work and his long hours away from home became part of family life.[18]

Second, industrial wage labor transformed the relationship between parents and children. In the early decades of industrialization, a large percentage of factory workers were immigrants—in 1900, for instance, 36 percent of all married men with children who were employed in manual occupations were immigrants—and parental authority was still unchallenged. Many immigrants held ideas about child-rearing that had been formed in the old country, such as the need for children to strictly obey parents and contribute to the family economy from a young age. Working-class children attended school only until their early teenage years, after which they took jobs. Parents and children sometimes worked in the same plant; textile mills were known to advertise for families rather than individual workers. Children were expected to turn over their pay packets to their parents unopened; their earnings could mean the difference between subsistence and abject poverty.[19]

But industrialization eventually led to an erosion of parental authority. Compulsory schooling laws restricted the ability of parents to send their children to work, and rising incomes reduced their motivation to do so. Moreover, attendance at public school, even for a limited duration, taught children to respect sources of authority beyond parents, including the school itself and the state. In 1892 a Baptist minister, Francis Bellamy, wrote "The Pledge of Allegiance," and soon millions of schoolchildren were reciting their loyalty to the flag and to the republic for which it stood—without regard to whether their parents approved of all for which it stood. During the Progressive Era (1890–1920), activists from the child-saving movement successfully pushed for legislation that raised the minimum age at which children could leave school and limited the number of hours that children could work. The child-savers' view of childhood as a time of education and protection from the adult world clashed with the view of the immigrant working class, and the child-savers prevailed. Nevertheless, change was gradual: in the 1920s, many parents still needed their teenage children to earn money and only 43 percent of nineteen-year-olds had completed high school. Yet by the 1960s, school attendance until age sixteen was mandatory, most parents had sufficient income to keep their children in school until high school graduation, and three-fourths of nineteen-year-olds had graduated. What is more, when teenagers worked, they no longer turned over their entire paycheck to their parents; rather, they began to consume on their own.[20]

Third, the growth of industrial wage labor altered the sense of time that the factory worker and his family had. In the preindustrial era, people's concept of work time centered on how long it took to do a particular task—plowing a field or feeding the animals. Task-oriented time did not depend on the clock; in fact, in the American colonies in 1700 only one in fifty white adults kept a watch, and only one in thirty-two had a clock. Rather, the markers of time were sunrise and sunset, calendars, and almanacs. With industrial labor, however, work began and ended on a schedule announced by the boss. On the assembly line, "scientific management" broke down tasks into short, repetitive movements measured to the second. The sense of time at the workplace shifted, in the terms of the historian E. P. Thompson, from "task orientation" to "timed labor." Time at home, however, was not as rigidly scheduled; wives who were caring for young children, for instance, were still oriented to tasks such as feeding and bathing. But timed labor intruded into the home as the family's daily routines accommodated the schedule of the factory. At Sparrows Point, as in many large enterprises, the plant operated twenty-four hours per day using a day shift, a night shift, and a 3:00 PM to 11:00 PM swing shift. Many workers were required to rotate among these shifts, often with little advance notice, and these changing routines disrupted family life.[21]

Finally, industrialization shaped how workers saw themselves—what we would call today their self-identities. Rather than defining their self-worth in terms of income, a domain in which they could never match professionals and managers, white industrial workers increasingly defined it in terms of morality, a domain in which they could surpass those above them. They were proud of their ability to perform demanding, repetitive industrial labor day after day and to support their families through their work—an identity that the sociologist Michèle Lamont calls the "disciplined self." This sense of self was focused on the workplace. To be sure, the disciplined worker felt responsible for his family's well-being, but once he was home his work was done. Until recently at least, he did not put one foot in front of the other and slog through the assembly line of dinner, dishes, baths, and bedtime stories. Instead, he relaxed. His worldview did not encourage him to spend lots of quality time with his children or to share intimacies with his wife. His hard work was done *for* the family but not *with* the family. Thus, the moral world of the working-class husband encouraged a very gender-segregated style of family life, with little overlap between what the husband and wife did.[22]

Yet by the 1960s, substantial numbers of working-class wives were combining domestic work with working for pay outside the home, often part-time, creating daily schedules that required organization and effort to manage. Wives had to cope with the constraints of their husbands' employment, which could include mandatory overtime, shift work, or worse yet, strikes and layoffs. Wives, however, did not aspire to the disciplined self. Their primary role was widely seen as supporting and comforting husbands and children. Paid work was seen as secondary and had to be coordinated with the time schedules of factory and school. Sometimes husbands objected to their wives taking jobs because it contradicted their sense of themselves as good providers. At first, the conflicts and double burdens that employed wives faced were theirs alone to bear and to resolve. But as their attachment to the workforce grew, and as feminist ideas began to diffuse, wives began to demand that their husbands alter their routines to help with housework and child care. The paid work that wives performed outside the home gave them a more independent sense of self. A renegotiation of marital roles began, and it is still in progress.

In all these ways—the movement of work to the factory, the restriction of wives to work that could be done at home, the lessening control over children, the pervasive influence of timed labor, and the importance of a disciplined sense of self—industrialization created and sustained the working-class family. Nevertheless, these families were not all the same. There were overlapping variations by place of birth, religion, and race. The values of the large number of immigrant families were influenced by the moral order in their countries of origin. Race also played a major role: until late in the story of industrialization, African American men and women faced very limited opportunities. Sparrows Point was one of the few steel mills to hire substantial numbers of black men for low-level positions (as opposed to relying on recent immigrants), but they were restricted to the dirtiest, hottest, and most dangerous jobs and blocked from moving to better positions. Blacks were also paid less than whites and, until the 1960s, lived in segregated communities near the plant. They did, however, out-earn most of their black friends and neighbors with the help of their wives, who worked outside the home more often than did the wives of white workers.[23]

Consequently, when I write about "the working-class family" in this book, I do not mean to suggest that all such families are alike. I use the term as what sociologists, after Max Weber, call an "ideal type": a description comprising the most important and visible aspects of a phenomenon, even if not every case has all of these aspects. Think of it as a conceptual model that helps us to understand the similarities and differences among the families of industrial workers over time. I make no restriction with respect to whether wives are working outside the home. In the nineteenth and early twentieth centuries, few of them would have been, but most were making financial contributions from inside the home. As we approach the present day many more of them would have been working for wages, although in the clerical and service sectors rather than in manufacturing.

CULTURAL SHIFTS

After 1975, as job opportunities in manufacturing and related industries declined relative to opportunities at the top and bottom of the labor market, important cultural changes occurred as well. Support for the male-breadwinner family plummeted. In the 1977 General Social Survey (GSS), 63 percent of women agreed that "it is much better for everyone involved if the man is the achiever outside the home and the woman takes care of the home and family." By 2011, only 26 percent agreed. Men were a bit more conservative, but their support dropped from 69 percent to 38 percent. Attitudes toward cohabitation have become much more favorable. When a national sample of high school seniors was asked in 1976 and 1977 whether they agreed that "it is usually a good idea for a couple to live together before getting married in order to find out whether they really get along," 33 percent of girls and 47 percent of boys agreed. When the question was asked of high school seniors in 2011, 67 percent of girls and 72 percent of boys agreed. Attitudes have also become more favorable to having children outside of marriage; in the 1950s and 1960s, it was a shameful event, but a few decades later it has become largely acceptable.[24]

As both the economy and the culture changed, so did the ways in which young adults formed families. In the midtwentieth century, marriage was the first step into adulthood. Couples did not live together until after their weddings. If a pregnancy occurred, it usually led to a marriage before the child was born, and if it did not, the child was seen as "illegitimate." In 1960, 95 percent of all children were born to married women; by the early 2000s, in contrast, the figure had dropped to 59 percent. Currently, marriage is often the last step into adulthood—something that one does after moving in with a partner, getting a job, renting an apartment, and even having a child. The belief has spread among all social classes that people should only marry when they have a steady income and maybe some savings. But most people think that it's okay to live with a partner until the relationship gets to the point where a marriage is viable.[25]

Here, however, the paths divide: college-educated young adults commonly postpone marriage and live with a partner while they go to graduate school or invest in careers, but they wait until after they marry to have their children. Only 6 percent in the mid-2000s were unmarried when they had a child. In contrast, high school–educated young adults are increasingly having children outside of marriage, the majority of them in cohabiting unions. In reality, amid all the concern about "out-of-wedlock births," it is not widely known that since the early 1980s the percentage of children born to women living alone has hardly increased. Rather, most of the growth in the share of children born to unmarried women has been among women who are in cohabiting relationships. And the biggest rise in births to cohabiting women has been among young adults who have a high school degree but not a bachelor's degree. Moreover, a substantial share of these cohabiting unions do not begin until after the woman gets pregnant. The grandchildren of the high school–educated couples who married in the 1950s because they got "caught" would today, upon learning of a pregnancy, either remain single or move in together.[26]

MARKETS AND CULTURE

The political scientist Charles Murray, in his widely read book *Coming Apart: The State of White America, 1960–2010*, surveys this landscape and argues that the decline of marriage and steady employment among the white working class has been solely due to cultural change. The globalization of the economy and the computerization of production, he declares, has had nothing to do with it. The problem, he concludes, is a decline in traditional values, most notably industriousness. Young men, he states, are not as industrious in seeking employment and sticking with it as were past generations. The percentage of men with no more than high school educations who are working or looking for work has declined, and applications for government disability benefits have greatly increased. Yet there are jobs out there, notes Murray, even if they do not pay as much as they used to, and young men should take them. He links the cultural decline to the expansion of the welfare state in the 1960s—his book begins with a description of November 21, 1963, the last sunny day in America, after which Kennedy was assassinated, Johnson became president, and the War on Poverty began. The enlargement of the welfare state that began under Johnson, Murray claims, encouraged people to depend on government benefits instead of working hard and made it easier for poor women to receive benefits from programs such as Aid to Families with Dependent Children (AFDC)—which Americans call "welfare"—and to therefore become more economically independent from men.[27]

Yet by 1996, the average thirty-year-old man with a high school degree earned 20 percent less than a comparable man in 1979, and the Great Depression aside, he belonged to the first generation of American young men to earn less than their fathers did. More important, the long historical view demonstrates that class differences in marriage have been tied to the extent of economic inequality in American society—closely for whites and to a lesser degree for African Americans—for at least 130 years. That is apparent in figure 1.2, which shows trends in the percentage of men in each of three occupational groups who were married in every census from 1880 to 2010 for whites and from 1900 to 2010 for African Americans. Unlike the

Figure 1.2 Married, U.S.-Born Men Ages Twenty to Forty-Nine, by (Nonfarm) Occupational Group, 1880–2010 (Whites) and 1900–2010 (African Americans)

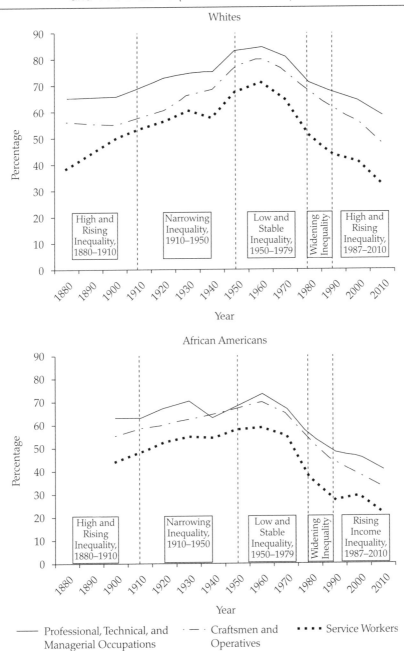

Source: Ruggles et al. (2010).

charts in figure 1.1, which were restricted to married men, these charts include men of all marital statuses and show the percentage of those who were currently married. I have excluded men with farm occupations and immigrants, and I have restricted the chart to men who were between the ages of twenty and forty-nine.[28]

Let's begin with the chart for whites, the group on which Murray focuses. Notice that, at all times, the highest percentage of married men are those with professional, technical, and managerial occupations (physicians, executives); men in service occupations (janitors, waiters) have the lowest percentage who are married, and craftsmen and operatives (electricians, machinists) occupy an intermediate position. Now let's look at the spread between the highest and lowest groups in each census year. In 1880 the difference between the highest and lowest line is twenty-seven percentage points. The spread then narrows and is at a minimum in the post–World War II period, following which it widens again. It does not again exceed twenty-seven percentage points until 2010.

Figure 1.2 therefore provides the important information that the current era is not the first time that white people in the United States have experienced a large marriage gap; rather, it is the *second* time. The first marriage gap occurred in the late nineteenth century, decades before the American welfare state was born during the Great Depression and a lifetime before Johnson expanded it in the 1960s. What these two eras have in common is that economic inequality was high and rising during both of them. To illustrate this point in figure 1.2, I have labeled five periods since 1880 in terms of trends in economic inequality. The periods are drawn from the work of the economists Claudia Goldin, Lawrence Katz, Robert Margo, and their associates, who have written widely about American economic history. It is common knowledge that economic inequality has increased in the most recent periods; the earnings gap began to widen after 1979 and then began to polarize—that is to say, the white-collar group atop the income distribution began to pull away from both the middle and the bottom—after about 1987. But the top was also pulling away from the middle and bottom during the first period, from 1880 to 1910.[29]

During this first period, the white-collar professional class solidified its gains in the labor market. For instance, the growth of the industrial economy increased the number of managers and executives; the extension of schooling increased the demand for teachers; and rising newspaper circulation (which quadrupled between 1880 and 1900) increased the demand for editors and reporters. The wages of the growing white-collar workforce rose relative to those below them. At the same time, the fortunes of independent craftsmen declined in manufacturing as large-scale factory production replaced their small operations. Master craftsmen of all kinds

—cabinet makers, shoe makers, candle and soap makers—either went out of business or hired more workers, produced larger quantities of goods, and turned into managers. Younger men who would have found positions as skilled apprentices and journeymen instead became factory workers. As a result, the share of workers in the middle of the manufacturing sector declined relative to the shares at the top and bottom. At the very top were "the captains of industry"—some of whom were referred to less flatteringly as "the robber barons." This was, after all, the era that Mark Twain called the Gilded Age. A century later, in a period that some are calling the New Gilded Age, we see a similar phenomenon. Economic inequality has widened as workers with bachelor's degrees have consolidated their positions in the knowledge industries and increased their earnings faster than those with less education. The middle of the labor market has hollowed out owing to technological change and the offshoring of production; low-skilled service work has expanded; and an elite—"the 1 percent"—has captured an increasing share of all income gains.[30]

What figure 1.2 demonstrates, then, is a strong association between the extent of economic inequality and the extent of marriage inequality among whites for more than a century. The marriage gap has varied directly with the earnings gap. In periods when earnings were more unequal, such as the first and last periods shown in the figure, the lines representing the percentage married for each occupational group are farther apart. When inequality was narrowing, as in the 1910–1950 period, so does the spread between the lines. When inequality was low and stable in the 1950–1979 period, the lines are bunched closest together and the proportions married reach their historical highpoints. During both Gilded Ages, young men with moderate skills may have had a harder time finding the kinds of occupations that could support marriage. In contrast, it was much easier in the low-inequality 1950s and 1960s for a young man in the middle of the labor market to land a job that could provide the foundation for family life.

To be sure, the parallel movements of economic inequality and marriage inequality do not prove that the former causes the latter. But it is hard to look at this chart and conclude that the state of the labor market has had nothing to do with the marriage gap among the middle class, the working class, and the poor in American history. To rescue Murray's contention that a lack of industriousness explains class gaps in marriage, one would have to come up with a plausible cultural story that fits not only the current gap but also the wide gap that existed in 1880. Yet no one would argue that men in the 1880–1910 period lacked industriousness and were unwilling to take low-wage work. To the contrary, they worked long hours for wages so low that families were often able to subsist only because of the economic contributions of wives and children. Moreover, the government social welfare programs that, according to Murray, create dependency among the poor, such as cash assistance for single parents, unemployment benefits, and food stamps, did not begin until the 1930s and therefore cannot be blamed for the differences that existed before then. What other, solely cultural explanations could be developed is difficult to fathom.

Murray's response to this line of criticism is, in part, to argue that the causes "don't make much difference anymore" in thinking about class differences in family life because they have been overtaken by changing cultural norms. It is true that by 2010 the spread of the lines, at twenty-nine percentage points, had surpassed the 1880 mark, suggesting that economic inequality is not the only influence on marriage inequality. In addition, by 2010 almost all of the lines had shifted downward compared to their 1880 values, suggesting a general decline in marriage. I would grant that, in a different sense, Murray is correct that cultural change has played an important role in working-class family life: even if it has not been the major determinant of class differences in marriage, cultural change has influenced what young men and women *who are not married* are doing. Single men and women in the late nineteenth and early twentieth centuries rarely lived with each other without marrying, and relatively few had children. They were much more likely to be living with their parents or to be boarding with other families. The norms against cohabitation and childbearing outside of marriage were too strong. But over the past several decades, these sentiments have weakened. Had norms not changed, the growth of childbearing outside of marriage that we have recently seen among today's unmarried low-educated and moderately educated young adults would not have occurred, even given the rise in income inequality. Moreover, these cultural changes, even if influenced by employment opportunities, could be deep enough to take on a life of their own, and they might not immediately respond to improvements in the economy. Certainly, cultural change is part of the story—but it's not the whole story by any means.[31]

We have seen, rather, an example of what social scientists call an interaction effect (or a synergistic effect): two factors uniting to produce an effect that is larger than either could have produced alone. The consequences of one potential cause—say, one's attitudes toward marriage and childbearing—depend on the level of another, such as the strength of one's labor market position. Childbearing outside of marriage has recently risen mainly among less-educated young adults who have experienced *both* a weakening job market *and* a growing acceptance of cohabitation and nonmarital childbearing. Among the college-educated, who have experienced the same cultural changes but have not seen a decline in career opportunities, no significant increase in childbearing outside of marriage has occurred. In interpreting this interaction effect, liberals may give more weight to the globalization and automation of production, which they see as the driving forces in the hollowing-out of the labor market. Conservatives, on the other hand, may give more weight to changing social norms, which they see as the major influence on nonmarital births. I cannot think of a feasible study that could definitively tell us how much importance to place on each of these two factors. But we can safely conclude that intellectual purists who insist that family changes are wholly a matter of cultural shifts, or conversely a matter of economics alone, are very likely wrong.

Figure 1.2 also displays the same information for African Americans, starting from 1900 rather than 1880 because so few African American men worked in higher occupations before then. The chart shows similarities with, and differences from, the trends among whites. As was the case for whites, the higher the occupation they filled, the greater was the percentage of African American men who were married throughout most of the period, though there were exceptions in some years; also as with whites, the percentages married were highest in the post–World War II period. But prior to 1950, the spread of the lines is smaller for African Americans—in other words, there was less difference before 1950 in the percentages of married African American men holding different occupations than there was among comparable whites. This smaller difference probably reflects the lack of opportunity for black men to attain truly middle-class occupational status. Black men classified as professionals and managers were more likely to have been funeral directors—one of the few professions open to blacks living in segregated communities—than corporate executives, and those classified as craftsmen and operatives were more likely to have been locomotive firemen who shoveled coal into steam engines than electricians or plumbers.

Moreover, as can be seen in the chart, African Americans also differ from whites in that the percentage married did not rise as high during the 1950s and 1960s and has fallen further in the most recent period, so that the proportions of married African Americans are now at historic twentieth- and twenty-first-century lows. The percentage married in the highest occupational group in 2010 was comparable to the percentage married in the lowest occupational group in 1900. Marriage rates have declined for whites too, but not to the same degree, and this difference has created the sharpest racial differences to be seen during the entire period. I have suggested elsewhere that African Americans have responded to the declining employment prospects of the most recent era by drawing more on extended family ties and relatively less on marriage than whites have done—a response that would be consistent with the greater strength of kinship ties among slaves (who were not allowed to legally marry) and in West African family structure.[32]

WHY IS THE MARRIAGE GAP A PROBLEM?

Some observers might say that there is nothing alarming about the working class's retreat from marriage. It's true that not everyone wishes to marry and that there is nothing wrong with family diversity. Moreover, we have seen that the United States experienced a large marriage gap in the late nineteenth century, only to see the gap narrow during the first half of the twentieth century. But the nineteenth-century gap did not lead to widespread cohabitation and childbearing outside of marriage, whereas the late-twentieth-century gap did. In some European countries, long-term cohabiting unions with children have come to function equivalently to marriages. (François Hollande, the president of France in the early 2010s, cohabited for nearly three decades with Ségolène Royal, a former presidential candidate, with whom he had four children before the couple separated in 2007.) But that is not the kind of cohabitation that is common in the United States, at least not yet. The United States has the shortest average duration of cohabiting unions of any Western country. Within five years after having a child, about half of urban cohabiting parents are no longer living together (whether or not they married in the interim). That is about twice the breakup rate experienced by children born to married parents. These breakups are often followed by another cohabiting union and perhaps another disruption. As a result, the children of cohabiting couples can see a bewildering number of parents, parents' partners, and stepparents enter and exit their homes in succession.[33]

The young adults without bachelor's degrees who are the heirs of the industrial working class today are not a cultural vanguard confidently leading the way toward a postmodern family lifestyle. Rather, they are a group making constrained choices. For the most part, these are people who would like to marry before having children but who think they are not economically ready. In contrast, college-educated Americans—the winners in our globalized and computerized economy—are still waiting until they marry to start having children. Consequently, one need not think that the working-class family was flawless in the past to be troubled by the existence today of a large group of moderately educated Americans who are increasingly disconnected from steady, decent-paying jobs and from marriage. Over the past few decades, as the social capital theorist Robert Putnam has noted, the social ties of the working class have declined as union membership has dropped and political parties have become less powerful. Now there is even less glue bonding them to the rest of society. As far back as the colonial era, marriage has been the traditional way in which individuals are connected with civil society. College-educated Americans remain tied into society in these and other ways, such as professional networks and memberships in clubs and organizations, but working-class Americans have fewer other sources of social ties.[34]

Both economic and cultural changes have been so great, and the diversity of pathways to family building have become so diverse, that it is doubtful that a coherent working-class family pattern exists anymore. In truth, it is doubtful that an industrial working class exists anymore, in the sense of a clear-cut group identifiable by the color of their shirts, the calluses on their hands, and the union cards in their wallets—or by their marriage to such workers. The best present-day analogues to the working class are men and women with a high school degree but no bachelor's degree because these are the people who, two generations ago, would have taken the industrial jobs that were plentiful. Their numbers are large: 55 percent of Americans between the ages of twenty-five and thirty-four have a high school degree but not a bachelor's degree. They constitute the vast middle of the American social hierarchy—trying to stay employed as the labor market changes, having an easier time when the economy is hot, as it was in the late 1990s, and a harder time when the economy is cold, as it was during the Great Recession of the late 2000s.[35]

What happens when the conditions that allowed most high school–educated Americans to connect to the rest of society through hard work and marriage no longer exist? The successful attainment of the disciplined self required not just an attitude but also a job—one that paid well enough and promised enough security that one could support a family through it. What happens when the disciplined self can no longer be attained? The successful assumption of the homemaker role required a husband with adequate, steady earnings. What happens when young women must enter the workforce while still retaining the primary responsibilities for the care of children? Will we see labor's love lost as the people we used to call the working class begin to devalue stable family ties? Will their multiple cohabiting unions and marriages affect their children's development? And what can be done to support a viable family system to supersede the old one?

These are the kinds of questions that American society is facing owing to the economic and cultural gap between a college-educated middle class that is managing to prosper in good times and tread water in bad times and a would-be working class that is declining in both good times and bad. These are also the questions that we examine in this book.

Chapter 2 | The Emergence of the Working-Class Family: 1800–1899

In NEARLY ALL societies in human history, there has been a division of labor between men and women, but both have done productive work. In the hunter-gatherer societies in which we lived throughout most of our evolutionary history, women gathered edible plants, which provided much of the food, while caring for young children. They nursed their children for a long time, thus reducing fertility (because nursing slows the return of ovulation), and carried them while foraging. Men's main job was to hunt and to defend the group against outsiders. Then we began to plant crops rather than move from place to place to gather food. In these agricultural societies, wives did numerous tasks such as keeping a vegetable garden, canning food, baking bread, making clothes, and tending fires—even helping out in the fields during harvest time—while men did most of the heavy labor such as plowing. Sons assisted their fathers and daughters assisted their mothers. The wives of urban craftsmen sometimes acted as assistants or coworkers.

When industrialization drew families to the cities, where factories provided the primary source of income, parents continued to carefully allocate the labor of husbands, wives, and children. That is to say, they still used family-wide strategies for maximizing their well-being. To be sure, families were not perfect little democracies; husbands had the authority, backed by law and custom, to make most final decisions. And their decisions were not necessarily in their wives' and children's best interests. Still, successful families allocated the wage work and home work of all household members jointly. Indeed, as noted in chapter 1, factory owners in industries such as textiles often recruited entire families. In the late 1800s, the Amoskeag Company, which had founded the city of Manchester, New Hampshire (naming it after the British city where the industrial

24

revolution began), and built one of the world's largest textile factories, began to recruit families, rather than just individuals, from nearby French-speaking Canada. Other mills did the same. The editor of a French-language New England newspaper testified before the Massachusetts Bureau of Labor Statistics in 1882: "I have a letter from an agent of the Boston and Maine Railroad who says he is ready to testify that since two years, no less than one-hundred superintendents or agents of mills have applied to him for French help, one mill asking for as many as fifty families at a time."

Among families in industrializing cities, it was a given that fathers would work full-time at the factories, and sons usually went to work sometime after age twelve. Unmarried older daughters usually worked as well. In some of the early mills, a majority of the workers were young un-married women. The Lowell, Massachusetts, textile factories in the early 1800s relied on "mill girls," young women from the surrounding New England farmland who lived in supervised boardinghouses and typically worked in the mills for several years before leaving. Mothers in white families who lived in cities with textile mills worked for short periods of time when the family income required it, but they mainly remained at home, where they earned money by taking in boarders or doing piece-work. Mothers who lived in cities dominated by heavy industry, such as steelmaking, rarely worked outside the home. Married black women were much more likely to work outside the home, many of them in domestic service to white families.[1]

Alice Lacasse Olivier, a French-Canadian who had worked at the Amo-skeag textile mills before her marriage, reminisced in an interview con-ducted when she was eighty-six about her family life while growing up. Although her story is about the early 1900s, it is probably similar to what mill workers in the 1800s could tell us if they were still around to talk:

My parents worked in the mill. They were immigrants from Canada. They were married in 1910, and I was born in 1915. After my parents got married, my mother just worked periodically, for two or three months at a time, when things would get too hard and my father didn't have any money. My father didn't really want her to work. That was a big issue because she always wanted to go in and earn a little money. But the minute she said she wanted to work, there would be a big fight. He'd say, "No, you're not going to work. You're going to stay home." And that's why she did other things. She'd make clothes for him, take in boarders, rent rooms. She used to rent one or two rooms for $12.00 a week to people who worked in the mills. Sometimes she'd also work little stretches at night, from six to nine, because we lived right in front of the mills. When there were big orders, the mills were always looking for people to work. But my father didn't want to keep the children. That was women's work; his work was outside.[2]

It wasn't that Alice's mother lacked for things to do around the house: she had twelve children. Just doing all of the housework was a demanding task for working-class wives. Today washing a load of clothes is not very difficult: you load them into the washing machine, set the load size and water temperature, and press start. But until the widespread adoption of automatic washing machines after World War II, the task was far harder. An article in *Home and Hearth* magazine in 1874, unearthed by the historian Glenna Matthews, helpfully describes a "simplified" method:

First, soak the clothes in cold water for six hours after rubbing the seams with soap.

Then wash them in tepid water and wring them out.

Then bring them to a slow boil.

Then rinse them in fresh, tepid water.

Then wring them out and put them in a cold rinse with light bluing.

This technique, according to the author, required "a very moderate amount of hard labor." Although that may have been true by late-1800s standards, it would seem like a lot of hard labor to anyone today. Moreover, the working-class wife (and it was nearly always the wife) who did the laundry may have also *made* the clothes, as did Alice's mother. The great growth of the ready-to-wear market did not occur until the 1880s and 1890s. Until then, the working-class wife bought cloth and sewed her family's clothes. Nor could she take advantage of those other twentieth-century labor-saving devices, the refrigerator and freezer, which meant that she had to shop daily for perishable food.[3]

On top of these time-consuming housekeeping responsibilities, the working-class wife was likely to be contributing to her family's earnings. She probably did not work outside the home most of the time—married white women typically did not—but there was a good chance that she earned money from within the home. For example, like Alice's mother, she may have taken in boarders. Renting a room in a family's house and eating meals with the family was the common way for single individuals to live when they left their parents' homes—or after they entered the country as immigrants. Few single individuals maintained their own household because cities did not have the large stock of apartment houses that we take for granted today, and also because incomes were so low that most single people could not afford to rent an apartment even if they could find one. After 1910, boarding began to decline as incomes rose, immigration slowed, more apartment buildings were constructed, and reformers, who were concerned about the moral hazards—especially to single young women—and the health risks of renting rooms to strangers, criticized the practice. Until then, taking in boarders was a major source of income for working-class families and a supplement to the earnings of some middle-class families as well.[4]

How did working-class families with modest homes and apartments squeeze in boarders? A woman whose father worked at the Sparrows Point steelworks explained to the anthropologist Karen Olson how her parents fit their two children, themselves, and four boarders into a three-bedroom house with one bathroom:

> We had boarders in our Sparrows Point home for at least seven years. Some of the boarders stayed with us for quite a while and I remember them well. We had three bedrooms upstairs and one was a right small room, and my sister and I slept in that room and Mom and Dad had a bedroom downstairs where the dining room should have been. The other two rooms were occupied by boarders.

So the husband and wife slept in the dining room, the two children were crammed into a small upstairs room, and the two proper bedrooms contained four boarders, double occupancy. The boarders rose early, bathed, and went to work before the children got up. Other Sparrows Point families exploited shift work by taking in men who worked at different times of the day and night and requiring them to share a bed. Homes were crowded, and privacy was at a premium.[5]

Some wives also contributed to the family's earnings by taking in piece-work—small-scale assembly work that could be done at home, often with children laboring as well. The family was paid by the number of finished goods they produced. For instance, Lizzie Kohout was listed in the 1900 census as a cigar maker, along with her husband John. They lived in a tenement house—a building housing up to twenty families—on the Lower East Side of New York City that was owned by the Harburger and Homan Cigar Company. She made cigars at home while caring for two boys, ages four and five. Other families assembled hats, shoes, or paper flowers. And often their contributions were ignored by the census takers, who did not consider home-based production to be work. Barbara Loukshes, an immigrant from Lithuania, was listed in the 1900 census as not having an occupation, trade, or profession. What she did have was eight boarders living in her home, all of them immigrants, and most of them working in the same factory as her husband. Without doubt they were paying for the privilege of boarding, and Barbara was cooking and washing for them.[6]

Wives such as these made critical, and often underappreciated, contributions to their families' standard of living at a time when the burden of meeting the daily needs of husbands and children for food and clothing was far greater than it is today. Many, perhaps most, working-class families could not have survived on the husband's wages alone. The Census Bureau listed most women without wage-earning, outside-the-home jobs as "not working," but that designation reflected a myopic view of work that left unseen the crucial caring labor and home-based earnings of working-class wives.

THE SUBSISTENCE IMPERATIVE

The division of labor in Alice's family reveals two imperatives—two pressing problems that had to be solved. The first was the imperative to provide enough income, food, and clothing for a family that, like many at the time, was barely subsisting. Call it the subsistence imperative. Alice's mother would rent rooms or work a few evening hours when necessary. The family was unusual in that, at their mother's insistence, they allowed their two oldest sons to stay in school and eventually become priests. As a result of that decision, however, the family gained no income from their sons, and consequently Alice was pressed into working at age twelve:

> By the time I was twelve years old, my father desperately needed money. He couldn't support the family by himself. Jackman's boarding house was right next door, and they offered my parents to give me a job, which was really illegal in a sense, because I was so young. I worked in the kitchen and I got $3.00 a week, which I gave to my mother, plus my board. . . . I worked an hour at noon and three hours at night, four hours a day. I worked six days a week.[7]

As Alice noted, by the 1920s compulsory schooling laws had deprived parents of the ability to augment the family's income by sending their children to work at young ages (although it is also clear from Alice's story that many families ignored the laws). Prior to the 1900s, in contrast, working-class families had often depended heavily on children's earnings. Textile mills were the largest employers of children; employers valued them for their speed and agility. Children also worked in coal mines (where they could help extract coal from narrow underground passages because they were small), as messengers and assistants, and at home doing piecework with their mothers and siblings. Sometimes daughters stayed home to do child care while mothers worked. "When my mother was alive," said another former worker for the Amoskeag Company, "she worked in the mill and I took care of the babies. At ten o'clock in the morning, my mother would go out and look across at our window to see if we were all right. We'd wave, and she'd wave."[8]

Child labor had been even more common during the early decades of industrialization in Britain and the United States, roughly 1780 to 1850. In an 1833 sample of textile mills in Manchester, England, 22 percent of the workforce was under age fourteen and 32 percent under age sixteen. Their eleven- or twelve-hour workdays were so tiring that supervisors had difficulty keeping them awake. A British factory overseer testified:

> I found that when I was an overlooker, that after the children from 8 to 12 years had worked 8 or 9 or 10 hours, they were nearly ready to faint; some were asleep; some were only kept awake by being spoken to, or by a little chastisement to make them jump up. I was sometimes obliged to chastise them when they were almost fainting, and it hurt my feelings; but the last 2 or 3 hours were my hardest work, for they got so exhausted.

"A little chastisement" could take the form of a blow from a rod known as a billy roller.[9]

The first textile mill in the United States, which opened in 1790 in Pawtucket, Rhode Island, had a labor force consisting of nine children ages seven to twelve, according to the historian Steven Mintz. The owner reported that in order to keep his young laborers awake, he would whip them with a leather strap and sprinkle them with water. Working conditions this appalling for children so young prompted reformers to advocate for laws to restrict children's working hours (but, initially, still allowing them to work up to ten hours per day) and to raise the ages at which they could commence work. New manufacturing technologies and changing labor needs also caused employers to hire fewer young children, and rising male wages enabled more families to keep their young children at home.

By the mid-1800s, the youngest children no longer worked in the mills, but childhood was still short for the working class: boys typically entered the mills between ages twelve and fourteen, beginning a life of industrial labor. Young girls were more likely to make contributions in the household, although textile factories employed them too. Very few working-class children of either gender attended high school. Children's labor remained an important part of family strategies for earning enough to live on.[10]

THE MASCULINITY IMPERATIVE

The second pressing problem that we can see in Alice's family's work patterns was the importance to her father of maintaining male power and self-respect. Call it the masculinity imperative. Alice's father saw himself as the decision-maker in the family. His wife wanted to work more often in the mills, but he was against it—you're not going to work, he told her, you're staying home. Men, by virtue of law, custom, and earning power, were the heads of their families. Under early American family law, which imported the practices of English common law, the husband and wife became one legal person upon marriage, and that person was the husband. He could make financial decisions for the family and even sell most of his wife's possessions. Only he could vote. Husbands were rarely prosecuted for hitting their wives unless they inflicted serious injury. Employers paid women less than men, on the theory that men were working to support a family but women were working for extras—which was plainly not the case in working-class families. Husbands were recognized as the head of their household, and on the whole they acted like it. During the nineteenth century, however, this legal power eroded somewhat; for example, wives were allowed to maintain control over property they brought to the marriage.[11]

In a predominantly agricultural society of smallholders, the basis of male authority—land ownership—was clear, stable, and unchallengeable. But as urbanization and industrialization proceeded, the source of male authority shifted to wage work, which was less stable and less clear—a paycheck versus a plot of ground. The greater insecurity of male authority may have fostered the need for a man to demonstrate manliness to his family, friends, and self. Said otherwise, industrial workers may have sought to preserve their unsettled self-respect by acting in self-consciously manly ways. They socialized with other men in taverns and other venues. Alice's father sold chocolate bars at the mills for a few extra cents and kept the money to pay for having beers with friends. By the standards of the day, he was behaving responsibly: many men deducted money for alcohol and tobacco from their paychecks before turning the balance over to their wives—who sometimes did not know how much their husbands were paid. Wives had no such prerogative: husbands expected that every cent they earned would go into the family fund. Alice's father also knew what a man didn't do: he wouldn't "keep the children," that is, care for them, while his wife worked in the early evenings, even though they needed the money she would have earned. That was women's work, Alice said; a father did his work outside the home. A man's place was in public—at work, in the town square, in the pubs and saloons. Had word gotten out that Alice's father was taking care of his children in the evenings, his honor would have been tarnished and his self-respect would have suffered.

Alice's father's preferences illustrate how working-class men affirmed their masculinity not solely by how they acted toward their wives and children but also by how they related to other men. The manliness of the working-class man had to be repeatedly, publicly validated. That is the odd thing about what we might call conventional masculinity: although it conjures images of strength, it's precarious. One's masculinity needs to be tested by other men and one must pass the tests—again and again. The anthropologist David Gilmore argues that in most societies men must meet markers of a successful masculine performance, sometimes by explicit rites of passage between boyhood and manhood, sometimes by day-to-day demonstrations that they meet the criteria of conventional masculinity. He cites the case of Alfredo, a man in southern Spain who owned a small grocery store. Alfredo disdained the public male camaraderie of drinking and spending, which he thought was a waste of time and money. So he spent most of his free time at home. Worse yet, he cooked. To other men in the town, Alfredo failed the tests of masculinity. What kind of a man was he, residents asked Gilmore, spending his time at home? Since he was not thought to be a real man, rumors spread that his daughters were not really his—that he had pandered his wife to other men. In the eyes of the community, Alfredo had failed Masculinity 101 because he had not separated himself from his wife and family and did not participate in the public world of men.[12]

Gilmore states that a man must typically prove his manhood in three ways: First, he must demonstrate his heterosexuality by impregnating his wife and controlling her sexuality. Second, he must provide for his family. Third, he must be able to protect them from harm. All the while, he must remain autonomous, socializing with men and resisting being drawn into the domestic life of the home. Accomplishing all this is not easy, especially for men whose labor is not highly rewarded. The industrial worker such as Alice's father was required to work long hours at tasks that were monotonous, alienating, and sometimes dangerous. (Industrial accidents were common, and their consequences were catastrophic. Another former Amoskeag worker said that her father had injured his finger while working in the bobbin shop and had been laid off, leaving the family destitute.

There was no workers' compensation, no unemployment insurance.) Doing so took stamina and self-control. The manly man therefore controlled his emotions and his urges in order to provide for his family.[13]

Conventional masculinity also required control over one's wife. Usually, that was accomplished through argument and authority—you're not going to work, you're staying home. But when argument failed, there was force to back it up. In the early years of the American nation, courts often recognized men's legal right to "chastise" their wives—to "improve" their behavior through physical punishment, as the British factory overseer did to his child workers—if their wives resisted their wishes or stepped out of line. That power was not unlimited, but it was recognized. By the late nineteenth century, judges had come to reject the idea that men had the right to correct their wives by hitting them and viewed such acts as moderate physical abuse; nevertheless, few men were prosecuted for this crime and fewer still were convicted. Judges cited the need to protect "family privacy" or "domestic tranquility," even though there was little tranquility in the homes of abusive men. Thus, assuring the orderly functioning of the husband-headed family was viewed as more important, within limits, than punishing men for beating their wives.[14]

Was there a femininity imperative? Yes, in the sense that a working-class woman was supposed to take care of her husband and children and run the household. Any self-respecting wife would want to show others, and herself, that she could do that. But the emotional duties that we think of as part of the nineteenth-century wife's role—nurturing, soothing, and even inspiring—were probably not as imperative for working-class families as they were becoming for the middle class. While the idea of an emotion-laden "women's sphere" was developing among the new middle class, most working-class wives were too busy and too poor to spend much time on it. With birth rates still relatively high (the typical white woman of prime childbearing age in 1880 had four children in her lifetime, and the typical black woman had seven), working-class women had too many children to care for and no servants to help. With so many families living close to the financial edge, these wives were earning money by cooking and washing for boarders or by rolling cigars. The core of their competence was domestic management—running a complex household enterprise with limited resources. Meeting this managerial responsibility, rather than providing moral support, was what the achievement of femininity was all about for nineteenth-century working-class wives.[15]

But whereas men had to pass masculinity tests in the eyes of other men, it's not clear that women had to convince other women of their femininity. For one thing, theirs was a private role, performed largely at home, rather than a public role that spanned work and home, not to mention the local tavern. So a woman's role was not as visible to others as a man's role was. For another, femininity was seen as natural—biologically and culturally given—even if in reality it was constructed with a great deal of effort. Eighteenth- and nineteenth-century writings are replete with references to this presumed naturalness of sensibility, sympathy, tenderness, and so forth. A writer in *Ladies' Magazine* in 1830 explained that women are "neither greater nor less than man, but different, as her natural vocation is different"—that vocation being domesticity. Consequently, the achievement of femininity may not have required the continual reinforcement that the achievement of masculinity seems to have needed. Fairly or not, women were assumed to be capable of running a household, while men's success in the labor force was more problematic: layoffs, injuries, strikes, economic downturns, or their own character could stand in their way.[16]

This contrast raises the question of why masculinity is so fragile. In much popular commentary today, gender differences are seen as having a biological basis in genes and hormones. Although there may be some biologically based gender differences—for example, men may be somewhat more predisposed to aggressive behavior, on average—it's hard to imagine that a genetically programmed characteristic would be as precarious as masculinity seems to be. If masculinity is such an important evolutionary trait, why is it so difficult to construct and so easy to shatter? It seems reasonable to suspect that there must be a substantial social component to it. Gilmore argues that masculinity tests are ways for young males to separate themselves from their mothers, who in nearly all cases were their first and primary caregiver. This psychoanalytic explanation has been most elegantly described by the sociologist and psychoanalyst Nancy Chodorow. Girls can maintain continuity in identification with their mothers as they mature, she writes, but boys must distance themselves in order to identify as men. Men must therefore do the work of separation, while women need only maintain connections. Masculinity tests are a way of doing that work.[17]

If you are partial to sociobiology, you might see the tests and rules of conventional masculinity as society's way of channeling the naturally more aggressive behavior of men onto constructive paths. Male camaraderie, with its drinking, fighting, and carrying on, provides a relatively harmless outlet for aggression that is more hazardous to express at work (because you might be fired for being insolent) or at home (because you might damage your marriage). The emphasis on self-control and hard work makes a virtue out of the necessity of performing alienating industrial labor. From this perspective, conventional masculinity is a way of imposing structure and discipline on men's lives and ensuring that they will take on difficult and dangerous tasks. If, on the other hand, you believe that gender is largely socially constructed, you might see conventional masculinity as a way to enforce a particular set of socially constructed attitudes and behaviors: heterosexuality, marriage, and a rigid division of labor between wage work outside the home and domestic tasks within the home. You might also see masculinity as a way to defend men's power over women and their privileges, such as drinking with buddies while their wives are cleaning the apartment and feeding the children. Other kinds of masculinity do exist, the social constructionists tell us, but they have been marginalized—working-class rebels who lacked self-control, for instance, or gay men who did not fit the macho image and who, until laws began to change in the 2000s, could not marry. Or at least, they have been marginalized until very recently. Today, as we will see, there are signs that working-class young men are developing a more emotionally expressive sense of self.[18]

A NEW SENSE OF TIME

During industrialization, working-class families also had to cope with an emerging, unfamiliar sense of time. It began with clocks.

Few people today think about what it means to have a day structured by the clock. Time just passes in an ordinary, predictable way. We never expect our sense of time to be any different, except, according to Einstein, if we find ourselves traveling at nearly the speed of light—which doesn't happen often, at least not in Baltimore. But clock time is actually new in human society. Before the inventor Eli Terry started his clock factory in Connecticut in 1806, clocks were large, heavy pieces of equipment that often stood six feet high and weighed over one hundred pounds, and few individuals except the wealthy had clocks in their homes. When Terry began to produce his clocks, people in his town were skeptical, according to an early history of the clock industry: "The foolish man, they said, had begun to make two hundred clocks; one said, he never would live long enough to finish them; another remarked, that if he did he never would, nor could possibly, sell so many, and ridiculed the very idea."[19]

Yet Terry produced 4,000 clocks over the next three years. Then, after perfecting the manufacture of a smaller clock movement that required only a twenty-inch-high case, Terry patented the first clock that could fit on a shelf. His innovation was soon copied by other clock makers in the area, and by 1820 Connecticut clock makers were producing more than 15,000 clocks per year.[20]

Terry deserves credit as an innovator in the making of clock mechanisms. But he had the good fortune—or perhaps was shrewd enough to notice—that the American economy was beginning to industrialize. Prior to this new era, people thought of time in terms of completing a task. Think of Terry in his workshop building his first prototype clock. Think of a farmer plowing a field or his wife sewing a shirt. These tasks took however long they took. This is not to say that people were unaware of time passing or that they had no idea how long they needed to spend on a task. They may not have had a Connecticut clock on their mantle, but they heard the rooster crowing at dawn, listened to church bells peal at noon, and watched sunset end the day. There was nothing leisurely about their lives; they worked hard. Still, their days were not organized around the minute-by-minute passage of time the way our lives are today. The sense of time that we take for granted as we check our watches, smartphones, and clocks several times an hour would have been incomprehensible to the preindustrial family.

As factory employment grew, however, workers needed to follow the clock. They were required to leave home and arrive at work at a particular time—say, the beginning of the day shift at 7:00 AM. At the plant, their duties were not structured around how long it took to complete a large task but rather around how long it took to do their small part of it. When assembly-line production became common in the early twentieth century, workers' duties would be timed to the second. Those who could not get to work on time, or who were too slow in doing their assigned tasks, were fired. To be successful in this environment workers had to develop a new sense of time—to make a shift from "task orientation" to "timed labor," in the words of E. P. Thompson (see chapter 1). During this transition, workers lost control over how they allocated their time. To obey their supervisors they had to develop a time discipline that had been largely absent from the preindustrial work world.

The ability to do timed labor isn't coded in our DNA because our hunter-gatherer ancestors had a task orientation to their labor. A hunt for game took as long to complete as necessary. The industrial revolution imposed time discipline on workers, who internalized it and reproduced it in their children by raising them to perform work on time, as instructed, without questioning authority. This transformation took decades in the United States as millions of immigrants arrived from different areas of Europe. Although some immigrants had industrial experience, most came from agricultural areas where task orientation was prevalent, and they needed to learn the new sense of time. Not until the 1920s, when immigration declined, was the transformation complete.[21]

Even our sleep patterns changed. In early modern Europe—up to about 1700—many people, if historians are to be believed, slept in two segments. Without gas lights in the street or at home, people tended to go to bed early and then wake up sometime after midnight. They would often stay awake for an hour or two, using the time for prayer, for contemplation (providing them with a better way to think about the meaning of their dreams perhaps), or for having sex. Then they would resume sleeping until morning. The historical record shows numerous references to a "first sleep" and a "second sleep." A character in a 1698 play says, "I believe 'tis past midnight, for I have gotten my first sleep." A medical book advises that to improve digestion one should lie on one's right side during "the fyrste slepe" and then "after the fyrste slepe turne on the lefte side." The advent of artificial lighting allowed people to be active later into the evening and began to erode the practice of segmented sleep. It largely disappeared in the 1800s, when the schedule of the urban, industrial workday forced workers to compress their sleep into a single, seamless period. Evening and night shifts in the factories further uprooted traditional sleep practices.[22]

At first, the home remained a place where the older sense of time still ruled. Wives' work was mainly task-oriented: doing the wash, cooking dinner, caring for young children. But the new sense of time inevitably seeped in. Breakfast needed to be served and dinner cooked on the schedule set by the factory. If the factory employed more than one shift, a worker might be required to rotate through them, and breakfast and dinner had to be rotated as well. If the household took in boarders who worked at different plants or at different hours, meals might have to be prepared more than once. Wives who took in piecework had to complete it by an agreed-upon time. As compulsory schooling laws raised the minimum age for leaving school, more children needed to be sent to school on time—clock time. Women's daily lives thus occupied an in-between space where task orientation and timed labor coexisted.[23]

THE IMMIGRANT WORKING CLASS

During the nineteenth and early twentieth centuries, wave after wave of immigrants entered the United States and attempted, usually with success, to take a place in the American working class. Between 1840 and 1860, 4.2 million immigrants entered the United States; about 40 percent of them were Irish, many of whom were fleeing the potato famine that struck Ireland in 1845. Immigration rose further after the Civil War: between 1865 and 1900, 12 million people entered the country, about half of them German and Irish and a million of them British. Late in the century, immigrants from southern and eastern Europe—Italians, Poles, Jews—began to outnumber the migrants from northern and western Europe. In addition, tens of thousands of French Canadians migrated to the Northeast to work in mills such as Amoskeag. Without immigration, industrialization would have proceeded much more slowly because immigrants, along with Americans who moved from the country to the city, were the workers needed by expanding American factories. Moreover, without substantial immigration, employers would have had to pay higher wages, reducing their profits. For instance, when Irish immigrants arrived in the 1840s, employers at the Lowell mills hired them at lower wages to replace the native-born mill girls. Overall, immigrants played a central role in American industrialization: even as late as 1920, 29 percent of the workers whom the Census Bureau classified as "operatives" (the category that includes many factory workers) were foreign-born.[24]

With the catastrophic failure of the potato crop emptying out entire villages, the Irish were more likely to arrive in family groups than were immigrants from most other nations. Young Irish women arrived with their families and frequently took jobs not only as mill workers but also as domestic servants. In fact, unmarried Irish women worked as domestic servants at higher rates than any other immigrant group. It was a demanding job, with long hours, and native-born white women disdained it. Twenty-five percent of all Irish immigrant women were working as domestic servants in 1855. In the 1600s and 1700s, domestic service had been a respectable and almost expected part of the life course for young adults, a role in which young men and women were tutored in the skills they would need to lead adult lives. Servants had been practically members of the family. But by the 1800s domestic service had become a low-paid service occupation.[25]

French Canadians, some of whom also arrived in families, held attitudes that allowed married women to episodically earn wages, as Alice's mother had done, or in some cases to work for wages steadily. Amelia Gazaille, who worked in the Amoskeag mills all her life, said: "My husband didn't like the idea of my working too much. I did the housework and let him help me. We both did it together. And when the children were too young, I worked and my mother took care of my children." Amelia made sure to mention that her husband did not like his wife working too much, thus allowing him to express the expected masculine opposition to wives' factory work. Moreover, Amelia saved face for her husband by defining his household tasks as merely assisting her ("I . . . let him help me"), implying that she retained the responsibility for household work. With these bows toward the expected roles of husband and wife, the couple embarked on a two-wage-earner marriage. They were unusual, however, even among French-Canadians. In 1900, 20 percent of foreign-born wives (most of them French-Canadian) worked outside the home in Manchester,

New Hampshire, and even those who did work tended to withdraw from the labor market when their children were older and could take jobs that would contribute to the family budget.[26]

The southern and eastern European immigrants who began to arrive in the last few decades of the nineteenth century were more resistant to wives and daughters working outside the home. In particular, Italian immigrants—or at least Italian men—seem to have been the most opposed to women leaving the home to work. In the southern Italian villages from which most of the Italians emigrated, the masculinity imperative featured a patriarchal code of honor that required strict protection of women's sexuality, which led to restrictions on the activities of wives and unmarried daughters outside the home. Families relied instead on the economic contributions of sons. Because lengthy schooling interfered with this family strategy, Italian immigrants saw it as unnecessary and were skeptical about the benefits of extended schooling and mandatory school attendance laws. School officials, in turn, were critical of what they saw as an anti-education bias among Italian parents, some of whom were not sending their children to school. The New Haven, Connecticut, superintendent of schools said in 1871 of the city's heavily Italian immigrant population (at a time when there was no statewide mandatory attendance law): "Every year it has become apparent . . . that parents [of unschooled children] to a considerable extent are insensible to the wrong they are permitting to be inflicted on their offspring."[27]

In the latter half of the nineteenth century, states began to pass laws that gradually raised the minimum age at which children could leave school. The higher school-leaving ages deprived immigrant families of a key element in their family strategies for earning a living because children could not be sent to work at an early age. For instance, one year after the New Haven superintendent made his comments, the Connecticut legislature passed a law requiring that children ages eight to fourteen attend school for three months of the year, six weeks of which had to be consecutive. Although this law may seem amazingly lax by contemporary standards, it meant that thirteen- and fourteen-year-old boys, who had been crucial wage-earners in many working-class families, had to at least temporarily withdraw from work. It also set the stage for laws that further raised the minimum age for leaving school. By 1900, school attendance was compulsory through age fourteen in many states—which is why Alice said that it was "really illegal in a sense" for her to have been working at age twelve rather than going to school. More generally, during the nineteenth century children's importance in the labor market declined throughout the United States and Britain, particularly among middle-class families, a phenomenon one historian has called the "adulting" of the labor force. Although children's work diminished as new laws gradually raised the minimum school-leaving age, other factors also were important: rising adult wages reduced the family's need for income from child workers, and changing production processes reduced employers' demand for child labor. In addition, a more sentimental view of children developed, according to which children were special beings who deserved a protected time to develop rather than being sent to work.[28]

Figure 2.1 shows how and when children's employment changed in the period between 1880 and 1950; the top chart is for whites, and the bottom chart is for African Americans. The figure displays the percentages of all ten- to fifteen-year-old children who were in the labor force (meaning that they were either employed or looking for work), classified according to the occupation of the head of their household (usually their father). I excluded household heads who were working on farms because child labor has a long tradition and a different character in rural areas than in industrial areas.

Looking first at whites, we can see that prior to 1900 children in the homes headed by craftsmen, operatives, service workers, and common laborers were substantially more likely to be employed than were the children of heads with white-collar occupations such as professionals, managers, clerical workers, or sales workers. In 1880 the children of families in the former group were more than twice as likely to be employed as the children of white-collar workers. The differences between the two groups remained large until the early 1900s, when employment began to decline steeply among all children. By 1930, compulsory school attendance laws and rising incomes had reduced employment among ten- to fifteen-year-olds to near zero. The gap in the use of child labor in the late 1880s and early 1900s between the working class and the white-collar middle class shows again that, as with the marriage gap (see figure 1.2), it was a period of substantial class differences in family life.[29]

African American children, the bottom chart shows, were much more likely to be in the labor force in the late 1800s than were white children: the proportion who were employed among children from homes headed by craftsmen and operatives and by service workers or laborers were well above the comparable levels among white children in 1880. (There were too few black household heads who were in white-collar occupations to provide reliable estimates.) Black children's employment dropped from 1880 to 1900 but remained substantial compared to white children's. After 1910, black children's employment resumed its decline, as mandatory school attendance laws limited the ability of parents to send their young children to work. And among both black and white children, boys were much more likely than girls to be employed. In 1900, for instance, 14 per-

Figure 2.1   Children Ages Ten to Fifteen Who Were in the Labor
Force, by (Nonfarm) Occupation of Household Head,
1880–1950

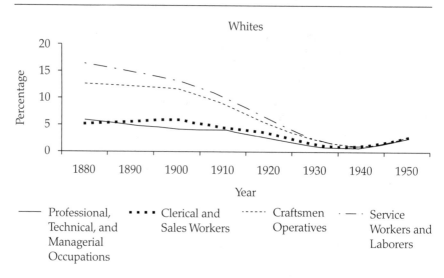

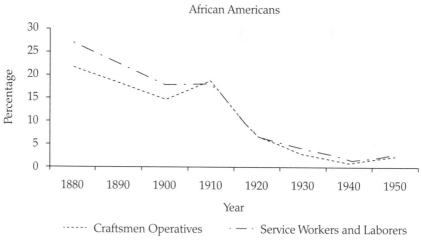

Source: Ruggles et al. (2010).

cent of white boys and 24 percent of black boys were employed, compared to 6 percent of white girls and 10 percent of black girls. Girls were more likely than boys to contribute at home and less likely to earn wages.[30]

Public education also had more subtle effects. Schools taught children basic literacy and numeracy, of course, but they did much more than that. First, they made children more independent of their parents. Being expected to obey their teachers and recite the Pledge of Allegiance to the flag taught children a valuable lesson outside of the three Rs: there were sources of authority in the world beyond their parents. Students realized that they didn't need to see their fathers as the ultimate source of power because there were also teachers, and teachers required you to do homework even though your mother would prefer that you help her with the piecework she had taken in that day. John Caldwell, a theorist of the decline in fertility in the twentieth century, has observed that even three or four years of schooling in a low-income nation can initiate a reduction in family size, because children realize that they are free to make decisions about their lives—including whether and when to have children themselves—and need not submit totally to traditional authority. Something similar may have happened in the United States: as the minimum school-leaving age rose inexorably toward sixteen, parents no longer had complete control of their children. An Italian immigrant barber told a researcher, "It is the American way; you cannot do a thing with your children in America. All you can do is have them arrested."[31]

Second, schools taught working-class children the discipline they needed to become industrial workers. Early public schools emphasized obedience, and a student who disobeyed was punished, sometimes even hit. Schools taught punctuality: students needed to report on time every day. Fixed-length classes and school days also taught students time discipline: for example, a test given in class had to be completed by the end of the class period. A critic described a day in the New York City schools in an 1893 report: "During several daily recitation periods, each of which is from twenty to twenty-five minutes in duration, the children are obliged to stand on line, perfectly motionless, their bodies erect, their knees and feet together, the tips of their shoes touching the edge of the board in the floor."

Working-class parents may have been unhappy about the independence that schools instilled in their children, but by and large they approved of the emphasis on discipline—it reinforced their belief that it was important for children to be obedient and self-disciplined. Schools, then, helped to reproduce the industrial laborers in the next generation. Parents thought that learning discipline was particularly relevant for boys, because of their future as wage workers, but considered it less important for girls. That may be one reason why some immigrant parents gave their daughters less schooling than their sons. Schools taught daughters independence that their parents did not want them to have and work discipline that their parents thought they did not need.[32]

THE EMERGING MIDDLE-CLASS FAMILY

The daily life of the working-class family, in sum, was distinct from older American family patterns in several ways: it depended on the wages of a husband who worked outside the home and who publicly displayed and defended his masculine sense of self; it relied on the supplementary earnings of children in the market and wives in the home; it followed a new sense of time; and its immigrant origins were diverse. It was also distinct from another family form that emerged at about the same time, if not a bit earlier: the middle-class family. The two models were not completely different. Like their working-class counterparts, most middle-class urban husbands worked outside the home. Initially, middle-class wives contributed earnings by taking in boarders, although their contributions lessened later in the century. Nevertheless, there were important differences between the working class and the emerging middle class in the roles of husbands, wives, and children and in the influential ideology that the latter developed to justify these roles.

The historian Mary Ryan provided perhaps the best description of the emergence of the middle-class family in her study of native-born Protestant families in the Utica, New York, area between 1790 and 1865. As commercial (sales and trade-based) capitalism grew in this previously rural upstate region, and as industrial capitalism arrived in the form of the first factories, Utica grew dramatically. A substantial number of managers, office workers, retail clerks, merchants, and other white-collar occupations were created. In fact, the term "white-collar" first entered common usage in the period of 1820 to 1850. These occupations were outside the reach of the immigrants who began to flood Utica to work in the factories, but they supported a relatively prosperous group of families—what we would term "the middle class." Throughout the rest of the nineteenth century, in Utica and elsewhere, the native-born population dominated the professions and higher-level white-collar occupations. Nationally in 1880, 93 percent of lawyers and judges were native-born, along with 91 percent of physicians and surgeons, 88 percent of teachers, and 76 percent of bookkeepers. In contrast, the native-born were much less prominent in industrial occupations: they constituted 61 percent of machinists, 56 percent of the general category of "operatives," 54 percent of all furnacemen, smelters, and pourers, and just 24 percent of textile weavers.[33]

As a result of its relative prosperity, the typical middle-class family did not have to worry about subsisting from month to month, as did many of the low-wage-earning immigrant, working-class families. Freed from the constant pressure to make ends meet, husbands and wives were able to turn inward to issues of personal life: privacy, domesticity, and the nature of the self. They were able to hold their children back from the work world longer than most working-class families could manage, to educate them more, and to teach them to adhere to middle-class values such as self-control. Increasingly, these families could afford to withdraw their wives from all income-earning activities. The percentage of professional and managerial households that had boarders dropped steadily from 1880, the first year for which good data exist, onward. It is possible that the drop had begun well before 1880, as wives focused on domesticity.[34]

Middle-class families, like working-class families, also had to adjust to a new sense of time. Lawyers had to get to the office on time, meet clients when scheduled, and show up promptly in court. Children had to get to school on time. But it was a less regimented sense of time than the working class experienced. A whistle did not blow at the start of the workday at the law office. The attorney did not lose pay if he was fifteen minutes late, and his workdays were not divided into precisely timed tasks like those that came to dominate the daily lives of factory workers. Therefore, middle-class, white-collar workers did not need to develop as rigid a sense of time discipline as industrial laborers needed. Nor did their families need to adjust to an arbitrary schedule that was set by an employer and subject to change with little notice.

Work was just as important to a middle-class man's sense of self as it was to a working-class man. Whether a man was a good provider was a similar test of masculinity up and down the class structure. But there were class differences in how men experienced work. Middle-class occupations were often more intrinsically rewarding than working-class jobs, and middle-class men invested their identities more heavily in them. They sought not merely to earn a living but also to move up in the world. The historian E. Anthony Rotundo found that nineteenth-century middle-class men described their personal goals using phrases such as "arrive at eminence and fame," "rise to wealth and honor," and "prepare myself for some station of respectability and usefulness." In short, they were ambitious—a trait that working-class men, who valued their bonds of solidarity with other workers like themselves, viewed with suspicion. Instrumental rather than uplifting, work for working-class men was to be endured—I get to work on time, I work hard, I bring home a paycheck. This instrumental attitude toward work was not as prevalent among men in the emerging middle class.[35]

Middle-class manhood was reinforced in public encounters with other men, as was the manhood of the working-class man. But public activities were more organized and formal among the middle class. To be sure, middle-class men frequented taverns, but men's clubs and lodges also grew in popularity in the nineteenth century. By 1900, Rotundo estimates, between one-eighth and one-fourth of adult males belonged to a lodge, with the proportion higher among middle-class men. The lodges featured male camaraderie and ritual and were criticized as undermining the family: "Every club is a blow against marriage, . . . offering as it does, the surroundings of a home without women or the ties of a family." Although it is hard from a contemporary perspective to see lodges such as the Benevolent and Protective Order of Elks and the Masons as antifamily, they did provide a setting in which men could reinforce their sense of manliness.[36]

In addition, middle-class families differed from working-class families in how they raised children. First of all, they had fewer of them. Women in Utica who began their families in the 1830s had an average of 3.6 children, compared to 5.8 children among women twenty years earlier. With fewer children and higher incomes, middle-class families could reserve more time and money for each child. They were the early innovators of the twentieth- and twenty-first-century strategy of low fertility and high investment. They also began to think anew about the nature of childhood. Whereas the father was considered the primary parent in the eighteenth century—he kept the children in the unlikely event of a divorce—mothers were now recognized as the more important parent. The idea that children had an inherently sinful nature was rejected; instead, parents viewed children as innocent and in need of nurturing and love, with mothers playing an increasing role in providing it. Middle-class parents also moved away from viewing childhood as a short period during which children could learn the basic skills they would need as adults and then, as early as age ten or twelve, become productive members of the family. Rather, they saw children as in need of more time to acquire the education and training necessary for white-collar occupations. Middle-class childhood therefore became a longer, protected stage of life during which children were shielded from the responsibilities of adulthood. Middle-class children often remained in their parental homes into their late teens or early twenties, while working-class children typically left home earlier.[37]

Prior to the emergence of the middle class, most parents emphasized obedience as a central value in rearing children—although the stern, disciplinarian father we associate with the Puritans had long since faded away. Among the new middle class, however, self-control became the paramount trait to cultivate in children. Ryan writes about the emerging middle class in Utica, New York:

The values that this elaborate system was designed to implant in the child's personality are almost too mundane and obvious to recount: the usual array of petit bourgeois traits—honesty, industry, frugality, temperance, and, pre-eminently, self-control. Already in the infancy of the young adults of the Civil War era, the literate native-born Protestants of Utica had worked out a set of strategies for the reproduction of a middle-class personality.

Instilling that middle-class personality meant raising children to be more self-reliant than in the past. The goal was for children to internalize the norms of proper behavior so that they could control their behavior without others having to direct them. In that sense, self-control required a view of the self as an independent entity capable of making choices and decisions, whereas obedience mainly involved doing the bidding of authority figures.[38]

The idea that the core of one's being involves an independent self that takes in information, reflects on whether and how to act on it, and changes in response to those actions is a modern one. One's sense of self typically coheres over time into a self-identity, a related concept. For instance, although there is nothing new about preferring to have sex with someone of the same gender, this activity only began to cohere into a self-identity as a "homosexual" (or its antithesis, a "heterosexual") in the nineteenth century. Prior to that time, one commonly acted on one's sexual preferences without much consideration about whether these actions created a basic sense of self that was fundamentally different from that of people who behaved otherwise. It's likely that this new, inward-oriented way of looking at oneself developed as rising standards of living provided people with the time to do more than work to put food on the table but also to think about larger questions of the nature of their lives. This perspective took root as more and more individuals experienced the luxury of cultivating their emotional gardens.[39]

We can see the start of this mode of thinking in how middle-class parents began to raise their children in the early 1800s. To be sure, the self-controlled, self-reliant personality that middle-class parents desired in their children was far different from the self of the late twentieth or early twenty-first century, with its penchant for expressing personal feelings and focusing on growth and development during adulthood—a cultural style sometimes referred to as "expressive individualism." Rather, what parents hoped to instill in their children in the early 1800s was a more constrained sense of self that was directed toward moderation in behavior and toward personal achievement, especially in one's work life. Ryan writes that the object of middle-class parenting was to produce a child not with "the spirit of a daring, aggressive entrepreneur but with, rather, that of a cautious, prudent small-business man." The model might have been Benjamin Franklin, with his maxims such as "early to bed, early to rise, makes a man healthy, wealthy, and wise." Franklin's autobiography is the consummate example of an older sense of self sometimes known as "utilitarian individualism": self-reliant, self-disciplined, and high-achieving. Middle-class parents of the early 1800s tried to instill that cultural style in their children. It would take a century and a half for the utilitarian sense of self to evolve into its expressive form. Meanwhile, working-class parents in the early 1800s held on to a more traditional set of values that placed much less emphasis on self-reliance and more on respecting and obeying authority. Thus, social class differences in child-rearing values—basically, a newer emphasis on autonomy among the middle class versus an older emphasis on obedience among the working class—first arose in the early 1800s, and they have remained visible ever since.[40]

The type of work that middle-class husbands did could be jarringly different from what traditional farm or crafts families did. Their work was done not for the family's direct use (such as growing crops) but rather for its exchange value—the salary it could bring in. This new commercial model of work was seen as potentially alienating in a way that agricultural labor was not—a cold, crass exchange of labor for money, much like the exchanges the working class experienced, but with greater financial rewards. Fortunately, it was thought, the family's higher income could be used to make the home a place where the white-collar husband could receive emotional support that would compensate him for his efforts. To accomplish this objective wives needed to be free from having to work outside the home so that they could instead focus on creating a setting where husbands could be morally and spiritually refreshed when they were not at the office. The wife's daily life revolved around this duty. It became her part of the world—her sphere of action—whereas the husband's sphere was the cold world of work. In this fashion, the doctrine of "separate spheres," with its sharp split between the moral natures of home and work, was born.

A certain amount of romanticism, perhaps even nostalgia, about preindustrial work contributed to these sentiments about the separate spheres. Family farms required dawn-to-dusk, physically challenging labor with a payoff that could be wiped out by drought, blight, or flood. Farm life was tough—most families lived close to the margin of subsistence—and many people were glad to leave it. Nor was wage work necessarily alienating. By contemporary standards, no one would want to work in a nineteenth- or early-twentieth-century textile mill, but some of the workers enjoyed it.

Mary Cunion, who started at the Amoskeag mills when she was fifteen, remembered:

> When I came in 1900, we worked from six in the morning till six at night. I worked solid. My aunt [who also worked in the mill] wouldn't allow any gallivanting around. Even on the weekends, I worked. But I liked it from the start. . . . I liked weaving. I liked watching the different boxes. . . . It's a very interesting job, weaving is. I think it's the most interesting work a girl can have. In fact, you never really learn it all.[41]

So there had to be something other than an objective analysis of the trade-offs between farm and factory work involved in the doctrine of separate spheres. It was, rather, an attempt to create an idealized version of masculine and feminine roles that reflected the values of the time: the man as producer, the women as nurturer; the man's world as profane, the woman's world as spiritual; the man's world as exhausting, the woman's world as renewing. The doctrine embodied a set of opposites that was consistent with the message of ministers at the time that the spiritual world was superior to the material world. The historian Nancy Cott, in her study of the emergence of the separate spheres doctrine in New England in the same period, quotes a New Hampshire pastor:

> It is at home, where the man . . . seeks a refuge from the vexations and embarrassments of business, an enchanting repose from exertion, a relaxation from care by the interchange of affection: where some of his finest sympathies, tastes, and moral and religious feelings are formed and nourished; — where is the treasury of pure disinterested love, such as is seldom found in the busy walks of a selfish and calculating world.

Perhaps the new separation of the venues for work and family life encouraged people to see men's and women's spheres as separate when, in fact, there was often an overlap. Even some of the middle-class wives of Utica worked outside the home. In addition, women's sphere may also have symbolized the preindustrial social organization that the new middle class regretted relinquishing—an older, task-oriented way of life that was less structured, less pressured, and more intrinsically rewarding, at least in retrospect. It may have been a way of keeping a valued part of the past alive.[42]

This was the middle-class vision of family life that, later in the century, the working class took as its goal. It restricted the lives of middle-class women and left husbands formally in charge. Yet it may have had some advantages for women. Appointing them as the guardians of moral values and giving them the major role in rearing children provided them with substantial influence. However circumscribed their women's sphere may have been, their control of it, with its claim to moral superiority, may also have allowed them to counter the authority of their husbands. Moreover, the ideology of the women's sphere may have created a consciousness of, and identification with, women as a group. Women established and maintained deep friendships with other women, reinforced by the segregation of their lives and by female rituals surrounding childbirth, weddings, illnesses, and funerals. Some joined together in public associations to promote values consistent with domesticity, such as greater devotion to religion, assistance for the poor, and enlightened child-rearing. These friendships and associations may have been a prerequisite for the development of feminist organizations in the nineteenth and twentieth centuries. Cott captures the dual nature of women's sphere in the title of her book, *The Bonds of Womanhood:* the bonds that tied women to the domestic sphere also bound them together in a subculture of sisterhood that prefigured their social and political movements decades later.[43]

THE MALE BREADWINNER IDEAL

The influence of the separate spheres doctrine soon spread beyond the middle class. As the working-class labor movement developed later in the century, its leaders adopted the doctrine as a justification for demanding that employers offer men a "family wage," that is, a wage high enough that it could support an entire nuclear family of husband, wife, and children without the wife having to work outside the home. Sometimes called a "living wage," it remained more of an ideal than a reality for the great majority of working-class families, but it exerted a powerful influence on their conceptions of what family life should be like. The goal of supporters of the family wage in the late 1800s and early 1900s was to have wives doing no work outside of the home, but workers' understanding of the prevalent social norms allowed wives to earn money through work *inside* the home, and as we have seen, many of them did. Jane Addams noted as much in an 1895 report based on visits to working-class families to whom Hull House had provided services:

> In this neighborhood, generally a wife and children are sources of income as well as avenues of expense; and the women wash, do "home finishing" on

ready made clothing, or pick up and sell rags; the boys run errands and "shine"; the girls work in factories, get places as cash girls, or sell papers on the streets; and the very babies sew buttons on kneepants and shirtwaists, each bringing a trifle to fill out the scanty income. The theory that "every man supports his own family" is as idle in a district like this as the fiction that "everyone can get work if he wants it."

As recently as 1920, the Women's Bureau of the U.S. Department of Labor reported in a study of four cities that if all the ways in which married women were earning money, including work in the home, were included, then married women would make up, on average, 50 percent of the labor force. The great growth in homemakers who devoted all of their time to housework, child care, and emotional support, never earning a dime, would await the midtwentieth century.[44]

Did this push for the family wage serve the interests of both married men and married women, or did it primarily serve the interests of married men by ensuring that their wives were economically dependent on them? Was it about the family's class position or the husband's position in the gender hierarchy? There is much debate in the historical literature on these questions. Early in organized labor's push for a family wage—around the late 1800s—class politics seemed to dominate. Workers demanded a family wage because they believed it to be in the interest of their entire family. And from the perspective of the waves of immigrant families formed during these decades, the family wage did look to be just. For one thing, housework and child care were so difficult and time-consuming that it seemed like a great advance to free wives from the additional burden of working for wages away from home. But gender politics was involved too. The demand for a family wage served to preserve men's sense of masculinity as industrialization proceeded. "Wages and jobs were at the center of the disputes between workers and their bosses," writes the historian Sonya Rose about similar struggles in nineteenth-century Britain, "but it was what wages and jobs meant to working-class men that was at the root of their strategies in these struggles." The movement for the family wage was also about ensuring that the average male worker could still pass the tests of masculinity.[45]

AFRICAN AMERICANS, WHITENESS, AND THE WORKING CLASS

As the American working class emerged, one group of laborers played an important but quite different role: African Americans. Prior to the Civil War, of course, most blacks labored as slaves on Southern farms and plantations. Although they were not part of an open labor market (except for a small number of free blacks in the North), their labor was nevertheless instrumental in starting the industrial revolution. The cotton they picked was shipped to the mills of the Northern states and to the Lancashire region of Britain, where it was woven into cloth. Cotton picked by slave labor and the technical innovations it spawned were so central to the initial growth of factory production that it is hard to imagine the industrial revolution occurring without it. Between 1785 and 1850, the amount of cotton imported in Britain rose from 11 million pounds to 588 million pounds, and the amount of cloth produced rose from 40 million yards to 2,025 million yards. Had the slave-labor-based plantation system not been in place, industrialization would probably have started later and proceeded more slowly.[46]

After the Civil War, the African American population remained largely agricultural: 88 percent of African Americans lived in rural areas in 1880, many of them working under the sharecropping system. But the urban population did increase, and black men and women in cities found their employment prospects to be limited. In Birmingham, Alabama, black men were hired in the iron factories, but only for undesirable jobs such as shoveling iron ore into hot furnaces. Their path to better positions was blocked: when employers needed more labor for skilled positions, they recruited skilled white workers from Northern mills rather than train black employees. Blacks were also able to find positions in the growing railroad industry as track layers, porters, and firemen. The fireman job—heaving coal into the steam engines—had been a stepping-stone to a job as an engineer, but black firemen were prohibited from advancing and white engineers expected them to run personal errands. In addition, white workers complained that the low-paid black firemen were blocking *their* chances for advancement. One employer, in response, justified the lower wages his company paid to black firemen in these terms: "The colored fireman is paid less than the white fireman. That would naturally follow from this circumstance, if no other: There are white firemen always on the road who are candidates for promotion to engineers. These white firemen outrank, so to speak, the colored fireman." In plain language, since black firemen were not allowed to become engineers, they should be paid less than white firemen who might someday become engineers.[47]

Black women also faced a much different labor market than did white women. They were basically shut out of industrial jobs and had little opportunity to do any work other than washing, cooking, and cleaning for others. Fifty percent of all free black women in New York City in 1855 worked as domestics; they were the only group to exceed Irish immigrant women in this regard. In general, married black women worked outside the home in far greater numbers than did married white women. For instance, 29 percent of black married women were listed in the 1880 census as being employed—that is, working outside the home—compared to 4 percent of foreign-born white married women and 2 percent of native-born white married women. Their work effort was partly a continuation of the lives of previous generations of black women under slavery—when work in the fields was mandatory—and partly a reflection of the need to supplement the incomes of black men, whose labor market situation was precarious. African American families may also have looked different from European American families in their division of labor, even had African Americans faced fewer labor market constraints after the Civil War. In West Africa, women often bore the major responsibility for cultivating food, and in many such societies women were active in marketing and trading. If there were cultural survivals from Africa in late-nineteenth-century America—a big "if" that has been debated by scholars—then it might have been culturally acceptable for African American women to work outside the home. Correspondingly, African American men might have been culturally inclined to allow their wives to work outside the home without feeling that their masculinity was threatened.[48]

In addition, the native-born whites and European immigrants in the working class began to exclude African Americans from advancement in a more fundamental way. After the Civil War, whiteness began to develop as a new panethnicity, a kind of overarching identity that gradually encompassed all of the European immigrant groups. In the minds of immigrants, this new panethnic identity began to be seen as a credential needed for membership in the working class. To be sure, talk of the "white race" was not new; Chief Justice Roger B. Taney's decision in the 1857 Dred Scott case, in which the Supreme Court ruled that freed slaves had no inherent right to citizenship, had included the phrase seven times. But Taney was referring to the original settlers, early immigrants, and their descendants. After the war, whiteness became an ethnicity that could be stretched and redefined. Most white individuals alive today do not see whiteness this way. Rather, they tend to see whiteness as the *absence* of ethnicity—as neither black nor Asian nor Hispanic. They see their skin as showing a *lack* of color rather than a particular kind of "colored." But whiteness did, and still does, take on the characteristics of a social category that is constructed by people based on what they perceive to be shared physical characteristics or regional origins.[49]

The expansion of whiteness was an ongoing project in the latter half of the nineteenth century and the early twentieth century. When Irish immigrants first arrived in the United States, they were not considered fully white. The neighborhoods where they first settled were sometimes the same neighborhoods where free blacks lived. The cover of an 1876 issue of *Harper's Weekly*, drawn by the famous editorial cartoonist Thomas Nast, shows two men on opposite pans of a balance scale. On the pan labeled SOUTH, a barefoot black man sits grinning at the man sitting on the pan labeled NORTH—an Irish man who is drawn with a darkened complexion, flat nose, and outthrust mouth. The two men, as the perfectly balanced scale shows, are equivalent. Even Jews were not considered white when they first arrived in large numbers in the late 1800s. An 1896 drawing shows Uncle Sam holding his nose as a swarthy, bearded immigrant with a skull cap approaches, his two suitcases labeled POVERTY and DISEASE, his scarf labeled SUPERSTITION, and a keg of beer on his back labeled SABBATH DESECRATION.

Irish immigrants, realizing that they needed to be seen as white to obtain jobs, commenced the process of joining the panethnicity. Even though they may not have been considered white at first, their European origins gave them options that were unavailable to blacks. The Irish gained footholds in certain occupations and then excluded blacks, realizing that to be considered part of the white working class they needed to work in occupations that only whites worked in. For example, in 1850 in Philadelphia, Irish laborers struck to demand the dismissal of a black laborer who was working alongside them. At a time when blacks were intimidated from voting, the Irish used politics to gain positions that provided patronage to their community. They saw the path to whiteness and took it, even though that meant avoiding or opposing the struggle of blacks for full citizenship. Sidney George Fisher, a Philadelphia diarist, wrote in 1862:

> The Irish hate the Negroes, not merely because they compete with them in labor, but because they are near to them in social rank. Therefore, the Irish favor slavery in the South, and for the same reason the laboring class of whites supports it—it gratified their pride by the existence of a class below them.

As Fisher's observation suggests, there was more to gain from being in "the laboring class of whites" than the simple economic advantages of higher wages and greater work opportunities. The direct financial advantage could not have been great enough to justify the animus shown by whites against black workers—being a white worker brought a psychological benefit as well. It was a whiteness premium that the African American sociologist W. E. B. Du Bois described as a "public and psychological wage," a way in which whiteness could function almost as a wage supplement.[50]

Needless to say, African American laborers were unable to join this new white working class. The labor union movement did not offer them much help. Unionists representing the white panethnic working class defined their self-worth by contrasting themselves with blacks. Admittedly, the tendency of white workers to define themselves in contrast to black workers was visible before unions became active. For example, by the early 1800s whites had imported the Dutch word "boss" to refer to their employers so that they would not need to use the word "master." For similar reasons, white domestic workers preferred to be called "help" rather than "servants." After the Civil War, as free blacks attempted to move into industrial jobs, white unionists had the choice of either embracing them as fellow laborers in the struggle against low wages and onerous working conditions or excluding them as competitors. For the most part, they chose the latter course. White industrial workers and their leaders expressed feelings of entitlement with respect to the labor market. They believed that they had priority in taking industrial jobs because they were superior to black workers, who, it was said, did not work as hard and were of questionable moral character. In an 1898 issue of *The American Federationist,* the magazine of the American Federation of Labor, a Southern white labor organizer complained that blacks did not have "those peculiarities of temperament such as patriotism, sympathy, etc., which are peculiar to most of the Caucasian race." A delegate to a 1905 convention of the Brotherhood of Railway Carmen, which did not allow black members, said: "God . . . made the Negro but he never made him to be a car worker. I do not believe the time will ever come when he should come into a union along with carmen. . . . When the time does come when I must sit down in social equality with the Negro . . . I want to be carried to the nearest insane asylum."[51]

White iron workers in Birmingham, Alabama, for example, worried that employers would use African American laborers to lower their wages, barred them from joining local lodges. The boilermakers' lodge announced that it would admit only "white, free-born male citizens of some civilized country." Many unions did not recruit black members, and even among unions that did, the local chapters were often segregated. When the American Federation of Labor (AFL) became the most powerful union organization in the 1890s, its leader, Samuel Gompers, urged its member unions to admit blacks so that employers could not use low-paid black workers to weaken the position of white workers. But the Federation did little to back up its rhetoric, and a number of important unions, such as the National Association of Machinists, were allowed to join the Federation even though they refused to admit black members. It was a fateful choice.[52]

In this way, "working-class" became a term that had the connotation of whiteness, which it retained throughout the nineteenth century and much of the twentieth century. Black industrial workers must be counted as members of the working class, but they were relegated to the margins of the labor market and faced substantial discrimination. By failing to make common cause with them, white workers pushed them into the hands of exploitative employers. Non-union black workers, with no other options for industrial work, sometimes crossed picket lines after being hired to work as strikebreakers, much to the anger of striking white unionists. Had blacks belonged to the unions, they would have sided with the strikers. Over time this system of privilege, in which the better jobs and the career ladders were largely reserved for whites, came to be seen by white workers as natural, the way whiteness itself seemed natural. They did not consider their status until their whiteness premium was lessened by legislation in the last few decades of the twentieth century. At that late date, the old, whiteness-based system had been in place so long as to be invisible to them, and the new equal opportunity laws seemed to white workers less like the removal of racial privilege and more like the imposition of reverse discrimination.

How the working class evolved with respect to race greatly affected black working-class family life, beginning with the subsistence imperative, which became even more urgent than for white working-class families. The exclusion of black men from all but low-wage jobs increased the economic pressure on black families and encouraged married black women to enter the labor market, where most of the occupations open to them were domestic service and laundry work. (As recently as 1940, six out of ten employed black women were working as domestics for white families.) Combined with the history of black women's work in the fields under slavery and in the sharecropping system, black working-class wives' employment set black families on a different course than the course followed by white families. The ideal of the homemaker who earns no money did not become prominent in black family life. One could argue that the homemaker ideal was never about black families—that it was developed by whites with white families in mind. In any case, it passed them by.[53]

If the subsistence imperative was more compelling for black working-class families than for white working-class families, the masculinity imperative, by contrast, was weaker. Prior to the Civil War, we know that at least on large plantations, slaves entered into informal marriages and created kinship bonds, even though they were not allowed to legally marry. But black slave husbands had not been able to fulfill any of Gilmore's three basic tasks of conventional masculinity. They could not protect their wives' childbearing capacity from sexual exploitation by overseers and masters. They could not provide financially for their families. And they could not protect their family members from harm, such as harsh punishment and being sold to other slave owners. After the Civil War, black working-class husbands could better protect sexual access to their wives, but given their restricted labor market position, they often could not provide economically for their families without their wives working as domestics or washerwomen. Moreover, their capacity to protect their families against the injuries of racism was limited. Black men were still blocked from achieving conventional masculinity after the Civil War—they could not pass all of the tests that defined a manly man.

The withholding of conventional masculinity opened space for black men to define themselves differently from white men and for black families to operate differently from white families. Whereas white men aspired to be autonomous workers who could shoulder the sole responsibility of providing for their families, black men were more likely to see themselves as part of a network of family and kin who provided mutual support. Whereas white men focused on their wives and children, black men had greater latitude to see themselves as connecting with, and caring for, a broader set of kin. Their labor market difficulties also allowed them to define themselves less heavily in terms of the jobs they held. Overall, then, the labor market challenges that black men and women faced provided the opportunity for a more flexible set of family roles, with less emphasis on the single-earner nuclear family than white men and women faced. It also offered the opportunity for a kind of masculine identity that was less focused on discipline and authority than was the case for white working-class men.

THE ROADS NOT TAKEN

By the end of the nineteenth century, working-class family patterns were well established. Among white married couples, husbands worked for pay outside the home. Many wives contributed earnings from work performed at home, and some wives worked sporadically for wages when the family's money troubles left no alternative, but the husband remained the main earner. Children still contributed earnings to the family pot as well, but compulsory school attendance laws had lengthened the number of years before they could work full-time. Among African American married couples, it was much more common for both parents to work outside the home, although many wives took in washing and sewing. Both black men and women faced limited labor market opportunities and lower wages than whites.

Leaders of the labor movement were by that time advocating for a "family wage" that would ensure that no wife need work outside the home. They were doing so on behalf of white workers, who constituted the overwhelming majority of the members of the leading unions. In fact, the labor movement largely excluded blacks. Even Gompers made it clear that he advocated recruiting blacks on pragmatic rather than moral grounds: "I strip myself absolutely from all sentimental considerations and base it upon what I am confident will best serve the interests of labor," he said in 1897. Black workers became, in the eyes of many white workers, the "other," the unmanly, the competition, the group against whom white workers measured themselves favorably. In the American West, the role of the "other" was also played by Chinese immigrants, who were subject to intense criticism from unionists. The Chinese had begun to appear in California in the 1850s, following the 1849 California gold rush. They were overwhelmingly male, and many of them worked as laborers in the building of railroads. White workers and labor leaders decried Chinese immigrants as threats to their livelihood because they worked for lower wages than whites received—a charge similar to what Eastern white workers were saying about blacks.[54]

If anything, the attacks on Chinese workers were more vicious than the attacks on blacks. In 1901 Gompers, who was "pragmatically" accepting of black workers, said of the Chinese that "every incoming coolie means . . . so much more vice and immorality injected into our social life." The word "coolie" implied that the immigrants were indentured servants sent from Asia to work for low wages, even though most had come as independent immigrants. Mexican immigrant workers were also excluded from membership in unions and decried by whites as low-wage labor. The similarity of attitudes toward black, Chinese, and Mexican workers makes one wonder whether white workers needed an out-group—whatever its racial or ethnic characteristics—to use as a rallying cry against the unfairness of employers. And one wonders whether factory owners also needed an out-group—to keep wages down and provide a supply of strikebreakers. Another possibility is that white workers disparaged nonwhite workers as a way of developing a contrasting, positive identity for themselves as, at the very least, respectable workers who would not stoop to low-wage labor. In this vein, the historian Alexander Saxton titled his book on Chinese immigrant workers *The Indispensable Enemy*.[55]

Labor unions also excluded women, not because they were outsiders but because men (and also many women) saw married women's proper place as in the home. They advocated for higher wages for male workers that would benefit the entire family and reduce the responsibilities of wives to a manageable level. But the campaign for the family wage was also a way of reinforcing the masculine achievement of being the sole provider for one's family. Moreover, it kept male authority and privilege in the home intact. Instead of urging equal pay for working women, unions endorsed "protective" legislation that restricted the hours women could work and outlawed night work or heavy lifting, on the theory that long, physically demanding work was dangerous to women's health and might damage their reproductive capacities. Thus, unions excluded most blacks and women, institutionalizing white male privilege in the workplace and in the home. The family wage movement incorporated both the class-based subsistence imperative and the gender-based masculinity imperative of the white working class.

Could the labor movement have made other choices? Yes, of course—at least in theory. The leaders of the nascent labor movement that grew after the Civil War could have incorporated black male workers into their coalition without disturbing their ideas about gender and the proper relations between men and women—that is to say, without weakening their ideal of masculine accomplishment. If incorporating black men on moral grounds was too difficult, unions could have included them on Gompers's pragmatic grounds. All they needed to do was define black men as equals in the workplace, as men who could achieve the norms of masculinity just as easily as they could, and as brothers facing a common antagonist in the capitalist factory owner. Instead, labor leaders viewed black workers as inferior, as incapable of achieving true masculinity, and as competition for jobs. They also may have received some psychological gain from excluding a group to which they could favorably compare their own tenuous class position. The historian David Roediger has advanced the controversial thesis that white workers projected onto blacks the preindustrial characteristics that they still valued but needed to reject in order to be disciplined industrial workers—contact with nature, a seamless work life and family life, a lack of self-control, and so forth. Blacks, he argues, became the displaced home for the anxieties of white workers. In any case, white workers and their leaders could not get beyond the racist sentiments that were embedded in American culture at the time. Instead, they created a white panethnicity that encompassed European immigrants but excluded African Americans, Chinese, and Mexicans, and they tried to restrict industrial work to those who had achieved whiteness.[56]

Unions could have incorporated women too. Here the issues were different than those raised by the possibility of incorporating black men. Although we can assume that no black workers shared the view of white workers that blacks should be disadvantaged in the labor market, many women did share the view that married women should withdraw from the out-of-home workforce. It was a view that remained popular through the midtwentieth century. Given women's low wages, advocating for a male family wage may have been the best short-term strategy for maxi-

mizing family income. Middle-class reformers liked the family wage because it promised to reduce the working-class family instability caused by
low wages. In fact, most interest groups liked it at the time. But the family
wage reinforced the idea that women should be paid less than men because their labor was less essential to family well-being. The labor historian Martha May writes:

> The family wage retained its power because it promised so much to so
> many: to reformers, order; to employers, profitability; to unionized male
> workers, access and job control; to the unskilled, the hope of better condi-
> tions. The ideology reinforced class-specific goals while providing social
> stability. The one group which obviously did not benefit from the family
> wage was working women. Not only were their wages reduced—or termi-
> nated—by the family wage ideal; there was also pressure from the definition
> of their work as unfeminine, selfish and detrimental to the social good.

The redefinition of married women's work as detrimental to family and
society, May argues, would prove to be as much of a problem for women
in the rest of the twentieth century as the low wages and job restrictions
that the family wage implied.[57]

What unions did was to use the culturally available models of class,
race, and gender of the era. This is not to excuse what they did, but rather
to explain it. In advocating for the family wage, unions advanced male
workers' economic interests, but they also were responding to the growing support for this idea, which had spread from the middle class to the
working class through the separate spheres ideology. Unions did not create the panethnicity of whiteness and the exclusion of blacks, but they
contributed to this movement. The social history of the nation—and of the
working-class family—would have been different had union leaders
fought hard to incorporate African Americans and women. Yet it would
have taken a huge leap into the future for the labor movement to have
done so. As it was, labor's advocacy of a family wage arguably increased
the well-being of many working-class families.[58]

The nineteenth-century developments we have reviewed—the subsistence imperative, the masculinity imperative, the altered sense of time, the
rise of schooling, the male-breadwinner ideal, the formation of a white
panethnicity and the exclusion of blacks, and the stance of labor unions—
set the stage for working-class family life after 1900. The twentieth century
began with three decades of income growth and relative prosperity and
then lurched into the Great Depression and World War II. These two seis-

mic events greatly affected working-class family life, as it careened in roller-coaster fashion through the 1920s, 1930, and 1940s before reaching its zenith in the 1950s. At midcentury, some commentators thought that a stable, long-lasting pattern of family life had been attained. But the 1950s proved to be merely the highest point on the roller coaster, which continued with a downward rush soon thereafter. It is to the first part of the twentieth-century story—the Progressive Era, the tumultuous Depression and war years, and the arrival at the top of the roller coaster—that we now turn.

Chapter 3 | Good Times and Hard Times: 1900–1945

Henry Brady, who was seventeen years old when he was interviewed during the winter of 1935–1936 by the sociologist Mirra Komarovsky, was the only person in his family who had a job. He earned $12 per week. His father, who had been a railroad engineer prior to the Great Depression, had been on relief for three years. His older brother didn't have a job, nor did his mother and two younger siblings. Once, according to his older brother, Henry was about to go out to see his girlfriend when his father said, "Why don't you stay at home—it costs too much to go out so often." Henry replied, "It's none of your business how much money I spend. It's mine. You keep your nose out of it." His father said nothing.

Henry told the interviewer: "I'm my own boss now. Nobody can tell me what to do or how to spend my money. Working makes you feel independent. I remind them who makes the money. They don't say much. They just take it, that's all. *I'm* not the one on relief. I can't help feeling that way." Henry added: "He's not the same father, that's all. You can't help not looking up to him like we used to. None of us is afraid of him like we used to be. That's natural, isn't it?"[1]

It may or may not be natural, but losing the respect of one's teenage children was a common occurrence among unemployed fathers in the 1930s. The Great Depression was a cataclysmic event in the United States in its depth and duration—far more severe than the serious recession of the late 2000s, which is commonly known, in reference to its larger, older cousin, as the "Great Recession." In fact, the two downturns are hardly comparable. During the Great Recession of the 2000s, the unemployment rate rose to 9.3 percent in 2009, peaked at 9.6 percent in 2010, and then declined gradually. That was enough to cause widespread financial hardship. Imagine, then, the consequences of unemployment during the Depression, which peaked at 23 percent in 1932 (and if we exclude farm labor, a much larger category in the 1930s than today, 32 percent) and then remained above 10 percent for nine years. Except for wars, it remains the greatest disruption the nation has ever seen.[2]

The Depression ended a period of substantial wage growth for American workers. The annual earnings of full-time manufacturing employees, for instance, rose by 56 percent between 1900 and 1928. Earnings also rose 57 percent for transportation workers, 43 percent for construction workers, and 55 percent for communications and public utilities workers. Meanwhile, the total fertility rate—the average number of children a woman could expect to bear during her lifetime if age-specific fertility rates were to remain unchanged—declined among whites (from 3.6 children in 1900 to 2.5 in 1930) and among blacks (from 5.6 children in 1900 to 3.0 in 1930), which meant that families had more income per child. We can think of the improving labor market of the 1900–1928 period followed by the Depression as prefiguring a cycle that would occur after World War II: working-class progress in the 1950s and 1960s would be followed by a decline—not because of a depression but because of the outsourcing and automation of industrial labor. To be sure, the era from 1900 through the Depression and into World War II is an important part of the story of the working-class family in its own right, but studying it can also reveal the factors in the post–World War II cycle that were unique to that later era and the factors, in contrast, that are likely to have an impact on families whenever there is a cycle of boom and bust.[3]

THE FAMILY WAGE

Although the movement for a family wage continued in the early twentieth century, only the most skilled and unionized workers achieved it. As in the late nineteenth century, both class and gender politics were involved. A spokesman for the American Federation of Labor said in 1919:

> The workers are tired of having them, their wives, and their children used as chips for our commercial, financial, and industrial gamblers. . . . What is the price we pay for children free from factory life, for mothers burdened by no duties outside the home, for fathers who have leisure for home and families? . . . The living wage is the right to be a man and to exercise freely and fully the rights of a free man.

One can see the subsistence imperative in the spokesman's complaint that working-class families were being exploited by irresponsible capitalists. However, one can also see the masculinity imperative in his belief that the battle for the living wage was about "the right to be a man." And what was that right all about? In part it was the right to be the head of the family; without doubt the family wage reinforced husbands' authority. It was also about the right to maintain the self-respect that came with achieving the goal of being a good provider.[4]

The most famous realization of the family wage occurred in 1914, when Henry Ford instituted a profit-sharing plan that virtually doubled the wages of most of his automobile assembly workers to $5 per day. Ford said that he wanted to create a larger middle class that could afford to buy his cars. There is no doubt that he also wanted to reduce the attrition in his workforce as the monotonous assembly line was being introduced. Keeping workers on the job longer would reduce his training costs and make the line run more efficiently. In addition, he wanted to keep the unions out of his plants, a goal that he attained for a time. But in order to receive the higher wage, employees had to meet Ford's idea of what a good family man's life should entail. He created an office with thirty to fifty investigators called, of all things, the Sociological Department (who says that sociology has no practical applications?) to determine whether each worker was qualified for the profit-sharing plan.[5]

To get the $5 wage, an employee had to fall into one of three categories: "All married men living with and taking good care of their families"; all single men over age twenty-two of "proven thrifty habits"; or men under age twenty-two and women "who are the sole support of some next of kin or blood relative." Other than those who were the sole source of support for someone, women were not eligible for the $5 wage. When he was asked in an interview in 1916 why women were not included, Ford replied: "There is no injustice there. . . . Women receive the same wages as unskilled male labor. But we believe here that a woman should be married and keep a home. . . . The normal business of women is keeping homes and raising children." Soon after that interview, Ford expanded the program to include women without dependents. But the number of women who were hired remained small. The company did not hire married women unless their husbands were unable to work, and it had a rule against hiring any woman whose husband worked in the factory. According to Ford's autobiography, as late as 1919 eighty-two women workers were fired when it was discovered that their husbands were also working at the factories.[6]

The investigators in the Sociological Department determined whether men were truly married by examining legal documents, insurance policies that mentioned both the husband and wife as beneficiaries, and baptismal records of children. (Ford's criteria apparently set off a minor boom in fraudulent marriages.) But a man needed not only to be married but also to be a good provider. One of Ford's closest advisers, Rev. Samuel Marquis, who was also an administrator of the Sociological Department, stated:

> We insist that a man shall provide generously in proportion to his means for his wife and children. Should he fail to do this, we may turn his profits over to his wife, until he learns to do the square thing. We impress upon a man's mind the fact that the one condition on which we will share profits with him is that he in turn will share them with his family.

Moreover, wives were not even allowed to earn money at home by taking in boarders, as they had commonly done for decades. According to Marquis: "Mr. Ford's idea is that a home in which there are roomers or boarders can never be a real home. We therefore insist that the wife of a profit-sharer be free to give her entire time to the home. Roomers and boarders must go or profits are withheld. Wives seldom object to this ruling." Full-time domesticity on the part of the wife was required; anything less would run afoul of the investigators. Moreover, the company believed in home-ownership. "We encourage better housing," said Marquis. "We take families bodily, if need be, and move them into better neighborhoods."[7]

No employer other than Ford had the messianic zeal to impose a vision of family life this strict and the resources to employ a platoon of crackerjack sociologists to enforce it. Yet Ford's preference for the family wage and the male-breadwinner family did not differ from the preferences of many of his workers. What was unique about his profit-sharing plan was the stunning steadfastness with which he enforced the emerging norms of the male-breadwinner family: All men and women should marry. Husbands should work outside the home. Their earnings should be sufficient to support their families, and they should devote most of what they earn to that obligation. Wives should not work outside the home, and furthermore, in a change from the past, they should not even earn money *inside* the home. They should be completely focused on home and children. If possible, married couples should buy their own homes.

These were the aspirations that many working-class and middle-class couples sought to fulfill during much of the century. They were also the norms that, after midcentury, many women reacted against.

FROM HOUSEWIVES TO HOMEMAKERS

Ford's insistence that wives stop taking in boarders reflected a nascent change in the concept of the male-breadwinner family. Throughout much of the nineteenth century, working-class wives had made financial contributions to the family pot through work done at home. The good provider did not want his wife to work outside the home, but his self-respect and the respect he saw in the eyes of other men remained intact if his stay-at-home wife contributed income solely through activities within the home. That way there was no public display of wives earning money. In nineteenth-century England, writes the historian Sonya Rose, a man did not need his wife to be devoted to full-time domesticity in order to feel that he had fulfilled his manly duties as the wage-earner; rather, he just needed her to refrain from working outside the home. In the United States, economic activities such as taking in boarders remained common in the late nineteenth and early twentieth centuries. A man was not threatened by having boarders in his home, nor by having his wife and children assembling hats or shoes from materials provided by a middleman. Families were living so close to the edge of subsistence that they needed more than one earner. It was also acceptable, even expected, for older unmarried children to work outside the home and contribute their earnings to the family budget.[8]

The common term for this type of home-oriented but economically productive married woman was "housewife." It is an old word; Shakespeare uses it eleven times in his plays. "Pray be not sick," says a disguised lord in *Cymbeline*, "for you must be our housewife." "Well or ill," replies a daughter of the king, "I am bound to you." The meaning of being a housewife changed over time as the industrial, urban population grew in Britain and then soon after in the United States. But at all times prior to the twentieth century, the working-class housewife was likely to be engaged in some type of income-producing labor. Middle-class families, in contrast, could sometimes afford to have their wives withdraw completely from income-producing labor. A woman in such a family was able to meet the ideal of the perfect wife who did not earn income at all—the logical endpoint of the separate spheres ideology. She might manage the household tasks, but the work was often done by servants, who were much more common than in the twentieth century. (In many major cities in the 1880 census, more than fifteen domestic servants were counted per one hundred families.) She devoted herself full-time to domesticity: raising children, managing the home, and providing emotional support and companionship to her husband. It was the highest form of the middle-class style of family life that had first emerged among native-born Protestants in the early 1800s.[9]

The idea of a wife who was solely involved with domestic activities was beyond the reach of most working-class families. Nevertheless, it was an influential model. And about 1890 a new word appeared in the English language that had the connotation of a wife who was fully immersed in domestic activities and who earned no income either outside or inside the home: "homemaker." We can see the emergence of the term "homemaker" with the aid of a massive data set of published words. In 2004 Google began a project to scan every word of millions of books, including more than 5 million published from 1810 to the late 2000s—about 4 percent of the books ever published. The resulting database can be searched for words or short phrases by year of publication. Figure 3.1 shows the frequency of the words "homemaker" and "housewife" per million words in books pub-

Figure 3.1   Number of Times the Words "Homemaker" and "Housewife" Appear per 1 Million Words in Books Published in the United States, by Decade, 1810–1819 to 2000–2007

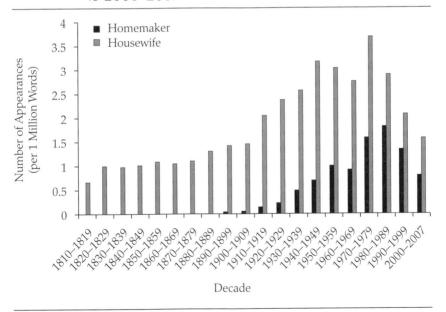

Source: Davies (2011) and Michel et al. (2011).

lished from the decade of the 1810s to the decade of the 2000s. For example, a phrase whose bar has a height of 1.0 appeared once per every 1 million words in books published in that decade. That rate of occurrence may seem pretty low, but there are lots of books and lots of words; what matters is the changing height of the bars over time. The figure shows noticeable and modestly increasing usage of the word "housewife" throughout the 1800s, but only a handful of instances of the word "homemaker" in books published in the United States prior to 1890—usage so low it registers as zero. After 1900, usage of both "homemaker" and "housewife" rose to a peak in the 1970s and 1980s and then declined. A similar graph of word usage in books published in Britain would show the same pattern at all times, but with a lower level of usage of "homemaker" than in the United States.[10]

The term "homemaker," then, is largely a twentieth-century Americanism. It has the further connotation of a vocation or profession, distinct from the mere laboring of the "housewife." That distinction is evident in one of the first uses of the term in a monthly magazine that debuted in October 1888, *The Home-Maker*, edited by Marion Harland. The first issue instructs the reader: "Home-making and house-keeping are not synonyms. It is possible to keep a house not wisely, but too well. If one must go to either extreme, let it be in making the home too comfortable." The work of the homemaker, the article makes clear, transcends the standard focus on upkeep and maintenance of the "ultra-particular" housekeeper. Rather, the homemaker operates on a higher level: creating a loving, comforting environment that exposes the family to art, music, and literature. In an 1899 issue of the weekly publication *The Outlook*, edited by Lyman Abbott, an influential Congregational minister and social reform advocate, an unsigned article entitled "The Home Club" comments on the homemaker:

> One is tempted to assert that such a homemaker's executive ability must be that of a railroad president, her financiering ability that of a banker, her diplomacy equal to that of a Minister to a foreign court; for the elements to be harmonized range from kitchen to nursery, with many outside interests that affect the home more or less closely. Perfect homemaking runs from plumbing to literature.

The reader is further told that perfect homemaking requires artistic taste, the ability to guide the reading of the household, and above all: "When all this has been attained, the highest is yet to be reached—the ability to love without reserve . . . to live each day with a dominating purpose to secure the happiness of each family member; and to do this, not as the servant, but as the queen." There is no mention of earning money in this lengthy description of the homemaker's responsibilities, and the reader gets the distinct impression that paid work of any sort would be beneath the dignity of the perfect homemaker.[11]

The historian John Gillis explained this linguistic transformation: "*Homemaking* came to mean something very different from *housekeeping*. A housekeeper could be hired; a homemaker could not." That is to say, a housewife is a just a worker, albeit one who specializes in work that is done at home, whereas a homemaker is also the moral center of one's family. Her work is symbolic, not just substantive, and it is conducted without money changing hands. Calls to professionalize this endeavor as an occupation through girls' education in "home economics" began at this time. The General Federation of Women's Clubs declared in its 1906 proceedings: "The vocation of homemaking will be infinitely ennobled in the eyes of our young people as soon as the great colleges place it on an equality with other vocations and offer special preparation for it."[12]

The existence of a homemaker, of course, presupposes a home, not just a house. The term "homemaker," in fact, reflects the emergence in nineteenth-century culture of the home as a symbol of the unity of the family—and of the wife as the heart of the home. A house is functional: it's a place where you live. A home is not only functional but also spiritual: it's a place where you belong. Houses are held together by wood and bricks; homes are held together by emotional bonds and shared values. The popularity of the new terms "homemaker" and "homemaking" increased as the idea spread that turning one's house into a home was a desirable goal. "Home had become a sacramental site," writes Gillis about changes during the nineteenth century, "complete with redemptive qualities previously associated with holy places." According to Gillis, "home has become perhaps the most powerful source of identity in the modern era." Henry Ford agreed, and he urged his workers to buy one.[13]

Why did the term "homemaker" emerge at the start of the twentieth century and not, say, in the midnineteenth century? I would argue that its appearance reflected the increasing standard of living that allowed more families to withdraw wives from all income-producing tasks. The economist Nancy Folbre has examined statistics on women's productive activities in Massachusetts, where the records are unusually detailed, from 1875 to 1920. She concludes that fewer and fewer wives were earning money in the home over this period. It became less common, for instance, for women and children to do piecework. In addition, although it remained common to allow nonrelatives to live in one's home for a fee, the nature of the arrangement shifted. The percentage of boarders who were not just sleeping in one's home but also eating their meals and having their clothes washed there decreased over time. Correspondingly, the percentage of boarders who were renting a room and eating elsewhere increased. Having a lodger in one's apartment required much less labor for the wife than did having full-service boarders.[14]

The rise of boarders eating elsewhere, as opposed to full boarding with meals, reflected the growth of inexpensive restaurants and cafeterias—which in turn reflected the rising incomes in the urban, industrial United States during this period. Joseph Horn and Frank Hardart opened the first automat in Philadelphia in 1902. It was a self-service restaurant in which the customer took a tray, exchanged paper money for nickels, and perused a multitude of small glass windows with food offerings behind them. The customer then made a choice, inserted a coin in a slot next to the appropriate window, opened it, and took the food. Workers behind the windows restocked them. This new way of buying meals seemed amazingly high-tech to the public, as well as affordable, and the automats became wildly popular: Horn and Hardart opened their first New York City automat on Forty-Second Street in 1912, and by the 1930s there were forty of them. They became icons of modern city living—even tourist attractions. I remember eating in one as a child while visiting New York with my parents in the 1950s. The automat and similar low-end restaurants provided food independence: no longer did you need to pay your landlady to cook your meals—and no longer did she have as many meals to cook. In the latter half of the century, unfortunately, the automats suffered from competition with fast-food restaurants; the last one closed in New York in 1991.[15]

In the early twentieth century, some of the better-off members of the working class were able to remove their wives completely from activities that earned money, at least until the Depression hit, so that they could approximate the homemaker ideal. Although the need for wives to earn money was receding, homemakers still had plenty of work to do in the home. The first electric refrigerators were not introduced until the 1920s, and only affluent families could afford them. Until then, iceboxes, and the almost daily shopping required to fill them, were the rule. The first electric washing machines were introduced in the 1930s, but were too expensive for families hit by the Depression. Being a completely domestic homemaker could easily be a full-time job. In fact, a writer in an 1889 issue of *The Home-Maker* lamented the passing of the loyal Irish maids "who only left to be married." Given the fast pace of late-nineteenth-century life and the need "to keep up with one's neighbors in social attainments, including dress and fashion, or on the higher plane of intellectual and cultural achievement," this obviously middle-class homemaker concluded that, "if ever capable, reliable service were needed, it is now."[16]

Most working-class families could afford neither to hire servants nor to completely forgo the wife's earnings in the early twentieth century. Nor were the roles of most working-class wives more spiritual than practical. Only high-wage workers could support families that met the lofty criteria of the perfect homemaker, completely immersed in domesticity. Moreover, in working-class families, most older teenagers still worked outside the home, as did Henry Brady, rather than graduating from high school, and they still gave most of their earnings to their parents. Not until the 1950s did wages rise high enough to allow families in which the wife earned no money inside or outside the home and teenagers earned no money beyond what they spent on themselves to become common among the working class. But the origins of the values that the working-class families aspired to in the 1950s lay in the homemaker ideal that emerged after 1890 among the middle class. That ideal evolved, in turn, from the nineteenth-century ideology of separate spheres.

PROTECTING MOTHERS AND CHILDREN

The division of labor in the family was also influenced by state laws enacted through the efforts of reformers during what came to be known as the Progressive Era, roughly 1890 to 1920. By the end of the period, forty-one states had enacted "protective" legislation that limited the number of hours that women could work, and many had restricted women's work at night or in unsafe conditions. In contrast, the courts struck down most laws that would have restricted men's work hours and working conditions. Other Progressive Era laws limited the amount of work that children could do and the age at which they could start to work. In hindsight, the limitations put on women's labor by protective legislation seem regressive rather than progressive: they hindered women's movement into the labor force and undermined women's quest for equality with men. Most of the legal inequalities between female and male workers would be lifted later in the century. But at the time, protective legislation seemed to be a social advance, and many of the leading intellectuals and activists of the day worked hard to promote it. Louis Brandeis, a leading progressive lawyer who would later be appointed to the Supreme Court, submitted a brief to the Court in 1908 urging that it uphold an Oregon law that limited women's work in factories, mechanical establishments, and laundries to ten hours per day. It was the first Supreme Court brief to rely on sociological and economic evidence and the testimony of experts rather than legal theory. In *Muller v. Oregon,* the Court upheld the state law.[17]

Protective legislation added legal support for the male-breadwinner family in two ways. First, and most directly, it limited the freedom of women to work outside the home. It constrained their earnings, which is likely to have reduced their authority and independence in the home, and reduced the competition for jobs that men faced in the labor market. A second, more subtle effect was to affirm a view of women as fragile beings whose reproductive capacities needed to be protected above all other interests. Brandeis wrote in his brief:

> Long hours of labor are dangerous for women primarily because of their special physical organization. In structure and function women are differentiated from men. Besides these anatomical and physiological differences, physicians are agreed that women are fundamentally weaker than men in all that makes for endurance: in muscular strength, in nervous energy, in the powers of persistent attention and application. Overwork, therefore, which strains endurance to the utmost, is more disastrous to the health of women than of men, and entails upon them more lasting injury.

The "anatomical and physiological differences" refer to women's reproductive organs. Brandeis quotes a British physician on the topic of working hours: "For women over twenty, nine and one-half hours is a reasonable time so long as they remain unmarried." Once they marry, however, they are at risk of becoming pregnant, and their working hours must be shortened to protect their reproductive organs. If husbands could not protect their wives by earning enough to allow them to remain at home, according to this line of reasoning, the state would now step in to ensure it.[18]

The women workers who were to be protected by these laws were sometimes called "mothers of the race," because their reproductive capacities were needed to produce the next generation. In 1900 a Pennsylvania judge wrote, in upholding a law restricting women's work hours, "Surely an act which prevents the mothers of our race from being tempted to endanger their life and health by exhaustive employment can be condemned by none save those who expect to profit by it." Precisely which race one was referring to was usually left unspecified. But it is clear from the actions of the reformers and the decisions of the courts that black women were not considered to be mothers of the race. The protective laws excluded most black women because they did not cover domestic servants and agricultural laborers, the two occupational categories in which the great majority of black workers were found. Indeed, throughout the decades leading up to World War II, African Americans were excluded from receiving the benefits of social welfare legislation. For instance, the law that created the social security program, the Social Security Act of 1935, originally excluded most agricultural and domestic workers from social security benefits. So did the Fair Labor Standards Act of 1938, which set the first national minimum wage. These limitations were compromises that Franklin D. Roosevelt felt he had to make in order to get the support of Southern representatives and senators, but they not only continued the exclusion of black workers from social benefits but also served to keep the black family outside of the framework of the male-breadwinner ideal.[19]

Between 1879 and 1909, the number of states with laws that established a minimum age at which children were allowed to work increased from seven to forty-four, and the age increased first to twelve and later to fourteen. By 1930 it was no longer the case that boys from working-class families were commonly taken out of school at age twelve or so and sent into the work world or that girls were taken out and assigned tasks at home. Instead, nearly all were remaining in school until age fourteen and a large and increasing share were remaining in school until age sixteen. The Fair Labor Standards Act also forbade the employment of children under fourteen and further banned the employment of fourteen- and fifteen-year-olds in certain industries, such as mining and manufacturing. There were various exceptions, including children working for their parents, working in retail trade, or working in agriculture when they were not required to attend school. But the act confirmed and codified several decades of change in children's labor.[20]

Support for the passage of these laws reflected the spread of new ideas about childhood; without the popularity of these ideas, it isn't clear that the laws would have been passed or that parents would have obeyed them. According to the sociologist Viviana Zelizer, a major shift occurred between the 1870s and the 1930s in how parents viewed children: early on, children were considered to be economically useful little laborers, but by the end of the period they were seen as economically useless dependents who were nevertheless suddenly *priceless*. They were priceless in two senses: First, by the 1930s they were without a price because they were no longer economic assets and, indeed, were moving out of the realm of waged work. Parents were no longer thinking of children under fourteen (and, increasingly, under sixteen) as sources of income. Second, they were priceless in the sense of being so treasured and cherished emotionally that no price could be put upon their great sentimental value. The parenting practices of the Utica middle class suggest that this transformation began before 1875, but it may have picked up steam at that point.[21]

Zelizer provided an example of the transformation. In 1896 the parents of a two-year-old child who had been killed by a train sued the railroad company. They requested damages not because of their emotional loss, mind you, but rather because the two-year-old had been economically useful, "going upon errands to neighbors . . . watching and amusing . . . younger child." The judge ruled, however, that the child was too young to have an earning capacity, and "hence the defendant could not be held liable in damages." The entire case was about what *price* to assign to the child's labor value. According to the judge, that price was zero; therefore, no damages could be collected. The family received no compensation for the death of their child. In contrast, when in 1979 a three-year-old child died from a lethal dose of fluoride at a city dental clinic, the court awarded the family $750,000. There was no mention of the boy's labor value; rather, the issue was how to compensate his parents for the emotional loss of this priceless child. The child's emotional value to his parents was immensely higher than what he could have contributed to the family income.[22]

These emotionally priceless children were remaining in school because parents began to see them as fragile beings who needed extended nurturing and support in order to become successful adults. In 1904 the psychologist G. Stanley Hall wrote a book about a new life stage that supported this view. He titled it *Adolescence.* Hall proposed that the teenage years are a time when young people need to develop their personalities and capabilities without interference from the world of work. In the past, childhood ended early and led straight to adulthood. Yet there is an intermediate stage of life, Hall argued, in which young people are neither children nor adults. It is a plastic and fragile period, he warned, in which the new powers that adolescents feel can be molded in positive or negative directions. Hall believed that adolescence is a biological stage rather than a cultural construct. Yet even a cursory examination of the history of childhood shows it to be absent prior to the nineteenth century and uncommon until the twentieth—an odd property for a biological given.[23]

In fact, it is likely that the concept of adolescence would not have flowered without the rising wages of the early 1900s, which allowed more parents to forgo income from their teenagers. Something similar to adolescence—but without the use of the term—was observed decades earlier, in the 1800s, in the lives of teenagers in well-off families headed by merchants or managers. Hall's book appeared at a time when the standard of living was high enough among a large group of middle-class parents that they no longer needed to have their teenage children work. Moreover, it was becoming clearer to parents that changes in the economy required that children receive advanced education in order to obtain the best jobs. The institution that would both insulate teenagers from the world of work and provide the advanced training was the high school. In 1900, 6 percent of seventeen-year-olds had graduated from high school; that rose to 16 percent in 1920 and 29 percent in 1930. By 1930, the secondary school enrollment rate of teenagers—the percentage of students between the ages of fourteen and seventeen who were enrolled in secondary school whether or not they subsequently graduated—was about 60 percent in New England and the North Central states, and 31 to 38 percent in the South. In fact, one high school opened each day, on average, between 1900 and 1930. Thus, by 1930 high school enrollment had become so widespread that, at least in the East, a majority of teenagers attended.[24]

As more teenagers attended high school, their role in the family changed from being a source of income to being an expense: it cost money to buy the clothes and supplies that they needed for school and to feed them. But parents received little money in return; unlike previous generations of children, the new sheltered children did not work and had no pay packets to turn over to their parents at the end of the week. A tidal shift had occurred in the economic relationship between parents and children. In the terms of the demographer John Caldwell, the direction of the intergenerational wealth flow changed. In the past, wealth had flowed up the generations from children to parents because the net economic benefits to parents exceeded the costs of child-rearing, but now, for an increasing number of families, wealth flowed down the generations as the costs of children exceeded the economic benefits. Caldwell developed his theory to explain the drop in birth rates that occurred in the latter half of the twentieth century in most of the less developed countries. Yet his theory might also have held earlier in the United States as fertility continued to fall during the late nineteenth and early twentieth centuries. "You just can't have so many children if you want to do for them," a woman in Muncie, Indiana, told the sociologists Robert Lynd and Helen Merrell Lynd in the mid-1920s. "We never thought of going to college. Our children never thought of anything else."[25]

CHILD-REARING VALUES

The Lynds began their in-depth study of Muncie—which they selected because it seemed to represent the typical American city—in 1924 and published the results in 1929 as *Middletown: A Study in Modern American Culture.* They divided the Muncie populace into a "business class," whose occupations involved working primarily with "*people* in the selling or promotion of things, services, or ideas," and a "working class," whose occupations involved working primarily with "*things,* utilizing material tools in the making of things and the performance of services." About 70 percent of the population, the Lynds claimed, belonged to the working class. This was, they argued, the fundamental dividing line:

While an effort will be made to make clear at certain points variant behavior between these two groups, it is after all this division into working class and business class that constitutes the outstanding cleavage in Middletown. The mere fact of being born upon one or other side of the watershed roughly formed by these two groups is the most significant single cultural factor tending to influence what one does all day long throughout one's life.[26]

One example of this cleavage, they submitted, was the difference in values about child-rearing between business-class and working-class parents. The Lynds presented mothers with a list of fifteen habits to be observed in the training of children and asked them to select the three most important ones. Mothers from the working class valued most highly "loyalty to the church" (selected by 56 percent) and "strict obedience" (46 percent). Business-class mothers also valued strict obedience (selected by 43 percent), but were much more likely to highly value "independence" than were working-class mothers (46 percent compared to 17 percent) and "frankness" (43 percent compared to 21 percent). In contrast, working-class mothers were much more likely to emphasize "good manners" (35 percent compared to 19 percent). The Lynds claimed that child-rearing preferences among both groups of parents had moved away from an emphasis on obedience and toward an emphasis on independence. One business-class mother told the Lynds:

> I am afraid that the things I really *have* emphasized are obedience, loyalty to the church, and getting good grades in school; those are the easiest to dwell on and the things one naturally emphasizes through force of habit. But what I really believe in is the slower but surer part of training that stresses concentration, independence, and tolerance.

A working-class wife offered this observation: "Obedience may be all right for younger children, but, now, take my boy in high school, if we tried to jerk him up like we used to be he'd just leave home."[27]

Child-rearing values were in flux, according to the Lynds. Not only were both classes moving toward independence, but "many parents are becoming puzzled and unsure as to what they would hold their children to if they could." Still, a sharp contrast existed: working-class parents were less likely to favor independence and relatively more likely to emphasize conforming to authority (obedience, good manners) than were middle-class parents, even if both were trending in the same direction. It was as if both classes were moving in parallel away from the pole of obedience while still preserving the relatively greater reliance on it among the working class. This differential resembles the contrast between middle-class and working-class parenting practices that emerged in the 1830s when the middle class first began to grow. The largely Protestant, native-born families of clerks and merchants raised their children to have a more self-reliant, independent personality. Thus, the distinctive class differences in child-rearing values that the Lynds discovered in the 1920s were about one hundred years old and dated to the emergence of the middle and working classes during the early days of industrialization.[28]

Yet the relatively high value on obedience among working-class parents reflected more than just the survival of preindustrial patterns of child-rearing: working-class children in the early twentieth century needed to learn to obey not only traditional sources of authority such as parents and priests but also a newer source—the factory supervisor. Indeed, changes in production processes made obedience more crucial than ever. During the early 1900s, the principles of "scientific management" were used to break down complex tasks into simpler, repetitive tasks that could be completed by a worker remaining in one place as an automobile or appliance rolled by as quickly as possible. "In the past, the man has been first," wrote the developer of scientific management, Frederick Winslow Taylor; "in the future the system must be first." Henry Ford introduced his first assembly line around the time that he started his $5 per day profit-sharing plan. The higher wage was one way to motivate workers to remain on the numbingly repetitive job. But workers had also been primed to follow their supervisors' orders by an upbringing that stressed obedience and conformity. Without it, fewer of them would have lasted on the line. In this way, the values that working-class parents passed on to their children helped to reproduce the next generation of industrial laborers.[29]

FROM AUTHORITY TO SENTIMENT

The changing social value of children was part of a larger, long-term transformation in family relations that favored love and companionship over authority relations—not only in how parents viewed children but also in how husbands and wives viewed each other. The prominent family sociologist Ernest Burgess, writing in 1945 with Harvey Locke, claimed that family relations were in transition from an old style in which families were held together by the authority of husbands and traditional norms to a new style in which bonds of companionship, sentiment, and love held families together. He called it a shift in the family from "institution to companionship." In the older style, family unity was achieved by "social pressure" of various sorts, such as laws, customs, and religion. Increasingly, however, family unity was achieved through the "mutual affection of husband and wife and parents and children." In the older style, the family was autocratic and patriarchal, with the husband as the unchallenged head, whereas the new family was more democratic and egalitarian. Within families, the importance of emotional satisfaction and personal happiness was increasing.[30]

Burgess located this change during the first half of the twentieth century, but it is clear from numerous historical works that the transition had been in progress since the American Revolution. The patriarchal authority of the colonial father had eroded throughout the nineteenth century in the emerging middle-class family. As one historian notes in a review, "Scores of studies have shown how colonial America's rigidly structured social relationships softened under democratic values that challenged older notions of heredity, status, and manhood." The result was "a widespread bourgeois embrace of affection and benevolence—rather than blunt coercion—as the proper approach" to authority relations. The sociologist Claude Fischer concludes in his broad cultural history that it is "highly likely" that more middle-class spouses expressed their love for each other as the nineteenth century progressed. This long, gradual change was the origin of the more democratic and egalitarian marriage that Burgess observed.[31]

Why, then, did Burgess believe that the change had occurred a half-century prior to 1945? Perhaps it was the shortsightedness of American sociology, a discipline that barely predated the century. The University of Chicago, where Burgess taught, founded the first sociology department in the nation in 1892. The Chicago sociologists of Burgess's era studied urban growth and development in their mushrooming city with little attention to how it was situated in history. Nevertheless, the rising prosperity of the first three decades of the century probably did accelerate the spread of the companionate model, in which husbands and wives were supposed to be each other's friends and companions and to derive pleasure from their relationships. The increased leisure of the middle class provided more time for companionship. Contraceptive usage increased, suggesting that sexual intimacy outside of the context of childbearing was becoming important to couples. Changes in family relations had indeed occurred during Burgess's life, but they had begun much earlier than he thought.[32]

In any case, Burgess was correct in noting that the companionate family was a largely middle-class phenomenon at the time. Drawing upon his celebrated concentric-zone theory of urban growth, Burgess theorized that the "semi-patriarchal" and "patricentric" (that is, institutional) family would be dominant in the immigrant neighborhoods and working-men's zones near the center of most cities, whereas the "equalitarian" family would be more common in the native-born, middle-class, apartment-house district farther from the center. Although boarding had declined substantially in working-class neighborhoods by 1940, a small minority of American households still had boarders, the presence of whom at the dinner table might cramp the companionate style. A Women's Bureau report estimated that about 75,000 families were still doing piecework in the 1930s. The Lynds found relationships to be tense in working-class families: "Among the working class leisure activities and other relations between married couples seem to swing about a shorter tether than do those of business folk. Not infrequently husbands and wives meet each other at the end of a day's work too tired or inert to play or go anywhere together."[33]

The job losses during the Great Depression must have caused further tensions in many families. It is likely that the full flowering of the companionate marriage among the working class did not occur until after World War II, if then.

THE UNEMPLOYED MAN AND HIS FAMILY

The rising wages of the early twentieth century came to a crashing end at the onset of the Great Depression in 1929. In 1931 Franklin D. Roosevelt, then the governor of New York, convinced the state legislature to enact the Temporary Emergency Relief Administration, which by the time it ended in 1937 had provided public assistance to about 40 percent of the state population. (It also became the model for the federal agency of the same name that Roosevelt established after he became president in 1933.) In late 1935, Mirra Komarovsky obtained from the agency the names of some of the families that were receiving relief in a "large industrial city just outside of New York City." She restricted her study to families headed by parents who were native-born Protestants with at least one child over ten years old. Furthermore, the fathers had to be skilled laborers or white-collar workers who had been unemployed for at least one year and who had been the sole earner in the family prior to becoming unemployed. She and her colleagues studied fifty-nine such families by conducting separate interviews with the father, the mother, and one child, usually the oldest. These were families that had been seriously affected by the Depression; they had been receiving relief for an average of more than three years. Prior to the Depression, the fathers held occupations such as carpenter, inventory clerk, traveling salesman, auto mechanic, painter, and truck driver.[34]

Overall, then, these were families that, prior to the Depression, had been relatively prosperous by working-class standards, at least compared to unskilled workers (eight of whom made it into the sample despite the author's desire to completely exclude them). Notably, the husbands' pre-Depression incomes were high and steady enough that their wives had done very little to earn income, even from activities within the home. In describing most of the families, Komarovsky made no mention of the wives bringing in money. There were no boarders except in the home of one family that began to take them in after the husband had become unemployed in 1930. The occupations in which women were clustered were relatively protected during the Depression compared to men's occupations because the service sector and light industry recovered faster than heavy industry, in which few women worked. Consequently, some wives had the opportunity to contribute income after their husbands lost their jobs. Still, few wives in Komarovsky's sample had looked for work. The exceptions proved the rule that wives' work violated social norms: one woman who was employed for a short time "showed great tact," we are told, "in making her husband's dependence on her as painless as possible. She let him pay the rent and disperse most of the money." None of these wives were taking in washing or doing piecework.[35]

Komarovsky's central question was this: What happens within the family when the sole provider can no longer provide? What happens to his relations with his wife and children, his authority, and his self-esteem? It was a question that seemed important given the number of husbands who had managed to be the family's only breadwinner in the early 1900s. Komarovsky was astute enough to realize that the loss of the family's earnings, although the main direct consequence of unemployment, was only one of the ways in which being out of work could affect a man and his family. She knew that, in addition, prolonged joblessness could affect a man's sense of himself and his authority within the family. Moreover, being deprived of his daily routine could make a man feel irritable, depressed, and out of sorts. (A daughter said of her father, "He used to be so good and kind, and now he is so mean and nasty.") In our terms, prolonged unemployment affected both the subsistence imperative and the masculinity imperative of a husband's role. As for subsistence, the father's unemployment put the ability to get enough to eat and to have adequate shelter in question. One family, the Johnsons, used to live in a "nice apartment with six rooms," but had moved three times and were now living at the end of a dark hallway in a four-room apartment where, during a New York winter, only the kitchen was heated.[36]

But in addition, a man's failure to provide for his family made him unable to pass a fundamental test of conventional masculinity. As the sociologist Jessie Bernard wrote in a 1981 essay: "To be a man one had to be not only a provider but a *good* provider. Success in the good-provider role came in time to define masculinity itself. The good provider had to achieve, to win, to succeed, to dominate. He was a bread*winner*." Yet this is just what men such as Henry Brady's father could no longer do. In describing his children's feelings toward him, Mr. Brady used the same terms as his son: "It's only natural. When a father cannot support his family, supply them with clothing and good food, the children are bound to lose respect. . . . When they see me hanging around the house all the time and know that I can't find work, it has its effects all right. I guess the children never expect to see me work again."[37]

Both father and son saw the husband's breadwinner role as the natural order of things, as if it were timeless and biologically given. Yet in preindustrial farm families, husbands and wives worked cooperatively to ensure the family's well-being. And if we were to fast-forward half a century from the 1930s, we would see that a majority of married-couple families now had two earners. Given some distance today from its reign, we can see that the good provider role—the successful breadwinner—was not as natural as it seemed to families during the Depression. Rather, it reflected a particular way of organizing family life in an industrial era: a division of labor with less overlap between the tasks of husband and wife than was the case before industrialization or, for that matter, after industrial jobs began to decline. It was a division that reflected the cultural ascension of the ideal of separate spheres. These large-scale cultural processes, however, were invisible to the Brady family; they were convinced that being the breadwinner was almost an inborn trait.[38]

In some of the families Komarovsky studied, the wives blamed their husbands for their unemployment and accused them of not looking hard enough for work. Some of the men refused to do housework even though they were sitting around the house most of the day—as if to demonstrate that they would not do women's work under any circumstances. Their sex lives often deteriorated: in twenty-two out of the thirty-eight families for which adequate information was collected, the frequency of sexual relations declined—including four families in which sex stopped altogether. In some cases, however, couples reduced sexual activity not because of emotional strain but in order to lower the chance that the wife would become pregnant. Without modern means of birth control such as the pill or the IUD, financially struggling couples did what they could to avoid having another mouth to feed. One parent said, "It is a crime for children to be born when the parents haven't got enough money to have them properly." In fact, the total fertility rate declined 13 percent for whites between 1930 and 1936.[39]

Not all families descended into negativity and recriminations. When the marriage had been stronger before the Depression, when husbands and wives had loving relationships prior to unemployment, and when relationships with children had been strong, families were better equipped to survive the hardships of the Depression. One wife said, "Why should I blame my husband for unemployment when I know that there isn't anything he wouldn't do for the family if he could only find work?" Another said, "Money isn't everything; when you get a husband who is as good to you as my husband is to me, you can certainly consider yourself lucky." This finding—that the negative effects of the Depression were weaker when the family's pre-Depression relations were stronger and more supportive—was also reported by other sociological studies done at the time. Economic crises do not necessarily split families apart; in well-functioning families, crises can draw them together.[40]

Moreover, the experience of contributing to the family's earnings can be positive. In the early 1970s, the sociologist Glen Elder studied detailed records on families living in Berkeley and Oakland, California, who had first been studied during the Depression. Elder found that older children in these families had often been called upon in the 1930s to take jobs in order to help out the family. They became important wage-earners, although not necessarily with Henry Brady's lip. Surprisingly, when they later reached adulthood, those who in adolescence had experienced hardship and gone to work were doing *no worse* in terms of income and occupation than were adolescents who had not experienced hardship. It was as if their participation in the family economy had made them more mature and responsible—personality characteristics that they later used to their advantage. What Elder called "the downward extension of adultlike experience" was the silver lining for them in the cloud of economic deprivation during their teenage years.[41]

Komarovsky found that the effects of the Depression on unemployed fathers' relations with their children depended on the children's ages. With young children, relationships remained much as they were before the Depression. It was among older children that the relationships sometimes deteriorated. Most teenagers left school soon after reaching the minimum age, and boys looked for work. During the Depression, teenage boys sometimes could find low-paying jobs such as messengers and stock clerks more easily than their fathers could find breadwinner-quality jobs. It was not uncommon for older sons to be working when their fathers were not. And in those situations, the status of the sons rose at the expense of their fathers' self-esteem. Komarovsky described another incident involving the Brady family: "The family was almost finished with dinner when Henry came in. Mr. Brady got up immediately and surrendered his place to him. There was no extra chair. Henry took the place at the table as a matter of fact without thanking his father for it."[42]

One might expect that the pervasive unemployment and economic hardship of the Depression would have made unemployed workers more receptive to critiques of capitalism. Indeed, strikes and labor unrest reached a peak in the mid-1930s that is still unmatched. Yet Norman Thomas, the Socialist Party candidate for president in 1932 and 1936, did not attract many votes. Most voters took to the Democratic Party rather than to the Socialists, electing Roosevelt in 1932 to replace Herbert Hoover and then reelecting him over Republican Alf Landon in a landslide in 1936. Among the men studied by Komarovsky, only about one-sixth showed any movement toward the left. Despite living through a massive failure of the American economy, some of the men blamed themselves for their predicament:

"I would like you to put it down in black and white," said Mr. Adams, "that I alone am to blame for my present state. The system is alright. It's me. I had plenty of opportunities to have a decent life among my own class of people. It was drink that ruined me."

Mr. Adams was critical of Roosevelt, whom he viewed as ruining the country by getting it into debt. Another man said, "Depression is just a handy phrase in the mouths of a lot of people who like to lay back and make the world give them a living." After one man denounced capitalism, the interviewer asked him who he would vote for in the next election. He replied:

It may seem funny to you after what I have said, but I'll vote Republican. You see, the Republicans are the moneyed people. They have got all the money, but now they hide it away. I think that if we put them back they will start the factories going. We will at least have a steady job.

Others found scapegoats among immigrants and African Americans. An interviewer reported on one man's comments: "'Just look at the streetcars in the morning,' said one of them. 'They are filled with Italians and colored people. The Italians, Irish, and colored people somehow get the preference.'" Immigrants and blacks, this man believed, weren't just competing for jobs but were actually getting preference over whites. Another man had heard a radio broadcast praising relief. The interviewer noted his angry reaction:

"Why, the colored people down south have more food than they ever had." He went on to say, "That certainly made me boil. Where do I come in to be compared with those colored people? They have always lived like animals. It may be good for them, but they can't class me with the colored."

This was his attempt to convince the interviewer (and himself) that although he was receiving relief, he was a better class of person than "the colored people" who were also receiving relief.[43]

WORLD WAR II

The production of weapons and other wartime supplies to aid the Allies began to pull the U.S. economy out of the Depression in 1939 and 1940, even though the United States did not formally enter World War II until the Pearl Harbor attack in December 1941. At first, as heavy industry and related sectors transitioned to war production, most of the new jobs went to men. But after 1941 the massive draft of young men into the armed services created opportunities for women to move into jobs that they had been effectively barred from entering before the war. The cultural climate suddenly changed from disapproving of women's work in industry to encouraging it in the service of the war effort, and the number of employed women increased 60 percent between 1940 and 1945.[44]

Women's contributions to the war effort were romanticized in wartime culture. In the best-known example, a popular song, followed by a Norman Rockwell cover for the *Saturday Evening Post*, made "Rosie the Riveter" the iconic image of the unexpected entry of women into jobs no one could have imagined them holding prior to the war. Among housewives who entered the workforce after the war started, the majority were concentrated in the manufacturing sector that produced the Rosies and other operatives. But just 26 percent of the women who were working during the war had been housewives prior to Pearl Harbor, according to a U.S. Women's Bureau survey conducted in ten war production areas in 1944 and 1945. The image of the middle-class housewife suddenly wielding a welding torch only fit a minority of wartime women workers. Another 18 percent were married women who had been employed before the war started. It's likely that most of them were from less prosperous working-class families. The rest were single, divorced, or widowed, and over half of them had also been working before the war. No doubt many of them were from less prosperous families too. Overall, the response to the wartime opportunities probably involved at least as many women from working-class backgrounds as from middle-class backgrounds, if not more. Many of the working-class women were able to increase their earnings and learn new skills. Women liked their new jobs; three-fourths of them told the interviewers that they planned to keep working after the war, and the ones who had been working before the war—who were probably needier—were more likely to say that they wanted to keep working after the war. In contrast, only 20 percent of the former housewives said that they planned to keep working.[45]

In fact, few women workers kept their wartime jobs. After the war ended, employers, with the backing of public opinion, laid off their female manufacturing workers and hired back the returning soldiers. Women factory workers had been seen during the war as exceptions during an extraordinary time to the rule that women should not do physical labor. The rule was reinstated in 1946. Still, the wartime influx of women may have had some persistent effects. Married women over age forty-five, for instance, remained in the labor market after the war ended to a greater extent than younger women did. These older married women were less likely to have had young children in their homes. Since older children were viewed as less in need of continual nurturing by their mothers, public opinion was less hostile to mothers seeking employment after all of their children were in school. In the 1950s, even as the homemaker became culturally celebrated, married women without preschool-age children moved into the labor force in increasing numbers. Black women also gained from their experiences during the war. They had long been working for pay, but their opportunities were mainly limited to domestic service. By 1945, the percentage of black women in factory, clerical, and professional jobs had increased, and they were able to hold on to their entry into these occupations. Between 1940 and 1950, the percentage of employed black women between the ages of eighteen and forty-nine who were private household workers declined from 58 percent to 49 percent—the start of a sharp decline that continued over the next few decades.[46]

FORESHADOWING THE POSTWAR RISE AND FALL?

In a sense, the rising standard of living of American families in the first few decades of the twentieth century, followed by the family hardships of the Great Depression, foreshadowed the boom and bust that would occur in the second half of the century: the post–World War II prosperity allowed many working-class families to achieve the middle-class style of life they aspired to, and then technological change and the offshoring of production eroded those gains and threw the working-class family into crisis. In the early years of the century, we can see developments that presaged the postwar period. First, rising wages after 1900 led more married couples to withdraw wives not only from out-of-home employment but also from earning money through activities in the home. Among the middle class and the most prosperous layer of the working class, the ideology of the "homemaker" devoted entirely to domesticity spread. Children were kept in school longer as the idea took hold that adolescence is a stage when children need to be protected. They became net financial drains on their parents and yet were valued emotionally all the more. Young adults married earlier: the median age at marriage dropped from 25.9 in 1900 to 24.3 in 1930 for men and from 21.9 to 21.3 for women. Relationships between husbands and wives continued to evolve toward an emphasis on love and companionship. Even though most working-class families did not have the financial stability to support a homemaker or to privilege emotional relations over daily practicalities, they seemed to aspire to the newer style of family life.[47]

Then came the Depression and the devastation of working-class men's earning power. Men lost self-esteem as they failed to meet the male-breadwinner standard. When their job searches became futile, they moped around the house, depressed and irritable. They lost moral standing in the eyes of their wives and children. "When a father cannot support his family," said Mr. Brady, ". . . the children are bound to lose respect." Despite the disintegration of the labor market, men tended to blame themselves for being out of work: "I alone am to blame for my present state. The system is alright. It's me." Or they blamed immigrants and blacks for taking away their jobs: "The Italians, Irish, and colored people somehow get the preference." We see variations on these themes later in the century. But let me also note some family changes that were *not* seen during the Depression. There is no evidence of a rise in cohabitation—living together outside of marriage—among young adults who felt they did not have the economic foundation to support a marriage. Rather, they remained in their parents' homes or boarded in someone else's home. And although statistics are sparse, there is little evidence of a rise in childbearing outside of marriage. The strong norm stating that marriage was the only permissible setting for sexual relationships and childbearing prevented these potential responses. Later in the century, when the industrial decline occurred, the cultural climate would be different. Alternatives to marriage would be much more acceptable, and the responses of young adults to economic uncertainty would encompass sexual relations and childbearing in settings that would have shocked the 1930s working class.

Eventually, the family hardships of the Great Depression were reversed by the increased demand for labor during World War II. Whether the remnants of the working class in the early twenty-first century can reverse recent trends and establish a viable style of family life remains to be seen. Let us hope it does not take a war.

THE FIRST CENTURY AND A HALF: 1800–1945

During the first century and a half of industrialization in the United States, roughly 1800 to 1945, clear differences in family life emerged between the working-class family and the middle-class family, and then, toward the end of the period, those differences began to narrow. Although family lives were altered up and down the social class ladder, in some ways the larger break with the past occurred among the emerging middle class. It was the middle-class family, not the working-class family, that first developed new ways of thinking about the roles of wives and children. These included the doctrine of separate spheres in the 1800s, which enshrined the home as the sentimental haven from wage labor, and the concept of the homemaker in the early 1900s, which glorified the woman who presided over the household as a sort of socioemotional manager who earned no money inside or outside the home. Middle-class women's roles became imbued with a moral significance that at first had no counterpart in the working-class family, in which wives were still running households without many modern conveniences, raising large families, and taking in boarders or washing or piecework. Middle-class women were elevated to a spiritual position that was seen as above the fray of making a living. Until the midtwentieth century, most working-class wives could not afford to be—nor necessarily wanted to be—above the financial fray. Still, these new ideas became powerful cultural symbols to which the working class aspired.[48]

The middle class also was the first to provide a long, sheltered period of development for children to replace the shorter path to adulthood that had been common in the past. In the early industrializing cities, children's earnings were crucial for working-class families, sometimes making the difference between having enough income for food and going hungry. Working-class parents, particularly those who had emigrated from rural areas of Europe, resisted sending their children to school for an extended period, preferring instead to send sons out to work at ages ten or twelve and to task their daughters with helping their mothers. The working-class child-rearing style emphasized obedience to authority. This style was not simply a link to the preindustrial past but also a functional way of preparing children for the industrial labor force. But a different conception of childhood arose among middle-class families, who were preparing their sons for white-collar occupations and their daughters to marry such men. In the nineteenth century, they began to withdraw their children from labor, creating a protected time that could be used for more schooling, and moved away from emphasizing harsh discipline and toward instilling in their children a sense of self-control.

Consequently, the newly discovered life stage of adolescence was, at the time of the publication of Hall's book in 1904, largely a middle-class phenomenon. In contrast, childhood ended earlier for working-class children and led straight to productive young adulthood. In fact, class differences in family patterns were probably greater toward the end of the nineteenth century than at any other time in the first 150 years. By the end of the century, the well-to-do, white-collar, urban middle class had been firmly established, but the conditions of working-class life remained difficult. Wages in the late nineteenth century were polarizing, as the earnings of white-collar workers pulled away from the earnings of workers in the middle and bottom of the labor market. In manufacturing, jobs for craftsmen disappeared as the workforce divided into managers and laborers. These developments created high and rising economic inequality between the middle class and the working class. The favorable economic conditions at the top allowed middle-class husbands to be the sole earners and enabled their children to remain at home and in school until the late teens or early twenties.[49]

But after the turn of the twentieth century, as income inequality lessened, class differences in the daily lives of working-class and middle-class families narrowed. Mandatory age-at-leaving-school laws required working-class parents to keep their children in school longer, and the rising wages of working-class husbands made the withdrawal of children from the labor force less of a hardship. Class differences in the percentage of children ages ten to fifteen who were employed diminished over the first few decades of the twentieth century; the new laws and rising family incomes virtually eliminated paid work by children under sixteen. As a result, over time, childhood and adolescence became more similar in nature in middle- and working-class families. And as rising wages also led more working-class wives to forgo earning money at home, they were drawn closer to the homemaker ideal and to the lives of middle-class wives. Fewer working-class households took in boarders after 1910, and class differences in boarding were eliminated by 1940. By 1945, therefore, the differences in family patterns across classes were not as sharp as they had been a half-century earlier. The working class was about to enter an era when it would come closer to the middle-class family ideal than at anytime before—or, it would much later turn out, anytime afterward.[50]

Racial differences narrowed somewhat too after 1900 as African Americans migrated from the rural South to Northern cities. Urban black families subsisted by pooling the wages of fathers and the earnings of mothers from domestic service or laundering. Eddie Bartee moved from West Virginia to Baltimore in 1918 to take a job at the Sparrows Point steelworks, then owned by Bethlehem Steel. Bartee fed pieces of steel into a machine all day long and died at age fifty of chronic asthma. His son told the *Baltimore Sun*, "Through all the tough times in the mills, all the dirty work, he never said how hard it was." Like most other black workers, he lived in a segregated area in Bethlehem's company town. His employment situation and his treatment by whites left much to be desired. But his wages lifted the family out of poverty. Relative to other opportunities open to blacks, Sparrows Point was good enough that his son and a grandson later worked at the mill. Still discriminated against, still paid less than whites, and hired for some of the least desirable jobs, black husbands and their families nevertheless began to enter the industrial working class.[51]

Yet the dividing line between laborers who were defined as black and laborers who were defined as white was a major cleavage in the labor market throughout the 150-year period. Who was classified in each category shifted somewhat over time as immigrants such as the Irish came to be seen as white, but throughout the period the descendants of slaves were set apart, restricted in the occupations they could enter, and sometimes excluded altogether. To the descendants of the early European settlers and of more recent European immigrants, the boundaries of the workforce—who could be members of industrial labor unions, for instance—were defined by race. (And also by gender: union leaders alternately considered women to be fragile beings in need of protection or competitors for jobs.) Workers from the broad panethnic category of "white" were included; blacks were either ignored or not welcomed. During these times, white industrial workers, exploited as they were by employers that demanded long hours and paid modest wages, compared themselves favorably to blacks. By doing so, they gained a whiteness premium that Du Bois described as a "public and psychological wage." It served the interest of factory owners to maintain this premium (which they did by not hiring blacks or by paying them less than whites) in order to keep actual wages down.[52]

Moreover, the gender ideology that supported the male-breadwinner family was advanced largely by whites. There was little sense that the idea of separate spheres applied to black families. Federal and state legislation to protect supposedly vulnerable female workers did not apply to most black women. This pattern of omission, combined with black women's history of work under slavery and in the sharecropping system—and perhaps also with cultural survivals from West African social organization—discouraged the male-breadwinner model in black families. The lack of statutory protection for black families also encouraged the sharing of scarce resources among a larger network of kin in order to reduce the risks of poverty. Black men's industrial employment began to rise after 1900, as Eddie Bartee's story illustrates, and then increased substantially after World War II. Then, in the 1970s, just as black men had finally begun to share in the financial benefits of stable factory employment in large numbers, the manufacturing sector of the economy entered a great decline.

Meanwhile, white working-class men and women in the first half of the twentieth century seemed to aspire to the middle-class family ideal even when they could not achieve it. One might wonder why they did. The male-breadwinner family was not "traditional" because it did not follow the preindustrial family pattern that united the husband and wife in joint production. Moreover, there were alternatives to the male-breadwinner model: husbands and wives could have both worked outside the home, even if wives withdrew temporarily from paid work while young children were present. That was, in fact, the model that many married couples would begin to follow in the 1960s and 1970s. Labor unions could have accepted women as members and fought to raise their wages to the level of men's. Husbands, in turn, could have done more child care—as, in fact, husbands in dual-worker married couples employed on different shifts in the late twentieth century would do—instead of acting like Alice Lacosse's father, who refused to watch his children from 6:00 PM to 9:00 PM while his wife worked in Amoskeag mills because "that was women's work."

Taking a cue from Alice's father, one could conclude that men in the industrial era seized upon being the only wage-earners as the key to achieving conventional manhood. Symbolically, the physical labor of the factory worker mimicked the hard work in the fields of the farming father. It was a way of continuing the man's role of being the main provider of food and shelter, of meeting the masculinity imperative. In addition, their near-monopoly of wage work gave men the means to maintain authority over their wives and children. In a money economy, the person who controlled most of the money had the power to enforce his wishes, and that power was widely accepted by wives and children. Restricting wage work to men therefore maintained the dominance of the husband in the household. Yet relying mainly on the husband's wages was a perilous strategy for industrial workers because layoffs, injury, or illness could disrupt the husband's authority and sense of self.

As the century progressed beyond 1945 this strategy would also fail to address the contradiction of restricting wives to the home even though labor-saving appliances were becoming affordable, fertility was undergoing a long-term decline, and demand for labor was shifting toward occupations that employed a high proportion of women. For a time, this contradiction was counterbalanced by the prosperity of the immediate post–World War II years and the baby boom that it spawned. But it would resurface in the 1970s and beyond.

Chapter 4 | The Peak Years, 1945–1975

IN THE LATE 2000s, the sociologist Timothy Nelson, who was writing a book on fatherhood in poor neighborhoods, began to interview low-income men who had children not currently living with them. In the course of the interviews, he asked them to talk about the characteristics of the ideal father. He had this conversation with Will, a twenty-four-year-old white man:

NELSON: Ideally what kind of dad would you like to be? If you could be a picture perfect dad, what kind of dad would you want to be?

WILL: Like Ward Cleaver.

NELSON: Like Ward Cleaver huh?

WILL: Yeah.

NELSON: Why is he so good?

WILL: Because. He is like the ideal dad. He was always smiling, always happy, never had a worry in the world, his kids were always happy and always cheerful, they had everything in the world. That's an ideal dad.

Nelson's interview with Nicholas, a twenty-six-year-old Latino with two children, included this exchange:

NELSON: How about your friends? When did they first become dads?

NICHOLAS: Young, eighteen maybe.

NELSON: Eighteen, nineteen. Were they married?

NICHOLAS: No.

NELSON: How about the associates [girlfriends] you have? Were they all young?

NICHOLAS: Pretty much yeah. Urban life makes you young and promiscuous I guess.

NELSON: Really?

NICHOLAS: Yeah.

NELSON: What do you think marriage should be like ideally?

NICHOLAS: Ward and June Cleaver.

NELSON: Ward and June Cleaver huh? And do you know marriages like that?

NICHOLAS: No.

Talk of the ideal mother occasionally elicited similar sentiments, such as this from Michael, a forty-one-year-old African American man with two children:

NELSON: So your own mother was the ideal mother you think?

MICHAEL: Yeah.

NELSON: Did no wrong?

MICHAEL: You seen *Leave It to Beaver*?

NELSON: I caught the re-runs.

MICHAEL: Like that.

NELSON: Wow. That's great. So she was there for you all.

MICHAEL: All the time.

NELSON: For each of you all.

MICHAEL: Yep.

In all, eight of the men Nelson interviewed spontaneously referred to the *Leave It to Beaver* television situation comedy. Its last new episode had aired in 1963, almost a half-century before the interviews were conducted and before any of the men were born. Since then, cable television channels have periodically rerun it.[1]

It's one thing to be nostalgic for a past that you have experienced—your teenage years, for example—but it's quite another to be nostalgic for a time before you were alive. Social psychologists who study consumer behavior are familiar with what they call "historical nostalgia": a longing for an idealized time that occurred before one's own lifetime. It reflects a desire, in the words of one researcher, "to retreat from contemporary life to a distant past viewed as superior to the present." Those engaging in historical nostalgia seek role models whose behavior they can aspire to. This description seems to fit the unexpected nostalgia that Nelson found for the idealized family life depicted in a 1950s and early-1960s television series. *Leave It to Beaver* portrayed a middle-class marriage in which the wife earned no money through work inside or outside the home. She was, to use the twentieth-century term, the homemaker. Why were these men nostalgic for the breadwinner-homemaker family, or at least its depiction on television, as opposed to the family of another era? What is it about Ward Cleaver as a father or June as a mother that these men long for but do not think they can attain?[2]

A large part of the answer lies in how effortlessly Ward fulfills his role as a good provider and a steady presence in his children's lives. What Ward does for a living doesn't matter—in fact, little is said about his job as an accountant or, in the series *Father Knows Best*, about Jim Anderson's occupation as an insurance agent. But both Ward and Jim certainly receive a steady paycheck, and their standing as the sole providers gives them respect in the eyes of their wives and children. That's an accomplishment that many of Nelson's subjects wished they could match but doubted their ability to do so. As another one of Nelson's subjects said ruefully of *Leave It to Beaver*, "But we don't live in that perfect little fantasy world."

Yet this longing for the 1950s family represents *male* nostalgia. In the hundreds of interviews that Nelson's collaborator Kathryn Edin has done with low-income women about family life, no one has ever mentioned *Leave It to Beaver*. While some men would like to play Ward's role, no women, apparently, want to be cast as June. The central contradiction of the kind of family that *Beaver* and *Father* represent is this: although the role of the father as the sole provider and head of the family seems fulfilling and even ennobling to many men, women are deeply ambivalent about the role of the stay-at-home, fully domestic mom. They admire the loving way in which the idealized 1950s mother cared for her children, but they reject the restriction of that mother to the household, the denial of her ability to pursue a career, and the presumption that her husband ruled the home. Some men today, especially those who find it difficult to live up to their image of what a father should be, may want to return to the 1950s as depicted on TV, but very few women do. The 1950s family was much celebrated during its reign; to some observers, it seemed like the highest form of family life, the perfect fit with a modern industrial society. But there were undercurrents that gradually eroded its standing, so that today, in retrospect, it is the outlier rather than the standard for family patterns over the past century.[3]

In addition, when we look back at the 1950s, we find an unprecedented—and since unmatched—period of American economic history. During World War II, the United States had ramped up industrial production to produce war matériel. After the war, the nation stood on the winning side with its industrial infrastructure intact. Unlike other victorious countries such as Britain and France, and certainly unlike defeated countries such as Germany, its manufacturing base had not been damaged by combat or aerial bombardment. Although its citizens' loss of life was tragic, the United States suffered a lower level of war-related deaths relative to its population size than did Britain, France, Germany, Japan, Russia, or China. As a result, the United States emerged as the dominant military and industrial power in the world. The era after the war became known as the Pax Americana—the American-enforced peace—owing to the nation's military might, its commanding role in shaping postwar international accords, and its assistance in the rebuilding of Europe through the Marshall Plan. Its place in the world economy was just as commanding: in 1948 factories in the United States accounted for 45 percent of the world industrial output, and in 1950 the nation's manufacturing exports constituted one-third of the world total.[4]

The dominant position of the United States in the world economy allowed industries to increase wages and benefits while still increasing profits. When the United Auto Workers (UAW) union bargained with the management of the automobile companies, it won contracts that included cost-of-living increases, annual wage increases, and benefits such as pensions and health insurance. At the same time, the unions conceded to management the right to make key production and investment decisions. Their 1950 agreement, which *Fortune* magazine called "the Treaty of Detroit," influenced collective bargaining in other mass-production industries. Walter Reuther, the head of the UAW, called it "the most significant development in labor relations since the mass production industries were organized." Productivity—the value of goods and services produced per hour of labor—rose owing to improved production processes, which further increased the size of the pie to be divided between labor and capital. The result was a period of wage and profit growth, employment stability, and declining labor unrest. The median level of wages and benefits earned by high school graduates increased from $24,145 in 1950 to $46,994 in 1973 (in dollars corrected for inflation). Income inequality among workers with different levels of education, which had declined from 1910 to 1950, remained low.[5]

During this postwar peak, African Americans shared in the nation's prosperity more than ever before. Black women, in particular, made dramatic strides in the labor market. The percentage of employed black women ages eighteen to forty-nine who were private household workers, which had decreased from 58 percent in 1940 to 39 percent in 1950, dropped to 13 percent in 1970. In contrast, the percentage in clerical occupations, such as secretaries or bookkeepers, rose from 1 percent in 1940 to 23 percent in 1970. The percentage of black women who were filling professional occupations such as nurses, teachers, and social workers increased from 5 percent to 11 percent from 1940 to 1970. Black men also made progress, though less so than black women. The percentage of employed black men ages eighteen to forty-nine who were working in the manufacturing sector rose from 15 percent in 1940 to 29 percent in 1970—virtually the same percentage as for white men in 1970. Blacks were finally able to move into clerical work, skilled manual work, and even some of the professions in substantial numbers. I spoke with an African American woman who grew up during the latter part of this era and whose father worked at the Sparrows Point steelworks. Her father earned a steady income, and her mother stayed home. She lived in a black working-class neighborhood in which there were many fathers who kept out what she called "the undesirables." Now, she told me, if she went back to the old neighborhood, she would find an area devastated by drugs and crime.[6]

THE DEMOGRAPHICS

This unprecedented economic climate, combined with a family-centered culture, brought forth family patterns that the nation had not seen before and may never see again. At the start of the twentieth century, the average man married at age 26 and the average woman at 22, an age gap of four years. These ages were typical of American marriages at least as far back as 1850. By 1950, ages at marriage had declined markedly: the median was 22.8 for men and 20.3 for women. Nearly half of all women married by the end of their teenage years or soon thereafter, a stunningly high number by comparison to the way young people lead their lives today. A woman who ended her education when she graduated from high school, as many did, was likely to get married quickly, often to her high school sweetheart. Women who went to college joked about getting an "MRS" degree by the time they graduated. A psychiatrist who contributed frequently to magazines wrote in 1955, "A girl who hasn't a man in sight by the time she is 20 is not altogether wrong in fearing that she may never get married." What is more, the percentage of people who ever married for those whose prime marrying years were in the 1950s rose to about 94 percent for men and 96 percent for women. Virtually everyone married, and they married young. Moreover, once married, they had children quickly and often. The length of time between marriage and a first birth shortened, as did the time between all subsequent births. Living together without marrying, which is common among young couples with children today, was unthinkable in most strata of society. Single-parenthood was similarly stigmatized except perhaps among the poor.[7]

The total fertility rate had been declining for a century or more prior to the 1950s. By 1940, it stood at 2.3 children per woman of childbearing age. Then, unexpectedly, it rose above 3.0 during the 1950s and early 1960s—the famous baby boom—before resuming its long-term decline. The period from just after the war to the early 1960s was the only period of sustained rising fertility in the nation's history. Why did young couples have so many children? One reason lay in the unique life histories of the generation who were in their twenties and thirties. They experienced the Great Depression as children or adolescents and then a world war erupted as they reached young adulthood. After enduring these two cataclysmic events, the "greatest generation," as they are sometimes called, was pleased in peacetime to turn inward toward home and family. Historical accounts of the era emphasize the importance placed by the Depression/war cohort on security and stability—characteristics that had been in short supply in their lives to date. Family life was the domain in which they found that security. Raising children provided a sense of purpose to adults who had seen how fragile the social world could be.[8]

A cultural climate favorable to family life helped to reinforce this worldview. For instance, *McCall's* magazine popularized the word "togetherness" in May 1954 to represent this "new and warmer way of life," which was to be experienced "not as women *alone* or men *alone,* isolated from one another, but as a *family* sharing a common experience." All manner of media extolled the virtues of marriage and childbearing. Moreover, conditions were favorable for family formation and fertility: unemployment rates were low, wages were rising, and the government had enacted the GI Bill, which offered low-interest home mortgage loans to veterans so that they could buy single-family homes. In addition, young adults in the 1950s had a demographic advantage: there weren't all that many of them. Because birth rates had dropped during the Great Depression, the size of the cohort born in the 1930s was relatively small; consequently, the number of people in their twenties in the 1950s was modest. Employers in the rapidly expanding American economy were forced to offer higher wages in order to attract new workers because they were in short supply.[9]

But just how common was the iconic *Leave It to Beaver*–like family during the postwar peak? The demographer Donald Hernandez analyzed

Census Bureau data to determine the percentage of children who were born into families in which (1) the parents were married; (2) all children in the family had been born within marriage; (3) the husband worked full-time, all year; and (4) the wife did not work outside the home. His answer: for whites, 48 percent in 1950 and 47 percent in 1960. So about half of white children began their lives in the idealized breadwinner-homemaker family. As their childhoods progressed some of them saw their mothers take jobs outside the home—especially after they and their siblings started school—and others experienced their parents' divorce or a father's unemployment. Hernandez estimates that for white children born in 1950, only about 26 percent lived in the idealized family throughout their childhood until age seventeen. Among African American children, the figures are much lower: 21 percent of black children were born into the idealized family in 1950, and 18 percent in 1960. Fewer than 10 percent lived in such a family throughout their childhood.[10]

Beyond doubt, these estimates show that it's an exaggeration to assert that most children lived in breadwinner-homemaker families in the 1950s. But they also suggest that it's inaccurate to conclude, as some writers have, that the breadwinner-homemaker family was a myth. Among middle-class whites, it's likely that a majority of children started out in the idealized family and that many of them continued to live in such a family at least until they started school. Among working-class whites, the percentages were probably lower but still substantial. The idealized family was a common setting for white children, even though many mothers took paying jobs at some point, some marriages ended in divorce, and some fathers were inadequate providers. Among black children, however, the idealized family was far less common. It is fair to conclude that it never took hold, as an ideology or a reality, as strongly as it did among whites.[11]

In addition, there were signs of changes in sexual activity and childbearing that would accelerate after the postwar peak. A rise in sexual activity among unmarried young adults appears to have gotten under way in the 1940s or 1950s, leading to a modest but noticeable increase among whites in so-called shotgun marriages. If a young man impregnated a young woman, he and she faced strong pressure to marry. If they did not, the young man would lose face and the young woman might be spirited off to a "home" for unwed pregnant girls to quietly have her baby, who would then be put up for adoption. There was also a modest rise in the number of women who were unmarried at birth. Among white women who were in their prime childbearing years in the 1950s, about 6 percent had shotgun marriages and another 4 percent were unmarried at the time of their first birth. Those figures increased to 11 percent who had shotgun marriages and 6 percent who were unmarried at first birth among comparable white women in the 1960s. Although the percentage of white mothers who were unmarried at their first birth was still small in the 1960s compared to recent figures (29 percent for whites in 2010), one can see the start of the sexual revolution—or as the demographers who produced these statistics put it, the start of what may have been a longer, slower sexual evolution. For African Americans, the trends were the same, but the figures were substantially higher. Among black women who were in their prime childbearing years in the 1950s, 11 percent had shotgun marriages and 26 percent were unmarried at the time of their first births. In fact, the number of unmarried-mother families has been higher among blacks than whites going back to 1910—and possibly further—and the differences have been too large to be just a result of higher death rates among blacks.[12]

Still, there had never been an era in which marriage was as dominant in adult life among whites, and there has not been one since. Even among African Americans, a majority of women in the 1950s were married at the time they had their first child. In the 1950s, more so than in any other decade, marriage was the mandatory first step into adulthood for whites, and it was commonly the first step among blacks. It was what one did prior to investing in one's career or getting an advanced degree or having children—and for many women and some men, it was what you did before you had sex. In 1957 a national sample of Americans was asked what they would think of a person if all they knew about him was that he was not married. Several options were presented, and about one-third of the respondents chose "mentally ill." There was no other acceptable way to live a conventional adult life. If you wanted to have children, if you required the respect of your community, or if you wanted to think of yourself as having a successful life, marriage was unavoidable. We know anecdotally that many men and women who, had they been born a generation or two later, would have come out as gay or lesbian instead entered heterosexual marriages. Their only other choice was lifelong singlehood—being a "bachelor" or a "spinster"—and the intense scrutiny that status drew.

GROWING UP IN THE 1950S

Social scientists often study aspects of social life they have personally experienced. However hard they may try to be objective, their own life histories may influence their conclusions. It's useful, then, for social scientists to disclose their own backgrounds, when relevant, so that the reader can make a fully informed judgment about the findings presented by the author. In that spirit, let me offer my experiences in the 1950s and early 1960s.

I was born in Connecticut in 1948, so I grew up during that period. My parents both came from large immigrant families that one could best characterize as working-class. My paternal grandfather was a house painter at a time when painters mixed their own lead-based paints. He died of lead poisoning in the 1920s, which forced my father to drop out of high school to help support his mother and brothers. My mother was one of ten brothers and sisters in a family that owned a grocery store and some residential property. She was a smart woman who never had the chance to attend college. Both of my parents worked during the Depression, contributing their wages to the family pot. During World War II, my father was granted permission to remain at home to support his mother while three brothers served in the army. After the war ended, my parents married, as did many of their friends and relatives; the national marriage rate spiked upward in the late 1940s.

In a story similar to that of many working-class married couples at the time, my parents managed to move up to what might be called the lower-middle class. My father found a steady job as a wholesale salesman for a regional beer company. My mother stayed home before I was old enough to attend school; she had health problems that prevented her from having more children, which made me an only child, a 1950s oddity. Once I entered elementary school, she took a part-time job as a secretary two days per week. They purchased a modest house in the suburbs when I was ten. Like the typical 1950s husband, my father read the newspaper when he came home in the early evening while my mother cooked dinner. He did, however, help wash the dishes, which was seen as a substantial contribution to the housework. My mother hung the wash out to dry on a clothesline in the backyard. We had a black-and-white television set. (Only one relative had enough money to buy one of the new color models.) We had two cars, purchased at a discount from an automobile dealership where my father's brother was the service manager and a friend was a salesman. With air travel still expensive and uncommon, we took driving vacations, such as an excursion to see Niagara Falls. I won a scholarship to attend college; without that money, I'm not sure how my parents would have paid for it.

I think my father was happy with his life. He was proud of his family and his accomplishments, modest as they now may seem. His job was not fulfilling (he didn't even drink), but he didn't expect it to be. It provided a reliable paycheck, health insurance, a few weeks of paid vacation, and the promise of a retirement pension. What more could you expect? I don't think, however, that my mother was happy, although she probably didn't realize it at first. In 1963 Betty Friedan would write a book about "the problem that had no name," the vague feeling of many 1950s wives that something was missing in their lives. That was the problem my mother had: her intelligence and organizational ability were underutilized. For her asthma, her allergist prescribed a medicine called paregoric, which was a mild opiate. I think it functioned as a primitive antidepressant. She felt constrained by my father's modest income, but the norms of the 1950s made it difficult for her to contribute much to it while she had a child at home. After I left for college, she began to work full-time and eventually became the administrator for a department at a dental school. When I married, my mother saw the opportunities that were open to a woman of my wife's generation, and I sensed that she now realized what she had missed. Had she been born a generation later, she probably would have been a manager or a lawyer.[13]

Nevertheless, I had a happy childhood and entered young adulthood in good shape, if a bit neurotic. And here, reader, you must decide whether my experiences have affected my analysis of the 1950s, for I will conclude that it was a good time to be a child, even if it was not the best time to be a mother. To be sure, I have not based this conclusion primarily on my own experiences. There are aspects of the era that could be expected to benefit children. For instance, we know that children in the 1950s were more likely to live with two parents than in any other decade in the twentieth and early twenty-first centuries, for two reasons: First, adult death rates had declined so much from nineteenth-century levels that fewer children experienced the death of a parent. Second, the divorce rate, which had been rising steadily since the Civil War, was unusually stable. Put lower death rates and stable divorce rates together and you get greater marital stability, and a stable home life is good for children, as many studies suggest. My parents remained married and healthy enough to celebrate their fiftieth wedding anniversary, as did many of their friends and acquaintances. Few in later generations will be as fortunate. Childhood scourges such as poliomyelitis were eradicated. In addition, high school graduation rates continued their long-term rise, and college attendance was growing rapidly as well: the percentage of eighteen- to twenty-four-year-olds attending institutions of higher learning rose from 14 percent in 1950 to 36 percent in 1970.[14]

Moreover, many mothers who were ambivalent or unhappy in their marriages appear to have still functioned well as parents. That's the impression one gets from detailed written comments by one hundred white middle-class mothers in New England who were first contacted in the late 1930s and then recontacted through the mid-1950s. One woman, for instance, was surely frustrated by her husband, who, she wrote, "has at times little control over his temper." He also had an inferiority complex: "I often keep problems to myself if I think he will 'blow his top' or 'feel inferior.'" Yet she added, "The kids and I are far happier with our lot" than was her husband. And she rated her marriage as "decidedly more happy than the average" because it brought her these benefits: "a home, companionship, children and, if they are happy and well-adjusted—able to care for themselves and their families—complete satisfaction. The children keep us so busy now, we have little time for much else." Elaine Tyler May, the historian who studied the records of these families, concluded:

> Women had to make different kinds of choices than did men. They gave up careers in medicine and the fine arts and activities they enjoyed, such as music and sports. In almost every case, they complained about the burdens of their household tasks, particularly their husbands' lack of help with the children. They also complained of their husbands' selfishness, demands on them, and need to be the boss. Yet in all these cases, the wives not only put up with these problems but claimed to be satisfied with their marriages. Why? What did they gain? Here women's responses were even more concrete than their husbands'. For these women, life was "economically comfortable and secure"; marriage provided "complete peace," a "stable, comfortable life," "status," and "stability, children, a nice home," which made them the "envy" of many of their friends.[15]

I would not minimize the sacrifices that these 1950s wives and mothers made, nor would I condone their husbands' lack of involvement in child care and housework. I do not endorse their husbands' need to be in charge and to have the household revolve around them. Moreover, I do not believe that these wives were as satisfied with their marriages as they claimed. To admit to being unhappy in one's marriage was threatening to one's sense of self given the dominance of marriage as an institution and the difficulties of divorce. Nor am I advocating for a return to the 1950s family. I merely claim that most of these mothers, like most mothers today, cared for their children well and provided secure, loving home environments. For some, pouring time and energy into child-rearing was a way to compensate for less-than-happy marriages. Granted, if very serious problems were present, such as spousal abuse, child abuse, or alcoholism, the mother's ability to parent effectively would have been impaired and her children might have been better served by a divorce. Yet what we know of 1950s families suggests that these seriously impaired families were a minority. Many more marriages functioned adequately from day to day owing to the forbearance of the wife. All things considered, children received good upbringings in these families and experienced stable, two-parent environments while growing up.

WORKING-CLASS FAMILIES

We know less about working-class families in the 1950s than we do about middle-class families because the former were less likely to be studied at the time and were less likely to have left a written record. But a few good studies were conducted. What researchers found was not always upbeat or reassuring. Mirra Komarovsky, as she had done during the Great Depression, interviewed families in depth. Of the fifty-eight native-born, Protestant married couples she interviewed in the late 1950s for her book *Blue-Collar Marriage,* she judged one-third to be unhappy. Wives expressed far more discontent than did their husbands. Their problems often reflected the difficulty of adjusting to new expectations for marriage. Wives accepted their role as full-time housewives but were frustrated by it, as modern conveniences left them with less to do. Isolated during the day, some expressed to Komarovsky a wish to get a job, if only to get out of the house. In these respects, they were similar to middle-class housewives. But in addition, some were frustrated by their husbands' modest incomes and wanted to contribute their own earnings.[16]

Moreover, many of the wives preferred a new style of marital communication that emphasized friendship and companionship and included mutual disclosures of thoughts and feelings. This emerging companionate style, however, didn't fit well with the existing male style: working-class men did not talk much about their feelings to anyone and limited most of their conversations to other men. In an Italian working-class neighborhood, according to another book, all the men would sit together in the living room at family gatherings and all the women would gather in the kitchen. Communication between the groups about such matters as when dinner should be served had the flavor of international negotiations, with emissaries shuttling back and forth. A study of autoworkers described after-work male camaraderie that involved drinks, pool, and much ribbing of anyone who was too beholden to his wife's needs to attend regularly. Yet suddenly, a new emotionally close style of marriage arose that challenged the older, patriarchal style that men found comfortable but that seemed unsatisfying and increasingly out of date to women.[17]

Even among the middle class, the companionate marriage may have remained more of an ideal than a reality for many couples as they negotiated relationships that fell short of what wives may have wanted. But at least the middle class had some experience with the ideal. Since 1900 or possibly earlier, the rising affluence of the middle class had created space (literally, as families stopped accepting boarders) for wives and husbands to work toward an intimate, companionate style. The 1950s, however, was the first time that prosperity had spread so broadly that many working-class couples could contemplate the newer, companionate style. Komarovsky found that the more-educated working-class couples—wives and husbands who had graduated from high school—had established companionate relationships more readily than the less-educated. Still, one-third of the couples she studied were not friends in a sharing, mutually disclosing sense.[18]

An even grimmer portrait of the working-class family was painted by the sociologist and psychoanalyst Lillian Rubin in her book, originally published in 1976, *Worlds of Pain: Life in the Working-Class Family*. The title says it all, but in case the reader misses the point, the front cover is graced by a blurb from a prominent historian stating, "One of the most devastating critiques of contemporary American life." Rubin grew up in a poor immigrant family in the Bronx during the Depression. "But for a girl of my generation and class, college was not a perceived option," she wrote in chapter 1 of the book. "Instead I went to work as a stenographer. . . . If a girl wanted more, she married up. Four years later, at nineteen, I did just that." In *Worlds of Pain*, Rubin seems intent on showing how difficult working-class life can be and how hard working-class women struggle to keep their families afloat. The men and women of the white, high school–educated couples she studied in northern California in the early 1970s married young (on average, eighteen for women and twenty for men), and 44 percent of them did so after they "got caught," that is, the woman became pregnant. Their marriages may have provided an escape from an oppressive home, but their immaturity hurt their ability to establish durable frameworks. Over time, the men grew comfortable, but their wives, like the wives in Komarovsky's book, grew frustrated with the lack of an emotional connection. The men, Rubin reports, simply did not have a language for this kind of communication, which constituted a new demand in working-class marriages.[19]

Wives accepted the authority of their husbands—Rubin wrote that "he won't let me" was a phrase she heard again and again—but were dissatisfied with it. She noted that, "despite the yearning for more, relations between husband and wife are benumbed, filled with silence; life seems empty and meaningless; laughter, humor, fun is not a part of the daily ration." Some women considered themselves fortunate if their husband was steadily employed, was not an alcoholic, and did not beat them. Like wives in the middle-class families, these women had to make adjustments, but they were closer to the margins of their existence. One woman told Rubin: "I guess in order to live, you have to have a great ability to endure. And I have that—an ability to endure and survive."

As for their work lives, working-class men valued jobs that provided the opportunity to be independent and to control the pace of work, such as truck driving or skilled construction work. But far too many had to accept "dehumanizing" work that lacked these characteristics. More than half of the wives were working outside the home, usually part-time. They said that they were working for the money, not for satisfaction; nevertheless, many of them found rewards in being "a valued and useful member of society." Even in the 1950s, then, there were fewer fully domestic housewives among the working class than among the middle class. The 1960 census data confirm that difference: among married women ages eighteen to forty-nine who were raising children under the age of eighteen, 47 percent of those whose husbands were craftsmen, operatives, service workers, or common laborers were in the labor force, compared to 38 percent of those whose husbands were managers, professionals, or clerical or sales workers.[20]

Rubin found that more married couples socialized together than was the case among the late 1950s couples studied by Komarovsky and others—one-third of them bowled together on Friday nights. But dinner parties were still practically unheard of, and women rarely looked forward to entertaining at home. As one woman explained: "I've never given a dinner party. I don't know that I have ever been to one. You know, every now and then—it isn't often because it costs too much and besides it's too much trouble—I just have people down for dinner, but it's not what you'd call a dinner party." In the most plaintive image in the book, Rubin notes the expensive campers that sat in the driveways of many of these California families: paid for by the husband working overtime, they were used only two or three times per year. The consumerism symbolized by these campers was a major problem, leading couples to rack up bills that made their financial status precarious. Overall, she concludes, "the affluent and happy worker of whom we have heard so much in recent decades seems not to exist." When she tracked down thirty-two of the families a decade and a half later, eighteen had divorced.[21]

The view from Sparrows Point was decidedly more mixed. The 1950s and 1960s were the steel plant's boom years, a time when employment surged to about 30,000. African Americans had long worked at the Point; as early as 1900, nearly one-third of the workforce was black. Their wives often worked for white families. "Well, of course," a white person from the area recollected to the anthropologist Karen Olson, "all of our mothers had black women come in and iron." During World War I, the segregated community of Turner Station had been established near the plant. It was a neighborhood of modest but well-tended homes that many of its former residents remembered fondly. By the 1950s, black workers at the Point were earning substantially more than many of their friends and relatives. In some black families, wives stopped earning money and became homemakers. Olson collected eighty oral histories centered on Sparrows Point; in one of them, a woman who grew up in Turner Station told her:

> I came from a block where most of the mothers stayed home. Most of the men worked at Sparrows Point, and the wives took care of everything that had to be done at home, including cut the grass, plant the flowers, make market, and have their dinner on the table when the men came home.

Still, it was more acceptable in black families than in white families for wives to work outside the home, and many black women did. A man who had been a mill worker told Olson: "My wife worked for Social Security [headquartered in Baltimore], as did the wives of lots of black steelworkers. We had a good life for ourselves. If the man worked at the Point and his wife worked for Social Security, we thought we had it made."

"We had it made." Here we see a glimpse of a more egalitarian kind of working-class family in which wives could make substantial economic contributions. Far from being threatened by their wives' employment outside the home, black working-class men accepted and even welcomed it. Their masculinity tests did not seem to require that they be the sole breadwinners. Another woman who grew up in Turner Station in the 1950s and 1960s recalled that "most of the women I knew worked outside the home. They were nurses, hospital workers, teachers, and domestics. In my own family, all of the women worked, and it was just assumed that women would work." During these peak years, for perhaps the first time in American history, black working-class couples could readily pool two steady incomes, or even rely on the husband's income, and achieve something close to middle-class status. Despite the restrictions and the discrimination—some black workers at the Point had college degrees but couldn't find jobs that paid as much as mill work—it was an advance.[22]

White working-class families at the Point also experienced gains during the peak years. Freed from the tiring task of tending to boarders and aided by labor-saving devices, many white wives felt less burdened. They also felt that they had moved up in the world. When Olson mentioned her interest in working-class life to her informants, they often rejected the label and insisted that they were middle-class. They pointed to their incomes, the homes they owned (homeownership rates increased in the area during the peak years), the family car, and their nice furnishings and clothes. The white mill workers' good jobs at the Point were secured in part by work rules that generally prevented blacks from competing with them for openings and promotions. The main mechanism was the "unit security system," and here is how it worked: The plant was divided into many units, some of them more desirable than others. Seniority was determined by the number of years a worker had accumulated in his particular unit, not in the plant as a whole. And seniority was important because it determined who was eligible for promotions, who worked days rather than rotating shifts, and who was laid off first when cutbacks occurred. Since blacks were only hired into less desirable units, that was where they acquired seniority. They could theoretically transfer to a white unit, but they would lose all seniority if they did. A twenty-year veteran in a black unit, should he transfer to a white unit, would have less seniority than a white worker who had been hired the day before. And he would have to brave the hostility of white workers who wanted to preserve job openings in their units for their sons, nephews, and friends. There were other restrictive conditions as well. "Our union did not represent blacks' right," a black worker at the Point said. "They let that discrimination go on."[23]

White workers were more insistent than black workers that their wives not work outside the home except during emergencies such as strikes. A white woman said:

> We never had any financial problems, but I think my mother suffered, because during a big strike in 1959 my mother was forced to go to work in the personnel department at Hutzler's Department Store. When my father went back to work she had to quit her job and I know she felt defeated. I remember her saying that the job at Hutzler's had given her her own identity.

White mill workers could also be autocratic at home; for instance, some did not allow their wives to drive the family car. Others complained if their wives did any activities for themselves. A woman who grew up during the era told Olson:

> I'm as independent as I am because of what I saw happen to my mother. My father was typical of many men in this community. He wouldn't let my mother work, not even a little job in a dime store. And she had to go to him for money for anything she needed, even groceries. I promised myself I would never let that happen to me.

A mill worker's wife who reared children during that era seemed to sum up what white working-class life was like for women at the Point:

It was hard and it was pleasant. It was good being able to stay home and raise my children, but Rudy, he didn't give me any extra money except the food money. It was like being an unpaid maid. If I wanted furniture I had to save up for it little by little from the food money. If I wanted some for myself, I'd have to put away a little each pay until I had enough. That's the way Rudy was, claiming it was his hard-earned money, and his father was the same way with his wife. So we had security with those wages from the mill, but Rudy and his father controlled every penny.[24]

THE SUBURBAN LOWER-MIDDLE CLASS

The sociologist Herbert Gans provided the most positive take on the working-class family during the peak years. Gans's main intellectual project was to demonstrate that the often disdainful view of the working class expressed by urban planners and social critics was mistaken and elitist. Gans had studied a neighborhood in Boston that planners had designated a "slum" and slated for demolition under the rubric of urban renewal. What Gans found was a thriving working-class Italian neighborhood whose residents enjoyed the neighborhood and did not want to abandon it. When, in 1955, the Levitt and Sons home-building company bought a large swath of suburban land not far from Philadelphia, where Gans was teaching, he bought a house in the giant development and in 1958 became an early occupant of one of the 12,000 homes that would constitute Levittown, New Jersey.

The Levitts had established their first Levittown in Long Island, New York. They built modest houses, largely for first-time home buyers who received low-interest, low-down-payment financing that was guaranteed by the Federal Housing Administration, often through the provisions of the GI Bill. The first Levittown became a magnet for cultural criticism. Aerial photographs printed in newspapers, magazines, and books showed thousands of identical homes arranged on curving, intersecting streets. Every so often one could see the outlines of an elementary school and a small shopping center. Levittown became a metaphor for the conformity and homogeneity that the critics claimed to find in the burgeoning suburbs. The cultural concern about conformity was not limited to the working class: in his best-selling 1953 book *The Lonely Crowd*, David Riesman found the inhabitants of middle-class suburbs to be oriented toward the standards of others rather than guided by their own standards—"other-directed" rather than "inner-directed." In a 1956 best-seller, *The Organization Man*, William H. Whyte Jr. diagnosed a crippling conformity to corporate norms and a corresponding lack of individual initiative among middle-class men. He criticized the suburban housing development as a "filiarchy" in which families organized their lives around their children and made friends with other families similar to theirs.[25]

What Gans claimed to find in his 1967 book, *The Levittowners: Ways of Life and Politics in a New Suburban Community*, was a well-functioning community whose residents were pleased with the upgraded standard of living that homeownership in the suburbs provided. There are many ways to live well, he argued: "In a pluralistic society, there is no single standard for the good life, and in a democratic one, people have the right to set their own. For example, if Levittowners report that they find their community satisfying, as they do, their opinion ought to be respected." As in Boston, he had shown, to his own satisfaction at least, that the residents of a maligned community did not share the unfavorable opinions of their daily lives that were common among the maligners. Their views of their communities, he asserted, were as valid as the views of the urban intellectuals.[26]

In about one-fourth of the Levittown families, Gans discerned the same working-class culture that he had witnessed in Boston and that the Lynds had seen in Muncie in the 1920s: these husbands and wives had less companionate relationships and engaged in fewer joint leisure activities than did middle-class couples and their child-rearing practices were more oriented toward discipline and obedience. But he reported that about three-fourths of the Levittown residents exhibited a cultural style that seemed a half-step up from the working class and a half-step below that of the college-educated middle-class professionals. He called it the culture of the "lower middle class," a term that first came into use in the 1940s. Its practitioners were high school–educated, skilled manual and white-collar workers and their families. Husbands and wives in these families were more likely to pursue leisure activities together than were working-class couples, and they had somewhat more companionate marital relationships. In rearing their children, they did not emphasize obedience as much as in working-class culture, but they still wanted their children to be taught to share their values. Although they were active in local organizations such as churches, the PTA, or the Scouts, they took little interest in local government or national affairs.[27]

It was to this lower-middle-class cultural style that the working-class couples who bought suburban homes in the 1950s assimilated. Postwar prosperity and government housing policies allowed millions of working-class families to achieve lower-middle-class status. For the first time, the subsistence imperative of working-class life was easily satisfied by most families. To be sure, they did not adopt the cultural values of upper-middle-class couples, who raised their children to be autonomous, did all of their leisure activities together, patronized the arts, and took a strong interest in national issues. They did not live in neighborhoods that appealed to the elite. Yet neither were they alienated and depersonalized by suburban life, according to Gans: "And if suburban life was as undesirable and as unhealthy as the critics charged; the suburbanites themselves were blissfully unaware of it; they were happy in their new homes and communities, much happier than had they been in the city." From this perspective, the suburbanization of the working class was one of the great achievements of the postwar peak. It not only boosted the standard of living and the happiness of millions of working-class families but also allowed many more of them to become homeowners, a status that had long been of great cultural significance and was a tangible marker of membership in the middle class.[28]

Yet it is also clear that the benefits and burdens of suburban middle-class life were not shared equally by men and women. Gans insisted that most men and women in Levittown were happy with their lives and free of boredom, loneliness, and mental health problems. Women, however, were disproportionately represented in the minority who did have such problems. Gans identified a "female malaise" that affected perhaps one-third of the women. He said that it reflected the general problems of family relations and not suburban living. But he then described several aspects of the malaise that did relate to suburban living: Some working-class women missed family and friends in Philadelphia from whom they were cut off, whereas others felt stuck as full-time housekeepers without a car and with neighbors they didn't know very well. (Most families had only one car, which the husband typically used to travel to work.) Some whose husbands had longer commutes felt lonely: "If you are alone here, you are alone. In an apartment you can walk out the door." Gans called it the loss of an "urban safety valve." As one woman said: "In the city I was able to go into town every once in a while, but here I can't. I get restless at times, fed up. Then I need a change, have to get out. Being with the kids all the time builds up tension and you get rid of it by going out and away from them." Despite Gans's position, suburban life does seem to have played a role in the "female malaise."[29]

The benefits of suburbia were also not shared equally by whites and African Americans. The Levitts had not sold houses at their other Levittowns to black buyers, and they announced that they would not sell to black buyers in New Jersey. The company's spokesmen explained that if they sold houses to black people, they would lose money, because fewer whites would want to buy their houses—unless all suburban builders sold to blacks. But when open-housing activists challenged the company, its executives gradually realized that they would lose in court. At that point, they voluntarily opened Levittown to black families, but only in new areas of the town that were still being built. Integration was achieved peacefully and the black families that bought homes were accepted by their neighbors. Yet by 1964, only about fifty black families resided in Levittown. The low numbers may have reflected the housing prices (which were out of the range of many black families), the reluctance of black families to move to an overwhelmingly white and potentially hostile neighborhood, or the preference of some black families for neighborhoods with a higher concentration of blacks. In any case, suburbanization in the 1950s and 1960s was a largely white phenomenon.[30]

WORKING-CLASS CULTURE

The working-class family was more than an economic category. During the peak years, it became a cultural phenomenon as well. That is to say, beginning in the 1950s, the concept of a working-class family became imbued not only with hard and fast characteristics, such as the occupation of the husband and the household and market work of the wife, but also with the softer cultural characteristics embodied in a new metaphor in American English: "blue collar." It was a play on an older metaphor, "white collar," used to describe clerical workers, whose clean white shirts became a symbol of their nonmanual jobs. In contrast, the iconic blue chambray shirt worn by many manual workers was designed to absorb the dirt and grime of physical labor—the very labor that became the center of the cultural concept. You might think that the phrase "blue collar" is as old as industrialization itself, but it is not: the term was hardly used before World War II. Figure 4.1 displays the number of times each of these phrases, "blue collar" and "white collar," appeared per 1 million words in all English-language books published in the United States in every decade starting in the 1810s.[31]

Let's start with the gray bars, which show the prevalence of the older metaphor, "white collar." As you can see, it had a small but noticeable presence in books as early as the 1830s. In that era, a small middle class of salaried managers, professionals, clerks, and bookkeepers emerged among native-born families. The usage of "white collar" grew slowly but surely through the 1800s and early 1900s. In contrast, the usage of "blue collar" is a much more recent phenomenon. Its prevalence, shown by the black bars, was negligible throughout the 1800s, and the term only began to be widely used in the 1950s, as the peak years began. If I were to include a graph of the prevalence of the related phrase "blue-collar family" in books over time, it would look similar to figure 4.1—emerging in the 1950s and peaking in the 1970s. I would claim that the appearance of the blue-collar metaphor in the 1950s marked the origins of the idea of the working class—and of the working-class family—as a cultural style, perhaps even a way

Figure 4.1   Number of Times the Phrases "Blue Collar" and "White Collar" Appear per 1 Million Words in Books Published in the United States, by Decade, 1810–1819 to 2000–2007

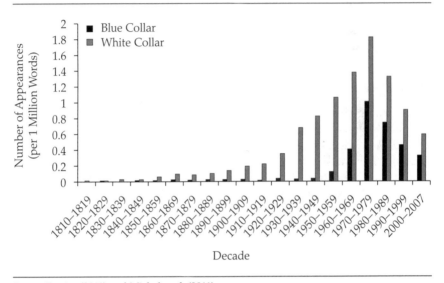

Source: Davies (2011) and Michel et al. (2011).

of life. It provided a label for a range of behaviors that went beyond whether or not a person was doing industrial labor. This usage reached a high point in the 1970s, just as the growth of industrial employment was slowing, and then it declined. The fact that the usage of "white collar" also grew through the 1970s and then declined suggests that the two metaphors had become linked. The distinction between blue-collar work and white-collar work had become part of the language and the culture.[32]

The "blue collar" metaphor had both positive and negative connotations. On the positive side, Americans thought of blue-collar workers as embodying virtues such as hard work and personal responsibility. Of course, working with one's hands had long been celebrated in America—think of the legend of John Henry the steel driver, building the railroads during the nineteenth century, or of Paul Bunyan, the giant lumberjack. And farm families had long been seen as hardworking: up before sunrise to feed the animals, working until dark to harvest the crops. But as the urban population soared and industrial employment grew as well, the factory worker, along with workers in related manual occupations such as construction, came to embody hard work. For the male industrial worker himself, the task was to somehow take pride in the performance of alienating, monotonous work, such as toiling on an assembly line, and to conceive of himself as successfully meeting the masculinity imperative of working-class life. The solution among white workers was to construct an identity that the sociologist Michèle Lamont calls "the disciplined self." It took a disciplined self to perform timed labor, hour after hour, day after day. It took a disciplined self to get up each morning (or each afternoon or night, depending on the shift), go to work, endure it, and bring home a paycheck at the end of the week. In other words, it took a disciplined self to be a good provider. Though Lamont interviewed steadily employed working-class and lower-middle-class men in the 1990s, the attitudes she found were probably representative of what similar men felt at midcentury. One said: "Family is very important to my life. You need to work to support your family. So, I don't worry about a job. I mean, I don't care what I have to do, I'll go out and do it to support my family." These men contrasted the integrity and trustworthiness of the manual worker with the untrustworthy nature of the upper-middle-class supervisor or professional, who were too ambitious, according to the men Lamont interviewed—too willing to cut social ties in their haste to climb the ladder of social mobility.[33]

This morally based sense of dignity was a reactive identity: it was not constructed by people who had the option of taking high-paying managerial or professional jobs or who could easily find meaningful work. Rather, it was constructed by people whose socioeconomic opportunities were circumscribed and who had to find self-worth in what was available to them. In addition, this sense of self was constructed in a social world in which manual work was not highly respected by the broad middle and upper classes. Many studies have shown that when asked to rank the prestige and status of occupations, people tend to rank manual occupations rather low. Manual workers know that; they give manual work the same prestige rankings themselves. The lack of respect and prestige given to the work they do produces "hidden injuries of class," in the felicitous phrase of Richard Sennett and Jonathan Cobb. Wounded by the disrespect for the kind of labor they valued and largely blocked from occupations at the top of the socioeconomic ladder, manual workers reacted by constructing an identity based on an alternative set of criteria in which ambition is suspect, how much you earn is not central to who you are, and being self-reliant and hardworking is valued above all. One worker said to Lamont concerning professionals:

They care more about showing off to other professionals. They have more of a contest with each other. I mean like "I've got a Jaguar," drive by to see his friends. As for me, I could not care less what the other guy thinks of me. Because if I feel good about myself, and my wife thinks good about me, and we're all happy, that's what matters to me. My family is what I center myself around. I'm not trying to keep a race with the Joneses, like that.[34]

The white workers also defined themselves by contrasting their capacity for disciplined work with the alleged lack of discipline among black workers—an attitude that we may recognize from the nineteenth-century organization of the working class around the concept of whiteness, which was stretched to accommodate European immigrants. One of Lamont's interviewees asserted, for example, that

blacks have a tendency to . . . try to get off doing less, the least possible . . . to keep the job, where whites will put in that extra oomph. I know this is a generality and it does not go for all, it goes for a portion. It's this whole un-employment and welfare gig. A lot of blacks on welfare have no desire to get off it. . . . I can't stand to see *my hard-earned money* [said with emphasis] going to pay for someone who wants to sit on his ass all day long and get free money.[35]

The tendency to contrast the virtues of one's group with the failings of an out-group is not unique to the United States. Lamont also interviewed working-class men in France. She found that white workers contrasted their positive qualities with the alleged lack of motivation of North African immigrants from the former French colonies of Algeria, Morocco, and Tunisia. North Africans are typically of mixed West Asian, sub-Saharan African, and European origin. In France, North Africans are not synonymous with blacks, many of whom have been absorbed into France over time from French colonies in the Caribbean or sub-Saharan Africa. Yet it is North African immigrants, not blacks, whom white French workers described in terms that were nearly identical to those American white workers use toward blacks. One French worker told Lamont:

Parasites . . . I hate all of them. All of those people who don't have a sense of responsibility. We work so hard to support them. When you look at your pay stub and see all that is taken away! How can I explain it?. . . They don't want to work. They only know the way to the unemployment insurance office, the ASSEDIC [*the acronym for this office, which he pronounces with a North African accent*].

The American and French cases suggest that working-class men commonly define their self-worth against an "other," an outside group toward which they can feel superior in their work habits and personal responsibility, be it African Americans or North African immigrants or, as in the late-nineteenth-century U.S. West, Chinese.[36]

Steadily employed American black workers, Lamont writes, respected the concern about discipline but displayed a moral sense of self that was centered on sharing with others in need—what she calls the "caring self." They frequently described their financial goals in altruistic terms. One black worker said that his goal was to "help people if I could. If you don't share it you lose it . . . because God will not bless you if you don't put it to good use." They were less likely than whites to describe themselves as feeling superior or inferior to others. When asked to describe the difference between the moral worlds of white and black workers, they said that whites were more individualistic and less caring, as in this man's comment:

> Blacks have a strong sense of family, a strong sense of togetherness. White people they don't take as much time with their families as we do. . . . They let their kids be much more on their own. Whites, their kids will go maybe to school away from home and might come home one weekend a year . . . and then when they're there, the parents are always going somewhere, and they have a babysitter, then they have a nanny.

Another said: "Black people are sensitive toward human needs because we are concerned humans, whereas the white people that I have met in my life seem detached from the human thing." This high moral valuation on sharing what one has with others could have prevented black working-class families from accumulating as much wealth as a comparable white working-class family during the peak years. But when the peak years ended and the fortunes of the industrial worker declined, the caring self may have made it easier for black working-class families to cope with that decline than it was for white working-class families.[37]

Not all of the cultural characteristics associated with the "blue collar" metaphor, however, were positive. The middle class's opinion of the working-class family was displayed in 1950s television series such as *The Honeymooners* and *I Love Lucy*. The former show began as a comedy sketch in 1951, ran as a half-hour situation comedy from 1955 to 1956, and returned as a periodic special program. It featured Ralph Kramden, a bumbling bus driver (played by Jackie Gleason), and his wife Alice (Audrey Meadows). Whereas middle-class sitcom husbands such as Ward Cleaver and Jim Anderson were wise, steady, good providers, Ralph Kramden was ineffectual, blustery, and undependable. And whereas middle-class wives were loving, warm, and deferential, Alice Kramden was wisecracking, sarcastic, and, all in all, fed up with her husband. Ralph was constantly coming home with harebrained get-rich-quick schemes, like buying 2,000 multifunction can openers that could core apples, scale fish, remove corns and selling them at a huge profit by hawking them in a television advertisement. But the self-professed king of his castle had to plead with his skeptical wife for the money to buy the can openers:

RALPH: Look, Alice, please, it's simple arithmetic. We buy something for ten cents, and we sell it for a dollar! It's that simple.

ALICE: If it's so simple, Ralph, why didn't the man who had these things in his warehouse sell them and make this big profit?

RALPH: Because he thinks small like you do. He thinks he's got to go from door to door to sell these things. That's where my great idea comes in. I go on television and in five minutes, I can sell the whole 2,000 of them. Look, how long do you think it would take that guy to sell 2,000 of these if he went from door to door?

ALICE: About one minute if this was the first door he knocked on.

RALPH: Oh, I'd like to belt you just once![38]

Gleason was always threatening to hit his wife (one of his tag lines was, "Pow! Right in the Kisser!"), but his threats were empty. In her commentary on 1950s television comedies, the historian Stephanie Coontz observes that working-class husbands—a category that also included Ricky Ricardo (Desi Arnaz) on *I Love Lucy*—could not control their wives. Gleason was also a disappointment to his wife and mother-in-law as a breadwinner. Moreover, he had no children. He therefore failed all the tests of conventional masculinity. While the real-life blue-collar husband saw himself as a dignified provider, the embodiment of masculinity, television saw him as far inferior to the white-collar husband in doing the things a 1950s man was supposed to do. Although blue-collar men exhibited a positive self-image that was grounded in their steady employment, middle-class culture promoted a different image: the bombastic working stiff who was not especially effective at doing anything. Here were the hidden injuries of class. Working-class viewers laughed at Gleason along with the rest of the country because it was all in good fun. Or was it? No one made fun of Ward Cleaver, and a half-century after *Leave It to Beaver* went off the air, young men struggling to piece together their family lives were still citing him as a role model. None of them mentioned Ralph Kramden.[39]

THE BEST OF TIMES AND THE WORST OF TIMES?

How should we judge the working-class family during the postwar peak? There was undeniably a best-of-times side. As the wages of industrial workers increased in the thirty years after World War II, husbands were increasingly able to support a family lifestyle that included a modest home, a car, ample food and clothing, and perhaps even a vacation trip using the camper sitting in the driveway; more and more working-class families had enough income and consumption to reach the lower rungs of the broad American middle class. Indeed, the postwar era was the only time when the American economy allowed large numbers of working-class families to attain something close to a middle-class lifestyle. It was also the only time when many working-class families could attain the culturally potent ideal of the breadwinner husband and the homemaker wife, at least during the years when they had preschool-age children at home. By the midtwentieth century, working-class wives' earnings from home production had diminished and, like their middle-class sisters, they now tended to specialize in housework and child-rearing when their children were young. Husbands took pride in their ability to support their families with only small monetary contributions from their wives until the children were older. Helped by government-subsidized mortgages and the interstate highway system, millions of young families moved to suburbs such as Levittown, where they seemed pleased with their environment, cultural critics notwithstanding. Even Lillian Rubin admitted to some positives: Work was readily available and wages were rising. A young man could graduate from high school and be confident of finding a steady job with decent wages and benefits. At home, men were drinking less and were less violent toward their wives than their fathers had been. And despite many husbands' befuddlement over the new companionate marriage, couples shared more leisure-time activities than their parents had.

It was also a good era for children. Dropping adult death rates and modest increases in divorce rates combined in the 1950s to provide children with stable, two-parent families on a level unmatched in any other decade in the twentieth or early twenty-first centuries. Moreover, the 1950s baby boom constituted the only significant rise in American fertility since at least 1800. Married couples had three children on average, and rising wages allowed parents to support these larger families. Few children lived with never-married or cohabiting parents compared to the current day because marriage was the only acceptable context for having children. Beyond the statistics, nearly all historical sources show that the cultural climate was focused on home and family more so than in any decade since. Perhaps this climate resulted from the experiences of the generation that was born during the Depression and fought in World War II, then may have been eager to focus on home and family. Rising prosperity may have supported this inward turn. In any case, children benefited from this familistic culture.

Yet to take a solely positive view of the working-class family during the peak years is to risk indulging in an idealized image that Coontz famously referred to as "the way we never were." There is certainly some justification for the worst-of-times arguments presented by authors such as Rubin. It seems clear in retrospect that the typical working-class marriage was better for men than for women. It allowed men the privilege of having children without providing much of the care they required. It preserved male prerogatives such as socializing after work at a tavern or going out for an evening with the boys, while their wives fed their children and put them to bed. As the sole or main earners, husbands controlled family finances and sometimes reserved funds for their own consumption before providing their wives with the rest. Wives had difficulty with such simple transactions as taking out a credit card in their own name. Many wives were caught between the cultural expectation that they should stay home and the desire for more income in a society experiencing a burst of postwar consumerism. White husbands felt that they had the authority to order their wives not to work outside the home, and some wives found this restriction to the home to be personally limiting.[40]

Work was hard, long, and alienating for many working-class men. Coming home tired and irritable, they were often returning to the only place in their lives where they could be in charge—a setting where they could compensate for the lack of authority and autonomy in the workplace. Some compensated by controlling their wives. Although most husbands were not violent, hitting one's wife occasionally was culturally and legally tolerated, and the concept of marital rape was unknown. Moreover, working-class men were not as comfortable as their wives were with the emerging companionate style of marriage. It required self-expression and self-disclosure, but many men were more comfortable with a style of marriage in which they had little to say about their feelings to their wives. There was also a downside in the 1950s family for men: although fathers were encouraged to be more involved in their children's lives, they could not become *too* involved, since a husband who stayed home to raise his children while his wife worked would have been ridiculed as less than a man.

The picture for African American families is also mixed. One might characterize the 1950s and 1960s as a period of constrained prosperity for them. Black men were finally able to obtain factory jobs in large numbers as employers' growing demand for labor trumped their reluctance to hire them. Black women, the majority of whom had worked as maids and laundresses as recently as 1940, shed private household work and moved into clerical and professional occupations. These were substantial occupational gains. Marriage was less dominant in the family lives of blacks than among whites, but it was still strong. In 1960, 62 percent of black men ages twenty to forty-nine were married (compared to only 26 percent in 2010). Twenty-two percent of births to black women in 1960 were outside of marriage—a much higher figure than for whites (2 percent), but a level that left more than three-fourths of births to black women *within* marriage. African Americans participated in the baby boom too. Their total fertility rate rose from 2.8 in 1940 to 3.9 in 1950 and 4.5 in 1960 before declining. Nevertheless, the constraints were visible: it was not until the mid-1960s that civil rights legislation provided African Americans with some relief from discrimination and segregation. It is unimaginable now (as well as illegal) that a major housing builder such as Levitt and Sons would announce publicly that it would not sell houses to blacks, but that is what happened in New Jersey in 1958. In Sparrows Point, black workers shared in rising wages but still earned less than whites, and many of them lived in segregated neighborhoods.[41]

THE CONTRADICTIONS OF THE 1950S FAMILY

The 1950s family was undermined by changes in the economy and in the culture that took place in the 1970s. But even had these changes not occurred, it is likely that at some point the 1950s family would have failed. It contradicted the historical development of American society in the twentieth century in too many ways. Consider the baby boom: The inward turn toward home and family encouraged couples to have unusually large families, but parents began to realize that child-rearing had changed irrevocably from the nineteenth-century model. No longer were children economic assets to their parents; rather, they were now economic burdens who required prolonged care and education in order to be properly launched into adulthood. Young couples soon resumed the century-long trade-off between quantity and quality: they chose to have fewer children and to invest more heavily in each of them. The total fertility rate peaked in 1957 at 3.8 children per woman and then began to decline; by 1972, it had fallen below the replacement level of 2.1 children per woman. The baby boom was not sustainable given the changing patterns of investment in children.

And as the birth rate began to fall, it became apparent that there just was not enough to do in the home to fully occupy the housewife except when her children were young and required time-consuming care. By the early 1960s, most households had hot and cold running water, refrigerators, and gas or electric stoves, and half had automatic washing machines. The Levittown houses came with modern kitchen appliances already installed. Families purchased vacuum cleaners and other labor-saving devices. Yet wives in the 1960s who were not employed outside the home spent as much time in housework as did rural women forty years earlier. For instance, despite the spread of automatic washing machines, housewives in the 1960s spent *more* time doing the washing than did women in the 1920s—probably because they had more clothes and washed them more frequently. In other words, consumption was greater (more clothes) and standards of housework had been ratcheted up (washed more frequently). But wives in the 1960s who did work outside the home did *not* spend more time doing housework than women in the 1920s, even on the weekends, when they were not at their jobs. It may be that housewives needed to demonstrate to their husbands and to themselves the value of their contributions to the family by filling their days with domestic activities, whereas wives who were also employed felt no such need. Merchandisers helped: Coontz reports that extra steps were added to some cake mix instructions to make wives feel more needed. But the basic problem remained: being a housewife was no longer a long-term, full-time job. It left women dependent on their husbands without a corresponding role that could fill their day. In response, many 1950s homemakers urged their daughters to pursue college educations and careers. A woman in the sample studied by the historian Jessica Weiss wrote: "They can make some impression or contribution to the world. . . . I want them to have some goal in life besides being a housewife. I'd like to see them make a living so the house isn't the end of all things." Another said, "I sure don't want [her] to turn out to be just a housewife like myself."[42]

Moreover, employment opportunities were shifting toward occupations that had come to be seen as women's jobs—most notably, clerical occupations such as secretaries, office machine operators, and (until their recent demise) telephone operators. As the twentieth century progressed, bureaucracies began to dominate both the private and public sectors of the economy: large corporations ruled industries, while federal, state, and local government employment grew. These bureaucracies needed clerical workers. In 1880, only 1.5 percent of workers held clerical jobs. Since then, clerical employment has become much larger: in 1930, shortly after the start of the Great Depression, 9 percent of all employees did clerical work; in 1950, near the start of the peak years, 12 percent did clerical work; and by 1970, 19 percent did clerical work. Most of that increase was specific to women workers. About 11.4 million more women, but only about 1.5 million more men, were working in the clerical sector in 1970 than in 1950. This growing demand for gender-typed labor pulled married women into the workforce and helped to undermine the single-earner married-couple family. It also led to another collar metaphor: "pink collar" referred to the world of female clerical workers. The term did not become common until the 1970s, following the large-scale movement of women into clerical employment.[43]

Paid work was least common when mothers had preschool-age children at home: in 1950 just 12 percent of married women with preschool-age children were in the labor force. Once all of a woman's children were in school, however, she was more likely to work at least part-time: in 1950, 28 percent of married women with children ages six to seventeen were in the labor force. Despite the home-centeredness of the era, married women's employment rates increased during the 1950s and 1960s. By 1969, 29 percent of married women with preschool-age children were in the labor force, as were 49 percent of married women whose children were all of school age. These increases were led in the 1950s and early 1960s by working-class and lower-middle-class women, who were less able to make ends meet on their husband's income alone than were wealthier women.[44]

To be sure, the main cultural message of the era to married women was that they should focus on domesticity. Nevertheless, the media provided qualified support for women who were working for wages. For instance, an article in the January 1954 issue of Ladies' Home Journal, titled "When an Older Woman Wants a Job," advised the reader that "a part-time job can bring a feeling of full-time usefulness and satisfaction." The word "older" in the title was meant to exclude women with young children, and the qualifier "part-time" acknowledged that women needed to retain time for their important domestic duties. Still, the fact that an article such as this one appeared at all in a mainstream magazine in 1954 is telling. The historian Joanne Meyerowitz found that popular magazines of the era expressed some ambivalence about full-time domesticity. They endorsed women's working if they did not have small children and celebrated publicly successful women. So, despite the glorification of the stay-at-home mother, a strong undercurrent of married women moving into the workforce could be discerned. Its causes were a mix of increased demand by employers for clerical workers, a desire to boost family income, and a search for a more fulfilling personal life.[45]

Because of all of these factors, it is likely that the 1950s male-breadwinner family would have sooner or later weakened even had labor market opportunities for men remained strong. How long it might have lasted, we cannot say. But in fact the labor market did begin to weaken in the 1970s as the offshoring and automation of production began to erode manufacturing jobs, with important consequences for family life. That is the story to be told in the next chapter.

Chapter 5 | The Fall of the Working-Class Family: 1975–2010

In 1983, TWENTY years after the television series *Leave It to Beaver* ended its run, Beaver Cleaver, now thirty-three years old, returned in a made-for-television movie on a cable channel, followed by a 1985–1989 series, *The New Leave It to Beaver*. Time had been unkind to Beaver: he was unemployed, he had trouble communicating with his two young sons, and his wife was divorcing him. He and his children had moved back in with his mother June. Ward had passed away, along with a generation of effortlessly successful breadwinners.

Many young adults, it turns out, were struggling in the 1970s and 1980s. The golden age of American capitalism had ended. Unemployment had increased, and wages were stagnant at best. American manufacturers, facing foreign competition, were demanding reductions in the benefits they had agreed to provide to workers, and unions were losing membership. Family life was changing too, and the marriage-oriented 1950s were beginning to seem like ancient history: age at marriage was rising, sex outside of marriage was increasing, cohabitation was becoming common, birth rates had fallen to their lowest levels ever, and—as the adult Beaver illustrated—divorce rates had soared. The new era posed challenges to young adults, many of whom were the children of the industrial workers of the post–World War II peak years.

By 1970, the combatants of World War II had recovered from the widespread wartime devastation and were challenging the dominance of the United States. Western Europe had established robust economic growth, and production in many Asian nations was rising. Rebuilding industrial capacity after the war, or building it for the first time, provided these countries with an advantage: factories could adopt newly developed production processes that were more efficient and required fewer workers than the older American factories. For instance, the Japanese steel industry took advantage of new technologies to produce steel more cheaply than most American factories could. In response, American steel factories were able to retool to some extent and, in doing so, to cut their workforce. The number of people employed in the American steel industry declined from 1.05 million in 1970 to 630,000 in 1990 and 477,000 in 2010. The same story was repeated in numerous other industries: foreign competition and more efficient production processes greatly reduced the number of workers needed. In addition, American corporations began to take advantage of the lower wages in developing nations by outsourcing their production to other countries. By the turn of the twenty-first century, the production of entire categories of goods had nearly disappeared in the United States. I tell the students in my large introduction to sociology course that I will give them a quarter for every piece of clothing they are wearing that was entirely made in the United States. I rarely lose more than the cost of a cup of coffee.[1]

Firms that were still producing goods in the United States generated some efficiencies simply by paying workers less in wages and benefits than they used to. In particular, mass-production industries abrogated the Treaty of Detroit. Beginning about 1980, automobile executives, facing foreign competition and higher energy costs due to price hikes by the cartel of oil-producing nations, demanded that the United Auto Workers give back some of the gains that the union had achieved. The firms threatened to close plants if the union did not comply, and the UAW agreed to hundreds of millions of dollars in givebacks. In one set of concessions to General Motors in 1982, annual wage increases were eliminated, some cost-of-living increases were deferred, and paid personal holidays were eliminated. One GM worker who took a buyout and left the company in 1987 told the sociologist Ruth Milkman:

> Let's face it. The auto workers just aren't what they used to be. They just don't have the power they used to, because there's not as many workers and there's always that threat, well, they can just pack up and leave—which is what they're doing. No one is listening to the union anymore. What are they going to do? They have no recourse. So I saw all that coming and I said, "I just don't want to be a part of this anymore."

Management's leverage was increased during the Reagan administration when the president crushed the air traffic controllers' union after an unauthorized strike in 1981 and appointed an anti-union management consultant as the head of the National Labor Relations Board (NLRB). Across the American industrial landscape, unions lost bargaining power and membership.[2]

The offshoring of production and the greater efficiency of the remaining American industries had two important effects on workers in the middle of the American labor market. The first was to decrease the percentage of all jobs that were in manufacturing and related manual work. Census data show that the percentage of workers who were classified as precision production, crafts, and repair workers and as operatives, fabricators, and construction workers—in short, what we might call blue-collar occupations—decreased from 28 percent in 1970 to 22 percent in 1990, and then to 17 percent in 2010. It was therefore harder to enter the industrial working class than in the 1950s and 1960s. A young man could no longer graduate from high school and walk into a decent-paying, secure factory job. (A young woman never could.) The share of blue-collar workers was shrinking relative to white-collar workers at the top and service workers at the bottom; the remaining industrial workers had a harder time finding and keeping jobs.[3]

The second effect was to raise the skill level that was required for many of the remaining blue-collar occupations. Consider workers who operate machinery in factories. The 1970 census counted almost 11 million of them, but there were fewer than 5 million in 2010, even though the total size of the labor force had expanded by about 50 percent. For example, during the same period the number of workers who operated lathe, milling, and turning machines plummeted from 345,000 to 14,000. Some of this drop undoubtedly occurred because production moved overseas, but some of it was due to the installation of computer-controlled labor-saving machines. After many manufacturers installed intricate machinery that performed the tasks that once required several workers to complete, only one worker was now needed per high-tech machine. But in order to control the machine, the worker needed the skills to program the numeric settings that determined precisely what it would do. These were skills that typically required advanced training after high school, often obtained in community colleges.[4]

While the number of workers who operated factory machines was declining, the number of professionals who *designed* the complex machines was rising. In 1970 there were only 3,800 computer programmers who designed machine tools that were numerically controlled by computers, but by 2010 there were 83,000 of them. This contrast between the burgeoning numbers of largely college-educated designers and the declining numbers of largely high school–educated operators is an example of what economists call the "skill-biased" technological changes in the American economy since the end of the postwar peak. In this usage, "skill bias" means that employers more highly value (are biased toward) people with greater technological skills and are therefore willing to pay them higher wages and salaries. Those skills are usually acquired through a college education. Opportunities have expanded for jobs in fields that government statistical agencies classify as "managerial" (such as advertising, marketing, and administration), "professional" (such as engineering and education), and "technical" (such as computer software development), and the vast majority of these jobs are held by individuals who have a bachelor's degree. Their share of the total labor force grew from 20 percent in 1970 to 32 percent in 2010.[5]

The occupations that are still growing despite not requiring high skills or much education tend to pay low wages. For instance, the share of service occupations grew from 14 percent in 1970 to 18 percent in 2010. These jobs include restaurant and hotel workers, janitors, and child care workers. What the service jobs experiencing growth have in common is that they provide assistance that cannot be outsourced to another country. Customers need their restaurants nearby; parents need their child care centers in the neighborhood. Moreover, these occupations provide the kinds of services that are in greater demand among the affluent. People with higher disposable incomes eat at restaurants more often and stay in hotels for business or pleasure. High-income dual-earner couples need to purchase child care services. Service workers also tend to perform tasks that involve what labor economists term "nonroutine manual operations." These tasks require complex eye-hand coordination that cannot easily be performed by a computer, such as gardening or waiting on tables. What we have seen, then, is a great expansion of the number of workers with higher-paying professional and managerial jobs and a modest expansion of the number of workers with low-paying jobs that involve serving other people's personal and family needs. In between, job opportunities are mostly shrinking.[6]

The metaphors that writers use to describe this situation—the hollowing-out or polarization of the labor market, or the hourglass economy—share the idea of a declining demand for labor in the middle of the labor market relative to demand for workers at the top and, to a lesser extent, at the bottom. To be sure, not all middle-skill jobs are in decline. With the growth in the nation's health sector and the increasing computerization of medical information, jobs for medical technicians and record keepers have increased. The number of radiology technicians increased from 69,000 in 1970 to 341,000 in 2010, and the number of health records technical specialists grew from 14,000 to 134,000. Operatives trained in computer-controlled machinery are in demand. The rise of online retailing has increased openings for drivers in shipping and delivery companies. In addition, law enforcement activity and rising rates of imprisonment have created an unfortunate increase in demand for police officers, prison guards, sheriffs, and marshals. But by and large, the middle of the labor market has been hit the hardest by the changes that have occurred in the American economy since 1970.[7]

The hollowing-out, nevertheless, has had different consequences for women than for men. The great growth of the pink-collar clerical work-force ended around 1990 as computerization began to replace more cleri-cal jobs. When I call Amtrak to make a train reservation, I hear a recorded voice saying, "Hi, I'm Julie, Amtrak's automated agent." Twenty years ago, a real person, usually a woman (hence the choice of Julie rather than, say, Jules), answered the phone. Unlike men, however, women workers were not pushed further into low-wage service jobs, some of which (cham-bermaids, home health care aides) they had long dominated. Rather, they were able to move into professional and managerial occupations—in part, by graduating from college in increasing numbers. As recently as 1995, young women and young men were equally likely to graduate from col-lege, but by 2013 young women had pulled ahead: 37 percent of twenty-five- to twenty-nine-year-old women had received a bachelor's degree or more compared to 30 percent of men of comparable age. In addition, women without college degrees increased their skills and seniority by vir-tue of remaining in the workforce longer than their mothers' generation had.[8]

In sum, the hourglass economy has limited employment opportunities for young men more than for young women. You can see the difference in figure 5.1, which shows the changes in real (that is, adjusted for increases in the cost of living) hourly earnings for women and men, by education, between 1979 and 2007. The bars that extend downward from the 0 per-cent line indicate a decrease in earnings; those that extend upward indi-cate an increase. Men who did not graduate from college—high school dropouts, high school graduates, even men who attended college but did not receive a bachelor's degree—experienced decreases in earnings, on average. But among women, only high school dropouts experienced a de-cline, on average, and that was a mere 1 percent. All other women experi-enced increases. As a result, among young adults without bachelor's de-grees, the earnings prospects for women and men diverged markedly. Women are still paid less than men, on average, but their earnings have been trending upward.

In theory, young women's improved earnings could have had one of two contrasting effects on marriage. First, their improved earnings could have made women more attractive as potential marriage partners because

Figure 5.1   Changes in Real Hourly Earnings, by Education, 1979–
2007

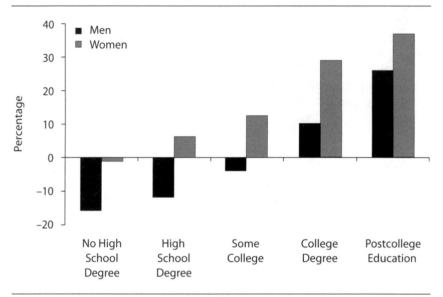

Source: Autor (2010). Reprinted with permission.

they could contribute a good income, therefore increasing their likelihood of marrying. We could call this an income effect: the more income women have, the more they marry. Second, women's increased earnings could have reduced their desire to marry by providing them with an independent source of income. We could call this an independence effect: the more income women have, the less they marry. In practice, among women without bachelor's degrees, the independence effect seems to have been stronger: between 1980 and 2010 these women became less likely to have ever been married. Perhaps the independence effect won out because so few young men had good earnings prospects that an acceptable marriage partner was hard to find and remaining single seemed the better option. The availability of cash assistance to low-income mothers from government social welfare programs may also have strengthened the independence effect. For instance, spending on the Earned Income Tax Credit (EITC), which assists low-income parents with children, rose sharply after 1985. In any event, an increasing number of young women without bachelor's degrees never married. They did not, however, forgo childbearing as much, leading to a rise in the proportion of children who were born to cohabiting couples or single mothers.[9]

Among women with a bachelor's degree, on the other hand, the income and independence effects have been more balanced. The decline in their rates of ever marrying has been more modest than among less-educated women. Highly educated women have had greater access to adequately paying, stable employment than have less-educated women. Many have used their stronger position in the labor market to live independently in their twenties without marrying or having children. But by the time they are in their forties, highly educated women are *more* likely to have ever been married than are less-educated women. This is a reversal of the educational differences in marriage that existed a half-century ago. It is as though highly educated young women have used their independent income to conduct a long, cautious search for a partner while also investing in themselves. But once they have found a suitable partner, highly educated women have used their earning power as an asset: it increases their attractiveness to potential spouses; it allows a couple to pool two incomes and attain a comfortable standard of living; it gives a wife greater bargaining power within the marriage; and it provides an escape mechanism should the marriage fail and the wife needs to support herself.[10]

THE CHANGING NATURE OF CLASS

How should we define the working class, or for that matter *any* class, after 1975, given an economy that has been transformed by the offshoring of production, computerization, and the resulting hollowing-out of the middle of the labor market? To this point, I have defined class largely on the basis of the occupations of married men: a working-class family consisted of a husband employed in a factory or at a blue-collar job, such as construction or truck driving, and his wife and children. But a sole focus on neither occupations nor marriage nor men is adequate after 1975. (And in truth it was not fully adequate even in the latter half of the postwar peak.) Complications include the shortage of the kind of industrial jobs that used to indicate membership in the working class, the decline of marriage as a marker of adulthood and parenthood, and the movement of women into the labor force. All these factors weaken the older definition. In the post-1975 hourglass economy, I would claim, education, not occupation, is the best indicator of class position. Education is paramount because it provides individuals with higher-level skills that give them a substantial advantage in the labor market. It is also important because of credentialism: an educational degree is a signal that employers use to determine whether a job applicant has the skills they require.[11]

We can see the importance of education as a marker of class most clearly with respect to the bachelor's degree, which is the closest thing to a class boundary that exists in the United States today, at least from the perspective of family life. In the 1980s and 1990s, the wages of both male and female workers with bachelor's degrees were rising faster than the wages of workers with less education. As a result, the financial returns to having a college degree, relative to a high school degree, rose as well. Since about 2000, wages have stopped rising for college-educated men and have slowed for college-educated women, perhaps indicating a moderation of the demand for high-skilled workers. Some college-educated workers, however, unable to find jobs that require their skills and pay accordingly, appear to be moving into middle-skilled jobs, displacing high school graduates. Those workers, in turn, may be displacing the least-skilled workers, forcing some of them out of the labor market entirely. This downward cascade of workers would still imply that college-educated workers are doing better than less-educated workers, but mainly because the latter have been crowded out of the jobs they used to hold.[12]

Moreover, individuals with a bachelor's degree have been progressively choosing spouses who also have a bachelor's degree, a matching process that has increased inequalities by separating college-educated young adults from the rest of the marriage market. A college education is also a marker of people's lifestyles: college-educated parents tend to rear their children in a way that continues to emphasize autonomy and self-development. And the family patterns of the college-educated, such as the percentage of women who are married when they have their first child, have become strikingly different from the patterns among the non-college-educated during the post-1975 period. In addition, education provides a measure of a person's potential labor market value, even when that person is unemployed or underemployed—two conditions that became more prevalent after the postwar peak.[13]

For these reasons, I think it is acceptable and even useful to think of people with bachelor's degrees as a separate class. In 2010, 65 percent of employed individuals with bachelor's degrees were in professional, managerial, or technical occupations, the occupational niches that have benefited from the transformation of the American economy. If we were to give them a name, we might reasonably opt for "middle class," with its connotation of a prosperous lifestyle, but that is not how the term is used in American political discourse these days. Rather, "middle class" has become an elastic term that covers almost everyone except the wealthy and the poor. In contrast, the term "working class" is shunned, as if it were pejorative. In his first six State of the Union Addresses, President Barack Obama used the term "middle class" ten times, but he used "working class" only once: in 2011 he described Vice President Joseph Biden, who was seated behind him, as "a working-class kid from Scranton." Obama's administration, like previous ones, has portrayed programs that would help low- and moderate-income Americans as benefiting the "middle class"—such as a proposal to expand Pell Grants for college tuition, which are awarded almost exclusively to students from families with modest incomes. When Americans are asked what social class they belong to in surveys that do not prompt them with a set of terms that includes "working class," few of them spontaneously say that they belong to the working class. Either we have all become middle-class or else no one wants to speak about the working class. I prefer, then, to refer to the group with bachelor's degrees as the "college-educated middle class," with the qualifier "college-educated" signaling that I am writing about a much more selective group of individuals and families than is commonly implied in conversations about the middle class. I also sometimes refer to this group simply as the "highly educated."[14]

Individuals in the middle of the educational distribution, those with high school degrees and perhaps some college attendance but not a bachelor's degree, have been hurt by the lack of opportunities in the center of the labor market. Few are in managerial or professional occupations; rather, they are spread out among production, sales, and office occupations, with some in low-paying service occupations. It's a diverse group, and hard to categorize or sort. An evident term for them is "working-class," but the problem with using that term—besides its disappearance from political discourse—is that it arose historically to refer to industrial workers and then, in the midtwentieth century, became associated with relatively stable, decent-paying blue-collar jobs. Today, however, a large group of moderately educated young men and women cannot break into the working class, defined in this sense. In an alternative world without offshoring and computerization, many would still be machine operators or crafts workers. In an alternative world in which American manufacturing remains dominant and American exports are still strong, many would be able to bargain for higher wages and benefits. In the real world, however, the defining problem of high school–educated young adults is that they cannot *become* working-class. Not coincidentally, it is the adults in this group who have experienced the greatest changes in family life since 1975.

One step below them are individuals who do not have high school degrees. They are concentrated in low-skilled occupations: in 2010, 41 percent of them were service workers or common laborers. Employment opportunities for them are not attractive: the jobs they can find often pay poorly and provide insecure employment. They therefore earn the lowest wages of any educational group. Since 1975, the family patterns of the two non-college-educated groups—the high school graduates and the high school dropouts—have become more similar to each other, and more dissimilar from the patterns of the college-educated middle class. As a result, the boundary between the two non-college-educated groups is not as sharp as the boundary between both groups and the highly educated. Instead of using the language of class, I refer to individuals without bachelor's degrees simply by their level of education—whether they have a high school degree or not—and I sometimes refer to the two non-college-educated groups together as the "less-educated."[15]

In addition, momentous changes in women's lives during the past half-century—the movement of married women into the labor force and the growth of single-mother families—have also made the relationship between family and class more complex. In the heyday of the male-breadwinner marriage, when most children were being raised by two parents, only one of whom was working outside the home, a family took the class position of the husband. But what is their class position when both spouses work? The lower a husband's income, the more likely it is that his wife out-earns him. The typical couple in which the wife has the higher earnings is more likely to be a construction worker married to a nurse than it is to be a pharmacist married to a corporate lawyer. When deciding what class they are in, both spouses consider the husband's and wife's incomes and weigh them about equally. But women and men diverge in their thinking about education and occupational prestige: women tend to consider theirs and their husband's more or less equally, whereas men tend to weigh their own more heavily. Consequently, in some dual-earner families, husbands and wives might not agree on the class in which they belong.[16]

The class position of an employed single mother would seem to be clearer: it reflects her position alone in the labor market. But class may work differently for single mothers—and for married mothers as well—than it did for workers in the past, when it was a concept largely associated with men's employment. For one thing, employed women may have a different set of interests and concerns. They may be more attentive to adequate arrangements for the care of children or the elderly since they are usually the primary caregivers. The male working class did not demand that employers subsidize child care because their wives were providing that care outside of the market. Since mothers entered the labor force, however, child care has become the most visible of a set of work-family issues that employers are called upon to address. Others include paid leave to care for a newborn child or a seriously ill family member and flexible working hours. None of these issues was prominent during the peak years. In addition, mothers' wages appear to decrease, on average, with each child they have—a property that several sociologists have called a "motherhood penalty." Although part of the drop reflects the lower work experience and seniority of mothers who take time off from work to care for young children, a substantial share of the drop in wages is not explained by less experience or seniority. It could be that some employers discriminate against mothers, or that women have different preferences for motherhood versus full-time employment. In these ways, issues of gender may modify the meaning of "class."[17]

FAMILY CHANGE, 1960–1980

The changing nature of class can help us understand recent developments in family life. But first, let us return briefly to the 1960s. Although social scientists thought that the family had reached a stable plateau, it had begun to change before they realized it. The birth rate reached its peak in 1957 and then began to decline. By 1970, it was down to its pre–baby boom, 1945 level. By 1972, it had reached an all-time low, and it kept falling throughout the 1970s. To some extent, the explanation for the decline is simply that birth rates were returning to their normal trend; from this viewpoint, it is the anomalous baby boom that needs explanation. But that's not a very satisfying interpretation of what was happening. The first few years of the decline occurred because couples were slowing down the pace at which they had children, which had accelerated during the boom. Then came an important technological development: the birth control pill. It was approved for use as a contraceptive in 1960 and became an immediate success. The pill provided the first reliable, medical means of preventing pregnancies and allowed married couples to space their children further apart or to avoid unwanted pregnancies. Advocates for more effective birth control methods thought that the pill would strengthen marriage since effective contraception would allow couples to have pleasurable sexual relations without the fear of an unwanted pregnancy and thus reduce the motivation for extramarital sex. "Marriages built upon the shifting sands of [sexual] fear, shame, and ignorance can never lead to happiness," wrote birth control activist Margaret Sanger.[18]

But reliable contraception had another effect: by allowing *unmarried* people to have sexual relations without fear of pregnancy, it contributed to a larger cultural phenomenon that began in the 1960s—the separation of sex, marriage, and childbearing. Until about 1965, they had been a package deal. Premarital sex had been slowly increasing since the 1940s, but it was still frowned upon. Cohabitation was still uncommon and disfavored. Then cultural norms began to change. Between 1965 and 1972, according to national surveys, Americans, especially young adults, became much more tolerant of premarital sex. The percentage of women under thirty who responded that premarital sex was "always wrong" declined from 50 percent to 17 percent over this seven-year period. What is more, the percentage of all births that were to unmarried women began to accelerate among those without high school degrees and to a lesser extent among those with high school degrees.[19]

The growing acceptance of premarital sex and (among the lowest educational group, at least) premarital births reflected a larger cultural change toward a more individualistic view of parenthood, partnership, and marriage. According to this view, sexual expression and parenthood are not bound by institutional rules but rather by personal preferences. Although marriage may be the preferred setting for raising children, mothers who choose—or have no alternative to—single-parenthood should be accorded the same respect as married mothers, and sexual relations between consenting adults are private matters that should not be under the control of the church or the state. Marriage and other intimate relationships should be evaluated on the basis of how personally fulfilling they are.

This new view was also evident in changing attitudes toward divorce. When a sample of white mothers in the Detroit area were asked in 1962 if they agreed or disagreed with the statement, "When there are children in the family, parents should stay together even if they don't get along," 51 percent disagreed—that is, they did not think that the parents should stay together. When the same women were asked the question in 1977, 80 percent did not think that the parents should stay together. The divorce rate rose greatly from the early 1960s through the 1970s for all educational groups. The rise was a result of a new view of marriage in which a spouse was justified in leaving a marriage if he or she no longer found it personally satisfying. In 1969 California enacted the first "no-fault" divorce law that allowed a spouse to obtain a divorce for any reason, even if the other spouse did not want one. Nearly all other states soon enacted similar laws.[20]

All of these changes began during the postwar peak. So did the increase in the percentage of mothers who were in the labor force—especially mothers whose children were all in school. These alterations of family life therefore cannot be ascribed to changes in the labor market—at least not at first. Liberal social scientists explained the decline of marriage among the less-educated by arguing that a growing number of heavily minority young adults—referred to initially as an urban underclass—did not have the skills or the social networks to compete in the labor market, even at the low-skill end. In this vein, the sociologist William Julius Wilson explained the sharp drop in marriage among African Americans as resulting from a shortage of "marriageable" men: men who had steady jobs with decent pay. Conservative social scientists rejected this view and proposed instead that the declining role of marriage among the poor reflected a greater dependency on government social welfare benefits. They noted the rise of federal antipoverty programs during the Johnson administration's War on Poverty in the 1960s and the great expansion in the late 1960s and 1970s in the number of single-parent families who were receiving cash benefits from the Aid to Families with Dependent Children (AFDC) program, commonly known as welfare. I would add that, in either case, the greater acceptance of cohabitation and single-parenthood also played a role.[21]

Another change that accelerated after 1960 was the growth of the Hispanic population. Just 3 percent of the American population was of Hispanic origin in 1960, and only half of them lived in metropolitan areas. Most immigrants were still coming from Europe. But in 1965 the United States passed the first of a series of immigration laws that increased the flows from Latin America, Asia, and Africa. For instance, a 1965 law established quotas for immigrants from various areas of the world, but promoted family reunification by providing generous numbers of visas for immigrants in the United States who had family members in their home countries. Since Latin Americans, and particularly Mexicans, had an established presence in the United States, they were able to secure a majority of these visas in order to bring in family members. Subsequent restrictions mainly increased the number of undocumented immigrants from Latin America.[22]

Meanwhile, in the 1950s and 1960s, Puerto Ricans, who are U.S. citizens and therefore free to settle on the mainland, began to migrate in larger numbers. They were motivated to leave the island because of widespread poverty, and they were attracted to the mainland because of the strong economy and the availability of inexpensive airfares, which allowed them to travel back and forth. The size of the Puerto Rican population residing on the mainland rather than the island tripled during the 1950s, with many settling in New York City. Puerto Ricans on the mainland have had levels of marriage and childbearing that are closer to those of African Americans. In 2000, 59 percent of births to Puerto Rican women were outside of marriage. Yet "outside of marriage" may have a slightly different meaning among Puerto Ricans and other Caribbean immigrants, who have a tradition of what are called consensual unions. These are long-term unions that have not been formalized by church or state but are nevertheless considered by the community to be like marriages.[23]

The large immigration flow and the higher birth rate among Hispanics boosted the Hispanic proportion of the U.S. population to 9 percent in 1990 and to 16 percent in 2010. Much of this great expansion, however, occurred as the industrial economy was declining. Foreign-born Hispanic men are still overrepresented in agricultural work, a long-standing source of employment for Americans of Mexican origin. In addition, Hispanics have relatively low levels of education: a lower proportion of Hispanic young adults are high school graduates and college graduates than is the case for African American young adults. Consequently, a larger share of young urban Hispanics must cope with the shrinking middle and the low-paying bottom of the hourglass economy.[24]

Reflecting their diverse origins, the family patterns of Hispanic immigrants and their descendants show great variation. Immigrant families from Mexico have had high marriage rates and birth rates. Foreign-born Mexican women between the ages of thirty-five and forty-four in 2000, for instance, had given birth to 2.7 children, on average, well above that of any other group. Birth rates among second- and third-generation Mexican-origin women are lower than among the foreign-born, although they remain somewhat higher than among non-Hispanic whites or blacks. Marriage rates have declined over time as well. Moreover, the percentage of Mexican-origin mothers who were unmarried at the births of their children doubled from 20 percent to 41 percent between 1980 and 2000, a percentage that sits between the levels for non-Hispanic blacks (69 percent) and non-Hispanic whites (23 percent).[25]

The marriage and childbearing patterns of Cubans, the most affluent Hispanic group, are closer to those of non-Hispanic whites. Cubans arrived in the United States with several advantages: they were initially welcomed as refugees, they had more education on average than did other Hispanic immigrants, and their skin color was lighter. Their marriage rates were higher and their birth rates were lower than those of the other major Hispanic groups. Indeed, the Cuban total fertility rate of 1.43 in 2012 was lower than the total fertility rate of 1.76 among non-Hispanic whites. Cuban Americans have used their marriage-based families to accumulate capital for the small businesses they have founded. Except for the Cubans, Hispanics in the United States are a disadvantaged population, with poverty rates well above those of non-Hispanic whites. With their relatively high birth rates (an overall total fertility rate of 2.19) and continuing Hispanic immigration, Hispanics have already become America's largest minority group, surpassing the African American population in size. Their success or failure in the labor market will be a major factor in how the United States adjusts to the new economy.[26]

FAMILY CHANGE, 1980–2010

After 1980, the typical age at marriage, which had begun to rise in the 1960s from an all-time low, continued its march to historic highs in the 2000s—an enormous six-year swing in a half-century. For men, age at marriage increased from a low of 22.5 in 1956 to 28.2 in 2010. The increase for women was similar, from 20.1 in 1956 to 26.1 in 2010. In the lengthened period of life prior to marrying, many young adults began to live with a romantic partner, a living arrangement that had become more socially acceptable. And since the 1980s, cohabitation has increased most rapidly among adults with high school educations. For instance, the percentage of nineteen- to forty-four-year-old women with twelve years of schooling who had ever cohabited more than doubled, from 32 percent in 1987 to 67 percent in 2009–2010. What is more, a growing number of the cohabiting unions included children. In the past, if a cohabiting woman became pregnant, she and her partner tended to either get married or to end their relationship. But today many more couples respond to a pregnancy by continuing to live together. Others respond by starting to live together: nearly 40 percent of the women who are cohabiting when they give birth did not start cohabiting until after they became pregnant. Only then did they and their partner decide to live together. Some are calling these last-minute coresidential arrangements "shotgun cohabitations," in reference to the storied shotgun marriages of old; today no one is holding a shotgun, however, and these relationships are not very stable.[27]

One might wonder why young couples would decide to continue to cohabit, or to begin to cohabit, but not to marry after the woman becomes pregnant. After all, isn't having a child a bigger commitment than marrying? This puzzle was addressed with respect to low-income, single women by the sociologists Kathryn Edin and Maria Kefalas. They interviewed many women who became pregnant but did not wish to marry the baby's father. In most cases, the women said that they would not marry until they found a man who had the potential to hold a steady job and treat them well. When they looked around, they didn't see many men like that, so they weren't sure they would ever find anyone to marry. Yet childbearing was such a central, deeply meaningful part of life that they would not think of having a childless life just because they couldn't find a marriage partner. Consequently, if they found themselves pregnant, they would prefer to keep the child and remain independent than to marry or to have an abortion.[28]

This logic has now worked its way up the ladder to all except the college-educated middle class. You can view the differences among education groups since 1980 more clearly in figure 5.2. It displays the percentages of children who were living with unmarried mothers—by which I mean mothers who were single or cohabiting—in 1980, 1990, 2000, and 2010, for whites and nonwhites. Let's start with the chart for whites. It shows these percentages according to the educational level of the children's mothers. Look first at the black bars, which display the living ar-

Figure 5.2   Children Living with an Unmarried Mother, by the
Mother's Education, 1980–2010

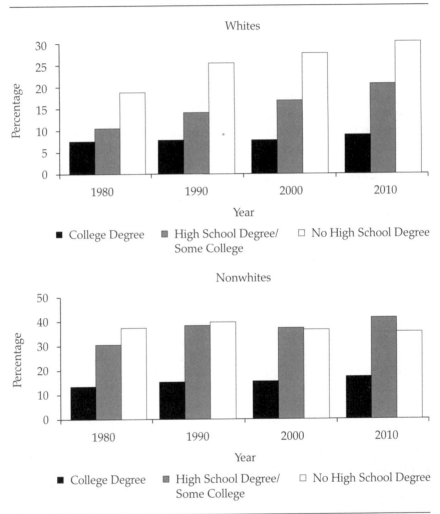

Source: My tabulations, pursuant to Stykes and Williams (2013), from the IPUMS data.

rangements of children whose mothers had bachelor's degrees or more, the group that I have called the college-educated middle class. You can see how short the black bars are compared to the gray and white bars, and you can see that the height of the black bars does not change much over time. This means that only a small proportion of children were living with an unmarried mother who was also highly educated and that the percentage hardly changed during the thirty years shown—it increased a tad, from 8 percent in 1980 to 9 percent in 2010. In fact, the black bars are so much smaller than the other bars, and they increase so little over time, that it is almost as if they have wandered in from another chart. The black bars demonstrate how different the family patterns of the college-educated middle class became over this period from the patterns of the less-educated among whites.

Now skip directly to the white bars. They show the living arrangements of children whose mothers did not have a high school degree. The white bars are always the tallest, which means that in each year the children most likely to be living with an unmarried mother were those whose mother was in the lowest of the three educational groups. Between 1980 and 2010, the heights of the white bars rose from 18 to 30 percent. Now look at the gray bars—those whose mothers had a high school degree but no bachelor's degree. Here we see the greatest proportional increase over time. The height of the gray bars nearly doubled, from 11 percent to 21 percent, in that span of time. The living arrangement of children in the middle group went from being closer to that of children with mothers in the highest group at the start of the thirty-year period to being closer to that of children with mothers in the lowest group at the end. The second chart in figure 5.2 shows the same information for nonwhites. All the bars are higher than among whites. Yet the story is broadly similar: the college-educated group, as was the case among whites, had by far the lowest percentage of children living with an unmarried mother, and the levels hardly increased between 1980 and 2010. Moreover, the percentage of unmarried mothers in the middle group had surpassed the percentage of those in the lowest group by 2010. For both whites and nonwhites, then, the living arrangements of children with highly educated mothers diverged more and more from the living arrangements of all children whose mothers did not have bachelor's degrees.[29]

The timing and size of this change suggests that something important was influencing the family lives of the non-college-educated after 1980, particularly those with a high school degree but not a college degree. It had to be something that had not been as important before 1980 and that was not affecting the family lives of the college-educated middle class. To be sure, single-parenthood and cohabiting-parenthood had become more culturally acceptable. But there is no reason to think that this greater acceptability would have affected only those without bachelor's degrees. That is to say, highly educated young adults also experienced the cultural shift toward the greater acceptability, and yet the percentage of their children living with an unmarried mother hardly increased. And if there were other cultural changes, such as a decline in the propensity to work hard, that change also should have affected all groups. Thus, cultural changes are necessary but not sufficient to explain the pattern we see in figure 5.2. For a fuller explanation, we need to find a development that mainly affected young adults without college degrees after 1980. The obvious candidate is the emergence after the mid-1970s of the hourglass economy.

A study of young adults in Toledo, Ohio, in 2002 showed how non-college-educated young adults may have factored the deteriorating economic situation into their decisions about cohabitation and marriage. Two-thirds of the young adults had a high school degree but not a bachelor's degree, and only 7 percent earned more than $40,000. The sociologists Pamela Smock, Wendy Manning, and Meredith Porter asked individuals who were cohabiting, or who had recently done so, what needed to be in place in order to get married. The overwhelming answer was financial stability. One unemployed twenty-nine-year-old, speaking of his own cohabiting relationship, said, "I don't really know 'cause the love is there uh . . . trust is there. Everything's there except money." Marriage requires a comfortable income, according to a thirty-six-year-old woman whose cohabiting relationship ended without marrying: "Money means um . . . stability. I don't want to struggle, if I'm in a partnership, then there's no more struggling, and income-wise we were still both struggling."[30]

These sentiments reflect a modification in young adults' view of marriage. A half-century ago, people got married in their late teenage years and their twenties, and afterward they rented an apartment and moved in together, the husband found a job, and they had children. Today most or all of those life events occur before a couple gets married. One marries when the rest of one's life is in order, including having access to decent-paying, steady employment, which can take some time—or may never happen. Living together and having children, moreover, are acceptable options, which they were not a half-century ago. As a result, many young couples today choose the lower-commitment cohabiting relationship over the higher-commitment marriage. By design, the former is easier to exit from than the latter.

When a wedding finally occurs, it is less a sacred event joining two families through the marriage of their children than a secular celebration of the achievements of the bride and groom. Increasingly, the couple plans for and pays for the wedding themselves, especially in less-affluent families. This celebratory aspect is important: many couples will not go ahead with a wedding until they have saved up for a proper one. A woman in the Toledo study, explaining why she and her partner were raising a child but had not married, said: "He gave me a ring, he asked me to marry him a long time ago. We talked about getting married, it's just we don't have anyone to pay for the wedding and I don't want to go downtown." "Going downtown" means going to city hall to have a civil ceremony—an unacceptable option to many cohabiting couples. Another woman said of her boyfriend, "He wants a big wedding and, you know, he wants the whole nine yards, but right now we can't really afford it." Marriage has become a capstone experience, the last brick put in place when all else is built, and couples want to celebrate it as such. If they can't, then they might as well continue to cohabit.[31]

When the sociologist Sharon Sassler and her collaborators interviewed thirty cohabiting couples they called working-class and another thirty-one they called middle-class in the Columbus, Ohio, area in 2004 and 2005, they found that the working-class couples were less likely to see their relationship as a precursor to marriage. Instead, they were more likely to say that they decided to cohabit because it was financially easier than maintaining two households. Four had begun to cohabit after the woman became pregnant. When Sassler asked the working-class couples how they would respond if they became pregnant now, the largest group said that they would be dismayed but would have the baby. Few said that they would marry because of the pregnancy. One woman who had already borne a baby with her partner said that he had asked her to marry him several times, but she had declined. "I want this to be because you are marrying me, not because you're marrying me because I'm pregnant." Another man said, "You need to have way better reasons than having a kid to get married." When asked what those reasons might be, he added: "Like 'I love you and I'm gonna love you for the rest of my life, and support you, and, you know, do whatever it takes to make it work.'"[32]

A half-century earlier, having a kid *was* a good reason to get married. In fact, you more or less had to. Today's non-college-educated couples seem to be saying something completely different: Not only is it unnecessary to marry just because you have had a child; that's not even a good reason to marry. Rather, it's better to wait until you are confident that two conditions hold: a strong expressive, emotional bond ("I love you and I'm gonna love you for the rest of my life") and an ability to sustain the marriage financially ("and support you"). This is the cultural context in which less-educated young adults are making decisions about marriage and parenthood.

The deteriorating employment opportunities in the middle of the labor market have undermined young adults' ability to meet the second condition—financial support. Fewer have confidence that they can make a marriage work economically. By itself, a stronger labor market would not lead every cohabiting couple with children to marry, because it would have little effect on their emotional bonds. But it would encourage marriage among couples who feel that they are emotionally ready to marry ("Everything's there but money") because it would provide them with a firmer financial base. In the polarized labor market that has evolved since 1975, some young adults may conclude that getting married anytime soon is unlikely. If so, they may use contraception less effectively, or not at all, and bring to term the pregnancies that may result. In this way, an altered cultural context and an altered labor market have combined to increase the share of children born outside of marriage among less-educated young adults.

DIVORCE AND THE LABOR MARKET

Meanwhile, the divorce rate, which peaked in 1980, has declined since then. But the decline has not been uniform: it has been steeper among the highly educated than among the less-educated. A thirty-year study of a national sample of adults who had reached their late forties and early fifties by 2010 showed a substantial educational gap in the likelihood of divorce: only 30 percent of the marriages of the highly educated had ended in divorce, in contrast to 48 percent of the marriages of those with a high school degree but no bachelor's degree and an even higher 58 percent of the marriages of those without high school degrees. Why might divorce have declined more for the highly educated? It's not clear that they are more culturally conservative with respect to family life. In 1982, as the divorce rate began to drop, the General Social Survey (GSS) asked a national sample of adults how important they thought family and children were as an aspect of life. Eighty percent of college-educated respondents under age thirty-five said "very important," which seems impressive until one learns that 90 percent of the non-college-educated said "very important." So there is no indication that the college graduates started off more conservative than the less-educated. And they did not, in general, become more conservative. In 2012 the GSS asked another national sample about family issues. Among those under age thirty-five, college graduates were far more likely to agree that it was okay for a woman to have an abortion if she wanted to for any reason (56 percent) than were respondents without college degrees (33 percent). And they were more likely to agree that same-sex couples could bring up a child as well as opposite-sex couples. Between the 1970s and the 1980s, however, they did become more likely to think that divorce should be made stricter, but so, to a somewhat lesser extent, did those without college educations.[33]

The most likely explanation for why college graduates are divorcing less is their position atop the hourglass economy. They are the ones who can still find steady, well-paying jobs. As highly educated people have become more likely to marry each other, they have largely separated themselves from the rest of the marriage market. In doing so, they are consolidating their resources, which often include two professional or managerial jobs, and building a solid economic floor for their marriages. In their more egalitarian style of marriage than was common in the 1950s, both spouses typically work outside the home. When marriages involve fewer economic difficulties, they engender less conflict between the spouses and are more likely to last. Since 1980, incomes in dual-earner marriages have far outpaced incomes in other family forms. For instance, between 1980 and 2012, the median income of dual-earner married couples increased 29 percent, while the median income of single-earner married couples increased by a negligible 1 percent and the median income of single-mother families increased 11 percent. It has been a relatively good period for the income-pooling married-couple family. They can use their combined incomes to purchase shared goods such as nice houses and automobiles and to pay for the leisure activities they do together. They can invest more money in their children's education and extracurricular activities. But it is mainly the college-educated who have been able to achieve this twenty-first-century style of consumption-oriented, stable marriage.[34]

THE CULTURE OF ANGER

The 1970s also marked a change in how blue-collar family life was portrayed in the media. While Jackie Gleason's Ralph Kramden character was often exasperated with his wife Alice, he was an optimistic guy, always convinced he had found a sure-fire get-rich-quick scheme. By the 1970s, a new trait had been added to the television personality of the white working-class man: anger. And what he was most angry about was race. Civil rights legislation and subsequent court decisions that sought to redress long-standing racial inequalities had him steamed. In *All in the Family,* the most popular situation comedy of the 1970s, Archie Bunker, portrayed by the actor Carroll O'Connor, became the bigot whom America loved. The first episode, which aired on January 12, 1971, entitled "Meet the Bunkers," included this exchange between Archie and his liberal son-in-law, Mike, who was played by Rob Reiner, with a telling commentary by Archie's scatterbrained wife Edith, played by Jean Stapleton:

ARCHIE: Well, let me tell you something. If your spics and your spades want their rightful share of the American dream, let 'em get out there and hustle for it just like I done.

MIKE: Yeah, but Archie, you're forgetting one thing. You didn't have to hustle with a black skin.

ARCHIE: No, I didn't have to hustle with one arm and one leg neither. So what?

MIKE: So you're admitting that the black man is handicapped.

ARCHIE: Oh no, no more than me, he's just as good as me.

MIKE: Now I suppose you're going to tell me that the black man has had the same opportunity in this country as you?

ARCHIE: More, he has more. . . . I didn't have no million people marchin' and protestin' to get me my job.

EDITH: No, his uncle got it for him.

Blue-collar workers at the Sparrows Point steelworks could certainly identify with Archie on that. In 1974, nine steel companies, including Bethlehem Steel, then the owner of Sparrows Point, and the United Steelworkers of America entered into an agreement with the U.S. government in an employment discrimination action brought by the Equal Employment Opportunity Commission. The consent decree, as it was called, changed the seniority rules at the Point from unit seniority to plantwide seniority. This ended the situation in which black workers, who were usually hired into units that had the least skilled and least desirable jobs, were effectively barred from transferring to other more desirable units when a job opened up. The consent decree also applied to the smaller number of female employees and led the firms to hire more women.[35]

The decree was issued at a time when the employment of steelworkers was already beginning to decline. Perhaps if the agreement had come a decade or two earlier, during the boom years of steel production and employment, the reaction of white steelworkers at the Point would have been less hostile. But with job opportunities decreasing, it became progressively harder for a white worker to find a job for a son, or a friend's son, or a nephew who wanted to work at the Point. The ending of the unit seniority system made it even more difficult because a black worker with several years of seniority at the Point could apply for an opening in another unit and would have priority over a white applicant with no seniority. To black workers the consent decree represented the end of decades of injustice and discrimination in hiring and promotion. White workers, however, felt as though their rights were being restricted in order to aid blacks. The unit seniority system had been in place for so long that it seemed to white workers to be the natural way for the plant to operate. They saw the decree not as the withdrawal of white privilege but rather as reverse discrimination. Some white workers refused to teach black or female transfers how to do their new jobs. A black man who used to work at the plant told the author Deborah Rudacille that some of his white friends grew distant after the decree.

> I had good white buddies that we worked together as a feeder, feeder helper, and floor hands, and when the consent decree came, they stopped speaking to me. They'd be working daylight and I'd be working three to eleven, and most of the time you came in you'd say, "Okay, we're running such and such a thing" or "Look out for this." If there was something going on that would make it easier for you, they'd tell you. No more.[36]

Women who started working at the Point also felt intense opposition from some of the workers. They posed a double threat to white men: a challenge not just to their jobs but also to their sense of masculinity. The presence of women disrupted the intensely masculine atmosphere at the plant. One woman steelworker told Karen Olson: "The men are out to impress each other. They talk different when women aren't around. They need to prove their masculinity. You'll find yourself talking about gardening with a man, but if another man walks up they catch themselves and start talking about 'let's go for a beer.'" The consent decree also provided employment opportunities to the growing number of single mothers. A thirty-year-old black single mother who lived in the all-black Turner Station neighborhood near the plant told Olson:

> Prior to working at Bethlehem Steel I was working as an assistant manager at Sambo's Restaurant, and I was working the graveyard shift. My daughter, Holly, was going on two, my former husband was completely out of the picture, and I was trying to get off welfare. I heard about jobs at the Point through the unemployment office. Bethlehem Steel was close to home, it was more money, and the benefits were good, including BlueCross/BlueShield. I was called down to Bethlehem Steel to be tested. From there I was hired as a bricklayer's helper in the labor department in March of 1979.

Nationally, the percentage of workers in the manufacturing sector who were separated, divorced, or never-married women with children under age eighteen rose from 3 percent in 1970 to 6 percent in 2010.[37]

The family issue that caused the most anger in the nation was school desegregation. In the 1970s, courts ruled that Northern cities such as Boston, in which neighborhoods were highly racially segregated, had to desegregate their schools by busing black and white students to different neighborhoods. When Boston and nearby suburbs began to bus students, racially motivated violence erupted. The issue of busing was particularly salient for white working-class families who could not afford to move to the wealthy, nearly-all-white exurbs that were beyond the reach of the busing orders. A worker at a Ford factory who had just bought a house in a working-class suburb on the edge of Detroit complained about a busing order to a *New York Times* reporter in 1972:

> "There are two things you buy a home for—how close you are to a school and how close you are to a shopping center," Mr. Burton said. "What burns me to the bottom of my bones is that I paid an excessive amount of money so that my son could walk three blocks to school. I'm not going to pay big high school taxes and pay more for a home so that somebody can ship my son 30 miles away to get an inferior education."

Mr. Burton told the reporter he planned to vote for George Wallace in the forthcoming Michigan Democratic presidential primary election. Wallace, the governor of Alabama at the time, had risen to prominence by opposing school integration. His stance appealed to white voters who felt powerless to stop a string of laws and court decisions favorable to blacks. The anger of many working-class whites has remained a part of American politics ever since the 1970s. The sociologist Michael Kimmel has labeled their attitude "aggrieved entitlement": a sense of outrage over the withdrawal of privileges—including the ability to send their children to a nearly-all-white neighborhood school—they had taken for granted. This sentiment has been compounded by the steadily worsening job market. As it has become harder for moderately educated men to fulfill the role of breadwinner, their despair has fueled their sense of outrage at perceived competitors in the labor market, such as blacks, immigrants, and women, and at a federal government they see as discriminating against them.[38]

LABOR MARKETS, CULTURE, AND FAMILY CHANGE

Since 1980, the college-educated middle class has been moving toward a pattern of partnering and childbearing that could be called neotraditional. Nine out of ten marry, and among those who have children, nine out of ten wait until after they are married. The likelihood that their marriage will end in divorce is well below that of their parents' generation. To be sure, there are important ways in which their family lives are unlike family lives in the past. A majority live with a partner, often but not always their future spouse, before they marry. They wait longer to marry, on average, than any generation since at least the late 1800s. Wives are much more likely to work outside the home than was the case a half-century ago. While all this may seem unremarkable, no expert predicted a sharp drop in divorce for any educational group back when divorce was at its peak in 1980. And none that I know of expected that college-educated women, who used to be less likely to marry than women without college degrees, would now marry just as often.

In the meantime, high school–educated young adults have moved since 1980 toward the type of family life that had previously been seen mainly among people who had not graduated from high school. Like the highly educated, they are postponing marriage, but they are not postponing having children nearly as much as the highly educated are. In a recent study of teenagers who had been followed into their late twenties, high school–educated women tended to start bearing children in their early to mid twenties, largely outside of marriage, and to be nearing the end of their childbearing period by the end of the study. Among women with a high school degree but no bachelor's degree, 69 percent of those who gave birth during this study had at least one of their children outside of marriage. It is now uncommon for high school–educated women to have all of their children within marriage—a stark change since 1980. They are increasingly bearing their children in cohabiting unions, some of which do not begin until after the pregnancy. These cohabiting relationships are very fragile. A well-known study showed that 48 percent of couples who were cohabiting at the birth of their child in urban hospitals between 1998 and 2000 ended their relationships within five years—a much higher breakup rate than among married couples. Consequently, the children who are born into cohabiting partnerships have a high risk of seeing their parents break up.[39]

Yet across the social hierarchy, there is little disagreement about the value of marriage. Young adults in all classes seem to value it highly. That is a bit of a surprise to experts, who, a few decades ago, thought that marriage was about to fade away. Regardless of educational level, most young adults would prefer to marry and to have their children after marrying. Regardless of educational level, they now see marriage as a capstone event in their lives, a step one does not take until one feels financially secure enough to bet that the marriage will be a success.

The big dividing line is what to do about children until one marries. The highly educated are much less likely to have children prior to marrying. Nonmarital childbearing is the key difference in the transition to adulthood between the college-educated middle class and the less-educated. The highly educated can foresee a favorable financial future in which to raise children—a future that includes finding a partner with

good economic prospects. In fact, they may already be living with someone who they think is a good candidate for marriage. They may also anticipate receiving financial assistance from their parents for a down pay-
ment on a home. They may expect to be earning enough to pay for child
care. Although they may not marry until after they complete graduate
school and establish careers, they are confident that the time to marry will
come. By the time they are age forty, the highly educated are more likely
to have ever been married than are those with less education. The less-
educated, in contrast, lack the confidence that they will be able to find a
partner who can also help to sustain a good marriage, and their doubts are
well founded. The financial stability that they consider adequate may
never appear. For the most part, they do not have parents who can aid
them financially. Many conclude that it would be a great risk to forgo having children in one's twenties just because they are not ready to marry. The
problem they see is that they may never be ready to marry and their opportunity to have children may be lost. So, according to this logic, if a
pregnancy occurs accidentally, or semi-accidentally, it may be better to go
ahead and have the child in a cohabiting relationship. This choice puzzles
college-educated observers because they see the advantages of waiting
until marriage. But so do the less-educated—they just do not see the likelihood of attaining a good marriage and will not start one until they are
reasonably sure of its success. Until about 1980, young adults with high
school degrees used the same logic as the college-educated: they, too,
waited until after marriage to have children. But now they use a logic that
is much more like that of those without high school degrees.[40]

These family patterns reflect major cultural changes since the heyday of
the 1950s families, for which some Americans seem to be nostalgic. The
place of marriage has shifted from the beginning to the end of early adulthood. Living together outside of marriage is broadly acceptable and unremarkable. Having a child outside of marriage may not be seen as optimal
but it, too, is acceptable. Dual-earner families are not just acceptable but
preferable because without two incomes, a family has little chance of attaining a prosperous standard of living. Family life is seen as a series of
choices that individuals should make according to their sense of personal
fulfillment rather than established norms. All of these changes are momentous in historical perspective. Ward and June Cleaver would be
shocked if they could see family life today. One could argue that the extent
of cultural change in family life since the end of the peak years is unmatched in any half-century in modern history.

Nevertheless, cultural change cannot fully explain the great changes
we have seen in the family lives of less-educated young adults over the
past few decades. To be sure, values such as a greater acceptance of raising

children outside of marriage appear to have changed earliest among the bottom group and then to have been adopted by the middle; some trickling up of cultural change has occurred. But why would the effects of those values have absolutely no effect on nonmarital childbearing among the highly educated, as figure 5.2 suggests? My answer is that the labor market did not deteriorate for them. In contrast, the less-educated were hit the hardest by the transformation of the American economy after the postwar peak ended. Even though nonmarital childbearing is more acceptable than in the past, only the less-educated have had an increasing proportion of their children outside of marriage because only they have experienced a falling probability of finding a financially suitable partner. Even though cohabitation is now respectable in most circles, only the less-educated have seen a sharp rise in the percentage of children born in cohabiting unions because only they have had to cope with a rapidly deteriorating labor market position.

The distinctive changes we have seen in the family lives of less-educated young adults today are the result of a globalized, skill-biased economy that has negatively affected those who, in an earlier era, would have flocked to factory jobs. Without doubt, cultural changes in American society have shaped the responses of less-educated young adults to this new economy. Neither cultural change nor economic change would have been sufficient by itself to produce a group of non-college-educated young adults who now have a majority of their children outside of marriage. Neither change would have been sufficient to erode the disciplined self that characterized the identities of white working-class men. Let us do the following thought experiment. First, can we find a historical setting in which the economy was very bad but norms about marriage and childbearing were more traditional? Yes, we can: the Great Depression. Despite a terrible job market in the 1930s, there was no meaningful rise in nonmarital childbearing because cultural norms had not changed. Now, can we find a setting in which the economy remained good but values changed? Yes, that has been the situation for highly educated young adults over the past few decades. Yet once again, there has been no rise in nonmarital childbearing, this time because economic opportunities have not declined for this population. Only among young adults who have experienced both a deteriorating labor market and a nontraditional culture do we see the kinds of changes in family and personal lives that characterize the less-educated today.

Chapter 6 | The Would-Be Working Class Today

With the collaboration of Timothy Nelson

THE FAMILY LIVES of young adults without bachelor's degrees, whom I have called the "less-educated," have changed greatly since the end of the post–World War II peak. They are the would-be working class—the individuals who would have taken the industrial jobs we used to have or married someone who did. Let me delve more deeply into how those changes have altered the way they lead their daily lives, including their attitudes toward the world around them, their self-identities, the values they are passing along to their children, and the instability and complexity of their families. To better understand these meanings, I suggested to the sociologist Timothy Nelson, an author of a study of low-income fathers, that he conduct some in-depth interviews. He and an associate completed thirty-three such interviews with high school–educated men in Boston, Chicago, and Cleveland who were between the ages of twenty-five and thirty-five and who had at least one child. We focused on men because they have been more affected by the decline of industrial jobs than women and because some commentators believe that men have become less willing to take the jobs that remain.[1]

Nevertheless, great changes have occurred in the work lives of less-educated women too. The proportion of these women who were participating in the labor force—which means working for pay or looking for work—rose dramatically between 1960 and 1990, when it plateaued. By 1990, 72 percent of less-educated women between the ages of twenty-five and forty-four were in the labor force, compared to 38 percent in 1960. The increase was greater among white women than among black women because the latter had long been in the labor force. In fact, by 1990 white women had caught up to comparable black women in the percentage of them in the labor force. During the same period, a noticeable number of wives began to out-earn their husbands. Among dual-earner married couples in which the husbands had average earnings, one out of seven wives had higher annual earnings than their husbands by the early 1990s. While less-educated men have struggled in the labor market in recent decades, less-educated wives have increased their work effort and their earnings. Moreover, the number of single mothers in the labor force has expanded greatly since the postwar peak. Of all less-educated working mothers in 2010, 41 percent were unmarried, a proportion that had risen sharply from 15 percent in 1960 and 26 percent in 1990. The old assumption that the working-class family is synonymous with the married-couple family no longer holds among the would-be working class. Some working mothers are cohabiting with a partner, and others have done so in the past or will do so in the future, but at any one time, most are unpartnered.[2]

As for our interviews with less-educated men, consider Frank, a thirty-three-year-old white man in Chicago who was living with a friend because he didn't have enough money to rent an apartment. After graduating from high school, he worked as a waiter for a few years, then went to bartending school and worked on and off as a bartender. For a time, he did valet parking several evenings a week. Frank's father was a firefighter, and he would have liked Frank to be one too. But, Frank said, "I had a little, um, a couple of run-ins with the law when I was younger. Nothing major, but I'm pretty sure it would have disqualified me." Besides, he told the interviewer, his father had been a firefighter for thirty-one years, and "I couldn't imagine doing anything for that long." Neither parent had encouraged him to go to college.

When Frank was twenty-eight, he moved into an apartment with his girlfriend, who soon got pregnant. By this time, he was working as an automobile salesman. A year after their daughter was born, however, they split up:

> You know, it's weird, uh, now that I think back on it, I can kind of pinpoint what happened. Before our child, our daughter, was born, her focus, all her attention was on me and vice versa. Then all of a sudden you throw a kid in the mix, and now my attention is all on him and her attention and we neglected each other. I think that's where it went wrong. And she met another guy. I wasn't looking for another girl. I was happy where I was.

He says he sees his daughter a lot: "She's the love of my life, she really is. Like I love this kid to death."

At the time of the interview, Frank was doing construction work three days a week for a contractor who paid him about $50 a day under the table. He also did disk jockey jobs on weekends when he could find them. Frank thinks that job opportunities come down to connections: "It really seems like it doesn't matter how great you are anymore, it's just who you know." When the interviewer asked if he thought there was a racial-ethnic component to job connections, Frank replied:

> Maybe. There's a possibility. It's interesting you said that because my dad was telling me a story about the fire department. How they have to take tests, right? Well, they had to make the test easier because of the blacks couldn't pass it. . . . And there was another time too, when there was a promotion and they had to promote the top five black people. So it didn't matter if you were higher on your test scores and you were white. Sorry, you know, so I think that right now they're really trying to push this equality thing, but it almost comes off as not being fair because they're pushing it. And to me, it shouldn't matter what color you are. It's who's better at the job, bottom line.

Frank was raised as a Roman Catholic, but he said, "I'm struggling with the whole God issue. I believe in a higher power, just not organized religion." Later in the interview, he said that he considered himself an agnostic:

> To me agnostic, it means, I guess it would mean I'm a seeker of the truth. I guess I believe in a higher power and I take a little from every religion. I believe certain things. I'm different. . . . Everything the Catholics say isn't true—and this is just in my opinion of course. But yet, some of the stuff they say, I believe. The same with the Muslims and that . . . I feel like they all have some truth in there. So I take what I feel is right.

Frank's world contrasts discernibly with that of Richard, a thirty-four-year-old white man living in a working-class suburb of Boston. He is married to his high school sweetheart and lives within a few miles of the house in which he grew up and in which his father still lives. He and his wife were engaged at eighteen and married at twenty-one. They had the first of their two children when they were twenty-four.

INTERVIEWER: Was it planned?

RICHARD: Um, yes, it was. I mean, we were married and the next step was kids, and it wasn't like "Okay, we have to have it now." It was just we knew it was coming. It was the next step.

When asked his opinion of cohabitation and marriage, Richard replied:

Somehow [marriage] changes the way people act or they have an expectation of something. So for her and I, you know, it works. I don't know if that's
because both my parents are still together, happily married. Her parents are
or were still together. Her father has passed away, but they were still happily
married. So I think that's what we saw, that's what we grew up with, it's just
that's how we are now, you know. But for someone in today's world, you
know, people live together for a lot of reasons, whether it's financial reasons
or they have kids or something. And that's great, whatever works for them
is good. You know, different strokes for different folks kind of. For me to
impose a judgment onto them, you know, it just doesn't seem right.

Richard loves spending time with his wife:

She's fun. We do everything together. There are couples that are like "Oh, I
don't want to go out with her." Or "I don't want to go out with him." But her
and I, we do everything together. We go food shopping together. We go to
the stores together. We shop together. She'll be like "Oh, you should wear
this," or I'll be like "You wear that," you know, so we have a good time together.

Richard and his wife take the children to Catholic religious school and
to mass every Sunday. When asked why that's important to him, he replied:

It gives the kids something to believe in. Kind of when we were growing up
the thought of Jesus looking down on you and watching you kind of put the
scare in all of us. So I think like 'cause nowadays there is so much on the
Internet and TV. Church just gives them something to ground to that's not a
cartoon, that's not a video game, something that's [part of] the past I grew
up on, it's continued the same to their age, so it's consistent. So I think that
will help them growing up to be the person that I am today and that I want
them to be.

Richard has worked steadily at maintenance jobs since he was fourteen.
He thinks there's as much opportunity to find jobs as in his father's generation. Recently he was hired for a maintenance position at a local university that comes with good benefits such as health and dental insurance,

supplemental life insurance, and a 401(k) account. He really enjoys the job. He has no regrets about not going to college, especially after watching his parents struggle to find the money to send his sister to college, but if his kids want to go to college, that would be fine. He added, "You know, my wife believes if you want to go to college [you] have to pay [your] way and get through. Me, I'm a little more, um, if they need help I'll help them whatever I can, do whatever I can." But the children would certainly be expected to help cover the costs.

Without doubt, Frank and Richard's lives differ in many ways. Above all, what is striking about Frank is his rootlessness—his lack of ties to institutions such as family, religion, and work. He is without a home at age thirty-three; he is a visitor in his daughter's life; he has cycled through a series of occupations, none of them very stable; and he is engaged in a quest for religious meaning that has taken him far beyond his childhood religion. The idea of impermanence is so ingrained in him at this point that he cannot even imagine a world in which a person keeps a job for three decades, as his father did. In trying to make sense of his chaotic work life, he blames a new social order in which African Americans get special treatment. Richard, on the other hand, remains rooted in his neighborhood and his childhood religious faith. He has been married since age twenty-one to a woman he dated in high school. He has been continuously employed in one field. He followed conventional norms by waiting until after he was married to have children—it was the "next step." He seems content with his life and the opportunities he has had.

It is nice to think that if everyone made the same choices as Richard, and not Frank, the problems of less-educated young adults would be solved. Yet Richard was the only man out of thirty-three who had a traditional working-class life: he had all of his children within marriage, and he had a continuous work history. A few came close. A thirty-five-year-old, married African American man in Chicago had been doing steady warehouse work for years, had only recently had a child, and attended church weekly with his wife. But he had also "gang-banged" from age sixteen to twenty-three, and he subsequently lost a job he had liked after his partying caused him to not show up for work. A twenty-two-year-old African American man in Chicago was married and had a young daughter, but he and his then-girlfriend had had a pregnancy that ended in a stillbirth prior to marrying. A white thirty-two-year-old Boston man, an Iraq War veteran, had married his girlfriend after she became pregnant and then had two more children with her. He was working at the time but also selling pain pills on the side; eventually he became addicted, he got his wife addicted, and his marriage fell apart. None of the other twenty-nine men had his first child in a marriage. In fact, most had never married. Frank's life story is much more typical of the group's than is Richard's. Admittedly, these men were not a random sample of high school–educated fathers; rather, they were volunteers who liked the idea of talking to an interviewer for two hours and receiving a $40 payment. As such, they were probably more down-and-out than the typical high school–educated dad. Yet national statistics confirm that marriage has faded as the setting for having children among this group. A few decades ago, a high school–educated young adult who had a child without marrying was an outlier, and such behavior was frowned upon. Now it is the young adult who has all of his or her children while married who is the outlier.[3]

Why was it so uncommon for these men to have continuous work histories and children within marriage? Undeniably, many of them had made unfortunate choices—dealing pills on the side, living the street-gang lifestyle, partying and not showing up for work the next morning. There is certainly a role for encouraging young men and women to make better choices than these. Yet some of these choices were made in reaction to a difficult labor market. Hector, a thirty-five-year-old Hispanic man in Chicago, framed drug-dealing as a response to not having a job:

> It's just that the point where you can't find a job is when the drug-dealing stuff starts, you know, 'cause, I mean, you can—there's other options. If you can't find a job, you can either, you can sell drugs. You can go robbing people. I'm not the robbing type. I don't, you know, burglaries—I never stole anything in my life.

I present Hector's reasoning not to justify drug-dealing as a nonviolent alternative to mainstream employment, but rather to show the context in which young men are making decisions. His thinking brings to mind the classic formulation that the sociologist Robert Merton first proposed in the 1930s. In an article that later influenced the architects of the War on Poverty, Merton argued that deviant behavior is most likely to occur when an individual shares the cultural goals of the broader society but lacks "access to the approved opportunities for legitimate, prestige-bearing pursuit of the culture goals." Merton was not trying to excuse or apologize for illegal activity, but merely emphasizing the pressure a young man might feel when he would like to take an approved path to a good adult life but cannot find it.[4]

The stories the men told did illustrate how much the job market for them has deteriorated. No job seemed secure. An African American man from Boston worked as an editorial assistant at a newspaper, but with newspaper circulation declining, his position was eliminated. He worked as a parking attendant at a local hotel, but was let go after the hotel installed automated parking equipment. He worked for a catering company, but it went out of business. At one point, Frank sold Pontiacs, but then General Motors terminated the Pontiac brand. Many men, like Frank, related complex job histories that seemed to involve little commitment by either the employer or the worker. For instance, a thirty-year-old Chicago man had been a telemarketer, an automotive body shop assistant, a fast-food worker, and a sous chef. On the employer side, workers are laid off as soon as conditions worsen. The pay is low and fringe benefits are often negligible. Employees who miss a day of work risk being fired. Small companies or individual contractors sometimes pay workers surreptitiously in cash so that they do not have to pay taxes. This arrangement gives workers more pocket money but creates no record of employment that can be used later to claim social security benefits. On the employee side, workers are ready to quit as soon as something better comes along.

It is as though the 1950s Treaty of Detroit, so lauded by Walter Reuther and other leaders of organized labor at the time, has been replaced by pervasive distrust. Whereas the 1950s workers, backed by their powerful unions, trusted management enough to pledge uninterrupted labor on the assembly line in return for good wages and the promise of retirement pensions down the road, today's workers and employers do not trust each other to pledge much of anything. The power of unions has faded: the overwhelming majority of less-educated young adults do not work in a place where a union has successfully organized. Absent an agreement between labor and management, young adults have neither the right to decent wages and benefits nor the obligation to be loyal workers. Employers have little responsibility except to pay the wage they offered in return for an hour's work. What has evolved in the market for non-college-educated labor after the breakdown of the Treaty is not war between employers and employees but rather mutual disengagement.

ARE LESS-EDUCATED MEN SIMPLY LESS INDUSTRIOUS?

Is part of the problem a reluctance among the men without bachelor's degrees to seize the modest opportunities that do exist? The political scientist Charles Murray argues in his influential 2012 book that the economic position of non-college-educated white men has declined because they do not want to work as hard as previous generations worked. He defines "industriousness" as the "bone-deep American assumption that life is to be spent getting ahead through hard work, making a better life for oneself and one's children," and he argues that among men of prime working age, industriousness is in decline. Let's leave aside the American exceptionalism rhetoric about whether working hard is unique to this country. There is, in fact, some evidence from surveys conducted over the past few decades that a belief in the importance of hard work has become less central in Americans' minds and, conversely, that Americans have come to be attracted to work that is less demanding. One such study, Monitoring the Future, has collected data on thousands of high school seniors annually since 1976. Another one, the GSS, has interviewed a national sample of adults every year or two since 1972.[5]

The Monitoring the Future study asked students to rate the importance of each of a long list of job characteristics. I compared the percentage who responded "very important" to these questions in the pooled responses from the 1980–1982 surveys to the pooled results thirty years later from the 2010–2012 surveys. Three characteristics pertained to the amount of leisure the job allows. The percentage who responded that "a job with an easy pace that lets you work slowly" was very important increased from 9 to 15 percent, and the percentage who considered it very important to have "a job where you have more than two weeks' vacation" increased from 18 to 29 percent. On the other hand, there was not much change in the responses concerning "a job which leaves a lot of time for other things in your life." I examined four questions pertaining to the intrinsic rewards of work, and the percentage responding "very important" declined over time for all of them: from 60 to 43 percent for a job "where you can see the results of what you do"; from 88 to 77 percent for a job that was "interesting to do"; from 72 to 66 percent for a job that "uses your skills and abilities—let's you do the things you can do best"; and from 48 to 43 percent for a job that would allow the respondent to "learn new things, learn new skills." Overall, recent high school seniors seem more drawn to occupations that ask less of them, such as those with a slower pace and more vacation time, and less drawn to jobs that have intrinsic rewards such as being interesting and allowing one to see the fruits of one's labor.

However, the Monitoring the Future surveys apply only to high school seniors. We can learn more about the adult population as a whole from the GSS, which in some of its waves has asked respondents who were in the labor force to read a card listing five characteristics of jobs and to rate them as "most important," "second most important," and so on. These questions were included in most of the 1973–1994 surveys, but unfortunately, not again until 2006 and (for half the sample) 2012. So the recent results may be less reliable. Nevertheless, they are worth a look, particularly for men, who are the alleged culprits for lacking industriousness. Among men ages twenty-five to forty-four, the percentage who rated the job characteristic "working hours are short, lots of free time" as most important or

Figure 6.1   Employed Men Ages Twenty-Five to Forty-Four Who Rated "Working Hours Are Short, Lots of Free Time," as Most Important or Second Most Important of Five Job Characteristics

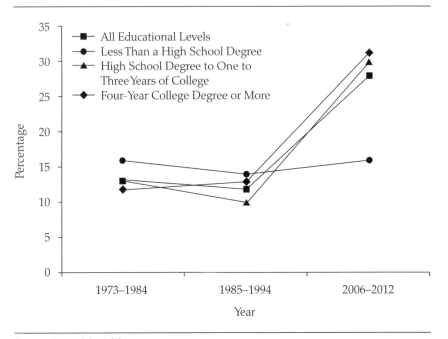

Source: General Social Survey.

second most important increased over time, especially in the more recent surveys. In contrast, the percentage who rated the characteristic "work important and gives a feeling of accomplishment" as most important or second most important decreased over time. The trends were very similar for women—this was not just a shift in values among men. As with high school seniors, American adults seem to have shifted toward valuing less-demanding work and away from the intrinsic rewards of work.[6]

Yet what is notable is that the shift in preferences shown by the GSS occurred not only among the less-educated adults whom some have labeled as not industrious enough, but also among highly educated adults. Figure 6.1 shows the percentage of twenty-five- to forty-four-year-old men who rated "working hours are short, lots of free time" as the most important or second most important job characteristic, by educational group. The line marked with squares shows the overall trend: an increase from 13 percent in the earliest period to 28 percent in the most recent period. As the line with the circles shows, however, the percentage choosing shorter working hours did not change among men without high school degrees; it was the same in both the earliest and latest periods. Rather than looking for shorter hours, many of them were probably looking for longer hours. The trend among the other two, more-educated groups—those with a high school degree but less than four years of college, as shown by the line with triangles, and those with four or more years of college, as shown by the line with diamonds—were almost identical, with a sharp rise among both. Men who had completed four years of college shifted toward preferring shorter working hours as much as men with less education.

How does this pattern of responses square with labor force trends? Murray points to the well-known drop during the past half-century in the proportion of prime-age men who are participating in the labor force— that is, who are working or looking for work. He argues that men's labor force participation declined because they generally are not interested in working as hard. Yet let's look at the falloff more closely. It was concentrated among men without bachelor's degrees. For instance, among men ages twenty-five to forty-four without bachelor's degrees, the proportion in the labor force declined from 95 percent in 1960 to 85 percent in 2010—a notable decrease indeed. Yet among comparable men *with* bachelor's degrees, the decrease in labor force participation was much smaller, moving from 97 percent in 1960 to 95 percent in 2010. This comparison raises a question: if being less interested in demanding work caused the decline in labor force participation, why didn't the participation of men with bachelor's degrees decline more? After all, they were just as likely as their less-educated brethren to shift away from preferring intrinsic rewards and toward preferring less demanding work. Yet college-educated workers are much more likely to put in long hours on the job than are less-educated workers. In 2000, 39 percent of employed men with college degrees worked fifty hours or more per week, compared to 22 percent of employed high school graduates. The number of hours worked per week by all dual-income, college-educated couples in the United States is higher than in Canada, the United Kingdom, France, and Germany.[7]

I submit that college-educated men are working long hours despite their preferences for easier employment because they are in high demand in the labor market, whereas less-educated men are not. Employers have sought to retain highly educated employees, whom they have trained and who have specialized knowledge, in the face of changing preferences. They have done so in part by emphasizing flexibility in the timing and place of work. Some large firms offer workers a choice of when to start and when to finish their days; some allow employees to work from home;

and a federal law requires them to offer unpaid leave to care for sick children or parents. Firms offer flexibility not just to parents but to childless workers who also want greater balance between their work lives and their personal lives. An army of nonprofit organizations, consultants, and academic researchers now marches under the banner of what used to be called "work-family balance" but is now referred to, in deference to the preferences of workers who do not have young children, as "work-life balance." In addition, high-tech firms that expect long hours provide amenities such as gyms and recreation rooms on-site in an effort to keep programmers and analysts near their desks. If you are a high school graduate who wants less-demanding work, you may be accused of a lack of industriousness, but if you are a college graduate with similar preferences, you may be seen as someone who wants a better work-life balance.

Said otherwise, one's labor market position still matters, despite people's changed attitudes toward work. In the privileged, highest-paying sector of the labor force, the growing interest in life outside of the workplace—the increasing preference for "leisure," if you will—has not led to a decline in hours worked. It is only in the non-college-educated sector of the labor force that the greater preference for leisure has corresponded to a decline in labor force participation. In this sector, demand is slack and employers have less incentive to retain workers, who are more interchangeable because they are in ample supply and require little specialized training. Small firms are much less likely to offer family-friendly programs. Low-paid workers cannot afford to pay for child care or to take unpaid family leave to care for a newborn. The men who were working less in 2010 were the ones who were not only moving away from a preference for demanding work but also facing an unfavorable labor market. In contrast, changing attitudes toward work did not correspond to declining labor force participation among men whose market position remained strong. The divergence between the labor force participation of highly educated men and less-educated men is another example of an interaction effect involving changing values and changing labor markets. Both cultural change and economic change contributed to the outcome; either factor by itself would have produced a weaker effect.

THE UNEXPECTED EMBRACE OF THE EXPRESSIVE SELF

The changes that have occurred of late in the values of young adults—the preference for less-demanding work, the heightened focus on self-development, the quest for a personally constructed spirituality—are not unique to them, or even to all of American society. These changes reflect a broader transformation of self-identity that has been observed throughout the Western nations. There are many labels for this cross-national development; here I call it a movement away from the "utilitarian self" and toward the "expressive self." The older utilitarian self was centered on qualities such as conformity to external standards—which included doing what your supervisor at work told you to do—and involved a focus on the material aspects of adult life, that is, on making a living and better yet on amassing some savings and moving up the economic ladder. It prioritized self-control and did not emphasize feelings and emotions. The utilitarian self therefore was consistent with industrial labor, which required self-discipline and the suppression of feelings such as alienation (my job is numbingly boring and unfulfilling) and anger (I can't believe my boss is asking me to take on this task). We can think of the disciplined self that Michèle Lamont observed among working-class men as a special case of the more general utilitarian self. The uncommunicative style of the working-class husband in the mid-twentieth-century family was based on this particular sense of self. The blue-collar husband carried into his marriage the self-identity he needed to be a successful industrial worker.[8]

In contrast, the newer, expressive self emphasizes one's feelings and emotional satisfaction and the pursuit of a personally meaningful life. It requires the active construction of one's sense of self through taking in what others are saying and doing and then modifying one's self-identity in response—a process that modernity theorists call "reflexivity." One needs to act autonomously in order to build one's expressive sense of self; it's not enough to respond automatically to other people's preferences and demands. The expressive self places greater weight on being sensitive to the emotional state of others (I can see that my wife is unhappy this evening; what should I do about it?), and encourages the expression of one's needs and desires to family and close friends (Here's the job I would really like to have; how can I get it?). One must be able to recognize and respond to the emotional cues that one's partner and children display and to verbalize and express wishes and feelings. One must be open to continual self-development rather than viewing one's life as settled once one reaches adulthood.[9]

The theorists of modernity who write about the expressive self and related concepts claim that hard work and material circumstances are less important to people today because, for the first time in human history, a broad swath of the population can take an affluent standard of living for granted. In fact, the political scientist Ronald Inglehart, one of the leading modernity theorists, writes of a transition from "materialist values" to "postmaterialist values" throughout the Western world as standards of living have improved. The newer set of values, which are the building blocks of the expressive self, are postmaterialist, or postmodern, in the sense that they arise and spread after the problem of providing basic goods and services has been solved. That is to say, only if people no longer need to worry about obtaining an adequate standard of living do their self-identities move away from utilitarian values and toward expressive values. Inglehart finds that more people tend to rate "leisure time" as important in their lives in societies that are closer to the postmaterialist pole than to the materialist pole. As for child-rearing values, in societies that are more postmaterialist, more people rate "tolerance" and "imagination" as qualities that are especially important for children to learn at home, and fewer rate "hard work" and "obedience" as especially important. Affluence, according to the modernity theorists, is a necessary condition for the emergence of postmodern values and the expressive self. It's easier to contemplate our preferences and share our feelings when we don't have to worry about putting food on the table. It's easier to consider a new career if we have some savings in the bank to support a transition.[10]

In most of Western Europe, the transition to the expressive sense of self seemed to gain momentum in the 1950s and 1960s among the highly educated and in the 1970s and 1980s among the less-educated. I think that the college-educated middle class in the United States began the transition at a similar time—that was the period when the companionate marriage of the 1950s evolved into the more individualistic marriage. And as their labor market position continued to be favorable, the highly educated moved further toward the postmodern pole during the rest of the century. They have used their affluence as a base for developing a new style of family life. It is still marriage-based, but unlike the older marriage bargain based on the husband specializing in paid work and the wife specializing in home work, both spouses are employed outside the home and they pool their incomes. In this way they solve the problem of affluence in twenty-first-century society and then move on to construct their expressive selves. They jointly invest in home and children. In the United States, though not in much of Europe, they are likely to retain ties to organized religion. We can see evidence that the highly educated are making this new lifestyle work in the sharp decrease in the likelihood that their marriages will end in divorce. The ties to orderly careers, stable intimate partnerships, and organized religion anchor the highly educated to the larger society despite the individualistic nature of the expressive self.[11]

What no one expected, however, was that less-educated young adults in the United States, many of whom are still struggling to ensure an adequate standard of living, would show signs of making the transition before they had attained affluence. While the older men who are still holding on to the remaining good blue-collar jobs by virtue of seniority may construct a moral world around the discipline of hard manual work and loyalty to family, the same logic is not evident among their sons and daughters. Instead, they appear to be organizing their worlds around personal growth and development, overcoming early trauma and pain, and surviving if not thriving as individuals. In most of Europe, extensive social welfare programs provide an economic floor for unemployed and precariously employed young adults, facilitating the shift in values, but that is much less true in the United States. What appears to be happening among less-educated young adults in America is the unprecedented emergence of a postmodern self-identity without economic security.

When the sociologist Jennifer M. Silva interviewed one hundred men and women in their twenties and thirties in Lowell, Massachusetts, and Richmond, Virginia, whose fathers did not have college degrees, she expected to find a group with a restricted emotional language and an emphasis on loyalty and discipline, but she did not:

> When I set out to discover how working-class men and women experienced adulthood at the level of the self, then, I was incredibly surprised to find that my working-class informants were absolutely fluent in the language of therapeutic needs, desires, emotional suffering, and self-growth. . . . Whether [poring] over self-help books to develop strategies to manage their attention deficit disorder, religiously attending Narcotics Anonymous meetings and learning to express themselves through art, attending obsessive compulsive disorder conventions at the suggestion of Oprah, or coming to terms with a pornography addiction, the men—and women—of the post-industrial class could not sound more dissimilar from the working class of a generation or two ago if they tried to.[12]

Central to these personal accounts, Silva found, were narratives of overcoming trauma and pain, such as childhood abuse or addiction. Such narratives were also evident in our interviews with high school–educated fathers. A white man in Boston had the phrase "my pain" tattooed across his neck. He explained: "I have a lot of, like my tattoo says 'my pain' because I grew up on the street my whole life. I don't want him [his son] to experience the pain I went through of neglect, someone not loving you, not being there." A black man in Chicago showed the interviewer a drawing on his wall that included four tombstones, each of which displayed the initialism "RIP" and the names of people who had "done him wrong" in his life, despite the fact that all were still alive: an old girlfriend, a rival, and his mother and father. Later in the interview, he said:

I was a bad child. I was pretty bad. I got into trouble every day. I got sus-
pended every day. We say it was—I seen psychiatrists, you feel me, to see
what was wrong with me. But now they found out my father wasn't around
and then I just kept using that. They kept trying to say that was an excuse. I
was just mad inside. I had a lot of anger built up and every time I'd release
it you do not want to be around me. So it took me years to develop that and
handle my anger in a proper way instead of just whatever around me de-
stroy it.

Others focused on self-development in order to repair themselves. When
a white Chicago man who said he was recovering from a history of alcohol
and drug abuse was asked whether he did any volunteer work, he replied,
"Right now I need to concentrate on me, you know." A white man from
Boston who was living in a halfway house described how his persistent
addiction problems had caused his girlfriend to break up with him and
led him to a treatment program: "She had to move on, I can understand
that, you know. She had to do *her* for a while, I had to do *me* for a while,
you know."

Several men had wandered away from their childhood religions and,
like Frank, had moved to a questing style of spirituality. In this mode of
thinking, religion becomes another avenue for self-development. A white
man in Chicago described his spiritual journey in these terms:

But you know, I used to be an agnostic. Then I was an atheist. Turned Chris-
tian. I was born Catholic. Studied Buddhists. Believe in karma. For some
reason, I know there's no God, but I believe there's karma. Like constantly,
when my son does something bad, something bad happens to him, I tell him
karma got him.

Many defined themselves as "spiritual but not religious." Over one-third
of the Americans who tell survey researchers that they are not affiliated
with a religion describe themselves as spiritual but not religious, and they
make up perhaps 7 percent of the U.S. adult population. They reject organized religion and focus instead on a personal spiritual journey. The sociologist Robert Wuthnow has described a shift in American religious belief
away from the "spirituality of dwelling" that was prevalent in the 1950s: a
religious home that provides familiar symbols and rituals. In its stead, he
writes, we have seen the rise of a "spirituality of seeking" in which individuals seek information on a variety of faiths: "Spirituality becomes a
vastly complex quest in which each person seeks his or her own way."[13]

Among the men we interviewed, those involved in recovery programs often ascribed a sense of spirituality to their self-help groups, as if the group process was a substitute for religion. For instance, the Boston man who said, "I had to do *me* for a while," was also one of the many men who described himself as more spiritual than religious. He told the interviewer that he recited the nondenominational Serenity Prayer many times a day to help him stay away from alcohol and drugs and that he regularly watched a popular self-help preacher on television. Of his recovery program, he said: "So a lot of people that are more spiritual are in the program. A lot more people that are in the program—Alcoholics Anonymous and Narcotics Anonymous is a spiritual program, it's not of any religion, creed, or any of all that good stuff they say, you know what I mean."

In this way, religion and the quest for self-development have merged in the minds of many Americans. This questing style may have become more common among less-educated whites over the past few decades. In the 1980s, the percentage of whites with high school degrees who attended religious services monthly or more often was nearly as high as it was among college-educated whites. But by the 2000s, attendance had declined among the non-college-educated, while showing little or no decline among the college-educated. The decline in feelings of spirituality, however, is smaller than the decline in religious participation. This increasing emphasis on a questing spirituality has helped less-educated Americans to pursue the same goal of self-expression and personal development pursued by the college-educated.[14]

In addition, the struggle of less educated men to come to terms with past losses and their focus on self-development can be seen as an attempt to acquire the emotional self-awareness and communication skills that industrial working men were said to lack in the past. Recall the difficulties that working-class couples—especially the husbands in those couples—had in adopting the emerging companionate style of marriage in the mid-twentieth century. A wife said to Lillian Rubin, "I keep talking to him about communication, and he says, 'Okay, so we're talking; now what do you want?'" The companionate marriage requires an ability to verbalize one's feelings and to share them. Working-class men found this requirement bewildering; it conflicted with the conventional masculine style of not expressing—and not even being fully aware of—one's feelings. Over the past few decades, an ever more individualistic style of marriage has emerged among the highly educated. In this new style, both the wife and husband work outside the home and both follow independent paths to growth and change over their married lives, sharing their feelings, supporting each other, and engaging in the joint project of raising children. The individualistic style of marriage raises the level of communication and coordination above the level required by the companionate marriage. To maintain an individualistic marriage, one must have an even greater facility with conceptualizing and expressing one's feelings and preferences than was required in the past.[15]

What we see in the tattoos of pain, the drawings of tombstones, the narratives of suffering and transformation, and the individually oriented spirituality of the twelve-step recovery group is an attempt among less-educated men to acquire the emotionally expressive capacities that were restricted, on the whole, to the highly educated a half-century ago. The decline of disciplined, industrial wage labor may have fortuitously freed men from the emotional constraints of conventional masculinity and allowed them to learn new forms of self-awareness and self-expression. From this viewpoint, the therapeutic language being acquired by less-educated men today may make them better attuned to the emotional requirements for successful contemporary marriages. The masculine imperative that was such an important aspect of the working-class family in the past, under which a husband needed to continually demonstrate his manhood, may be weakening. The sociologist Eva Illouz argues that middle-class men have been moving toward a new type of masculinity: a style of emotional awareness and self-expression formerly associated with a feminine self-identity. This new masculinity is more consistent with the individualistic marriage because of its emphasis on communication skills, and men who adopt it may be more successful in maintaining their marriages. Many college-educated men have made the shift, but we may now be seeing the first significant movement away from the industrial-era masculine identity among less-educated men.[16]

We need further confirmation of the apparent movement to a newer sense of self among the less-educated. Certainly, older attitudes still have power: both young men and young women think that a man must have steady employment to be considered a good marriage partner. Moreover, cohabiting relationships remain brief among the less-educated, and marriages are often brittle. The extent to which the newer attitudes have spread is unclear. But if the movement is indeed widespread, it may be an important development in the history of masculinity. Such a movement could reduce social class differences in the conduct of family life. With this newer identity, men might no longer need to fulfill the conventional masculine imperative to shoulder the entire burden of earning a living and display their manhood by being the taciturn authority figure at home. With the easing of the masculine imperative, they would be freer to be loving, nurturing figures in the lives of their partners and children. This development is still nascent. Nevertheless, the dominant mode of male thought and action among the less-educated—what the sociologist R. W. Connell calls "hegemonic masculinity"—may be eroding. Increasingly, what is holding back less-educated young adults from establishing the emotional style of marriage that is common among the highly educated appears to be economic security rather than gender ideology.[17]

CHILD-REARING VALUES

Given the shifts we have seen, what values are less-educated parents passing on to their children? Class differences in child-rearing values and practices appear to have continued their long-term shift. In the early 1800s, the emergent middle class began to socialize their children to be autonomous as well as obedient. Middle-class parents wanted their children to show self-control—the ability to internalize behavioral standards and make one's own decisions about how to act. An autonomous personality fit the demands of the growing white-collar professions, which required employees to show self-direction and to act on their own without constant supervision. In contrast, the continuing emphasis on obedience among working-class parents provided their children with the discipline to obey factory foremen and work under close supervision. These differences in child-rearing values reflect the differences noticed by the Lynds in Muncie, Indiana, in the 1920s between the "business class" and the "working class."[18]

A half-century later, sociologists once again asked Muncie mothers about child-rearing values. They found that the importance of strict obedience had declined even further among the mothers in both the business class and working class, while the importance of independence had increased among both. In the 1983 wave of the GSS, the last source of nationally representative data on the topic, only 19 percent of parents without bachelor's degrees rated "obedience" as the most important value in child-rearing. Other studies have reported similar findings. This shift from obedience and conformity to independence and self-direction is consistent with the changing requirements for jobs. Thus, the values that parents instill in their children both reflect their own experiences in the labor market and also prepare their children to be successful workers. Parents may not do this preparation consciously; rather, their experiences at work may subconsciously color the way they think about the social world, change their thought processes, and subtly influence how they conduct their family lives. In any case, as parents' job experiences change, so should the way they raise their children.[19]

Nevertheless, social class differences in child-rearing values still exist.

In the 1983 GSS, just 6 percent of parents with bachelor's degrees ranked obedience as the most important value. The sociologist Annette Lareau intensively studied a small group of families in 1989 and 1990 and found that middle-class parents invested time and money in developing their children's capacity for independent thought and action, a style she calls "concerted cultivation." Working-class parents were more likely to emphasize the need to keep children safe and healthy, with less attention to personality development, a style she labels as the "accomplishment of natural growth." White and black parents showed similar class differences. The middle-class style of cultivation entailed verbal reasoning and negotiation between parents and children; organizing out-of-school activities and transporting children to and from them; and intervening in schools to ensure that their children were treated well. The "natural growth" style, on the other hand, entailed verbal directives issued to children without much questioning or negotiation; unorganized, free-flowing out-of-school time; and reluctance to confront and question authorities such as teachers. The result was that middle-class children developed an "emerging sense of entitlement," which we might view as encouraging independent acting and thinking—just the kinds of skills that can be used to obtain and succeed at a high-paying job. Working-class children, in contrast, developed an "emerging sense of constraint," in which they were more deferential to, and distrustful of, authority figures, which left them less well prepared to act independently but perhaps better prepared for manual and lower-level white-collar jobs that involved close supervision.

The financial contributions of parents to their children's schooling and development have become larger and more unequal over the past few decades as the income distribution of the population has become more unequal. A report based on annual surveys of consumer expenditures since 1972 showed that parents at all income levels spent more on their children in the 2000s than in the past, with more of their spending now focused on child care and preschool activities for young children and postsecondary education for adult children in their early to mid twenties. All parents may feel the pressure to provide a more advantaged start to their children's lives and to ensure that their children continue their education after high school. But the report showed that parents with high incomes had increased their expenditures the most. Increased financial support is a way for affluent parents to pass along their advantages to their children. As the income gap increases between the families of the highly educated and the families of the moderately educated, differences in expenditures could be a key way in which family inequality is maintained.[20]

FAMILY INSTABILITY AND COMPLEXITY

Due to the changes in the family lives of young adults without bachelor's degrees, the United States is moving even further ahead of the rest of the developed world in a category no nation wants to lead: the most unstable family lives. We have seen that, between 1980 and 2010, the proportion of children living with a single or cohabiting mother rose sharply among the less-educated. Moreover, at the start of this period the living arrangements of children whose mothers had a high school degree but not a bachelor's degree looked more like those of the children of the top educational group, but by the end of the period their living arrangements looked more like those of the children of the bottom group. Their position dropped because an increasing percentage of moderately educated mothers were having their children within cohabiting relationships or as single parents. The cohabiting unions had very high breakup rates that contributed to higher levels of instability—about half broke up within five years of having a child. As I wrote in my 2009 book *The Marriage-Go-Round*, children in the United States experience more turnover in their family lives than do children in any other wealthy country. More parents, parents' partners, and stepparents move in and out of their households than in other countries.[21]

This churning of the household has long been the distinguishing characteristic of American families. It relates to the high value Americans put on marriage and their tolerance of divorce. Marriage has always been at the center of civil society in the United States, and divorce has been more acceptable than in many European countries. Catholic countries forbade divorce during most of the nineteenth century—and in some nations into the twentieth century—and the Church of England prohibited it until 1858. Today American levels of divorce remain high by Western standards, in large part because of the tendency of Americans to use personal fulfillment as the key criterion for whether their marriages are successful and to feel justified in ending a marriage if they are not sufficiently fulfilled. To this already high level of turnover we must now add children who live with parents who are cohabiting. By the late 1990s, 18 percent of newborn children in the United States had parents who were cohabiting at the time of their birth, the vast majority of those parents without bachelor's degrees. Many studies have shown that young children who experience more transitions by their parents in and out of cohabiting relationships and marriages show more problem behaviors, such as being disobedient and destroying others' things, and also have poorer school-readiness skills, such as the ability to pay attention.[22]

A related characteristic in which the United States also appears to have the unfortunate lead in the Western world is in the percentage of parents who have children with more than one partner—what demographers call multi-partner fertility. Mothers in the United States with one child are much more likely to have a second child with a new partner (rather than the same partner) than are mothers in Australia, Norway, or Sweden. Growing up with parents who have children with more than one partner appears to be an additional source of risk for unwanted outcomes. One study showed that, independent of the amount of instability in a house-hold, an adolescent who is living with a half-sibling (meaning that his or her mother bore a child by another father) is more likely to use drugs or to have sex by age fifteen than a comparable adolescent living with a full sibling. Whereas multiple marriages and cohabitations create family in-stability, multi-partner fertility creates family complexity: half-siblings or step-siblings living in one's home, or half-siblings from a nonresidential father's new marriage who live in the father's new home. Some of the children in a complex household may have an active noncustodial father who visits regularly and has health insurance that covers his children, while other children in the household may rarely see their father. The youngest child in the household may have the advantage of living with two biological parents while older children do not.[23]

There is yet another cause of family instability that has unfortunately increased: the rising rates of incarceration. As is well known, the number of people incarcerated in jails and prisons has skyrocketed since about 1980, owing in part to laws that mandated longer prison sentences for drug-related offenses. Nationally, over half of all prisoners have children under age eighteen. As a result, American children are at an increased risk of having a parent in prison. The problem is worst for children with par-ents who have not graduated from high school. By one estimate, at current rates, 15 percent of white children and 62 percent of black children in this group will have a parent in prison before they reach age eighteen. The numbers are also high for the children of parents with high school educa-tions: 4 percent of white children and 16 percent of black children of par-ents with a high school education will experience a parent's incarceration before they reach age eighteen. The imprisonment of fathers—most pris-oners are men—leaves mothers to raise their children without any contri-butions from them. Some mothers compensate by repartnering, which may help economically but also increases the complexity of their families. In addition, incarceration raises the risk that the marriages of imprisoned men will end in divorce.[24]

We cannot be sure that family stability and complexity cause the prob-lems that studies find in children. It could be that the cause-and-effect ar-row runs the other way: parents with problems such as depression or sub-stance abuse may be more likely not only to have children who develop problems but also to lead unstable, complex family lives. Most likely, the arrow runs both ways: instability and complexity are sometimes symptoms of underlying problems that cause the behaviors we see in children and are sometimes the direct cause of them. Nor is complexity always harmful. The sociologist Frank Furstenberg has noted that in some non-Western societies, such as those that allow polygamy, families can be quite complex but function well, albeit with large power differentials between men and women. For instance, the availability of multiple caregivers could be beneficial to children when an African man heads a compound with dwellings for two or three wives and their children, or when a rural East Asian patriarch lives with his sons and paternal grandsons and their wives and children. In these settings, the rights and responsibilities of each married couple and their children are clear. But as Furstenberg also cautions, these kinds of societies tend to have well-understood norms about how family members are supposed to behave. Today American society lacks these kinds of rules. And the sheer speed at which parents, partners, and parent-figures arrive and depart from households would make following rules difficult even if everyone knew what they were. At what point, for instance, does a man who has moved in with a woman and her children become authorized to act like a parent—to supervise and discipline the children? Does it matter whether he has children from his previous relationships living elsewhere? Or whether the biological father is still in the picture? The short-term cohabiting unions that are spreading among less-educated young adults are making the task of stabilizing these complex families even more difficult.[25]

THE DIVERGING EXPECTATIONS OF WHITE AND BLACK WORKERS

Among less-educated workers, racial tensions remain. White workers, without realizing it, are drawing upon a long history of animosity toward black workers. To be sure, the overt racism of late-nineteenth- and early-twentieth-century industrialization—a time when white unions largely resisted the incorporation of African Americans—has greatly diminished. Civil rights legislation, changing attitudes, and increased education are among the factors that have improved the relative position of African American workers. No one could imagine a union leader today issuing the kind of blanket denunciation of the "Negro race" that was common in 1900. Nevertheless, there is still a connection between whiteness and the working class. Resentment surfaced when the privileged position of whites in the industrial workforce was undermined by equal opportunity legislation and court decisions. As the reaction to the 1974 consent decree at the Sparrows Point steelworks showed, whites were angered by legal rulings that dismantled discriminatory workplace practices that had been in effect for so long that they seemed timeless and natural. They viewed the opportunity to move up to a more desired position or to get good entry-level jobs for their sons and nephews—an opportunity long open to whites but for the most part closed off to blacks—as a basic privilege of being a factory worker. The leveling of this opportunity and others caused dismay and anger among whites. The sociologist Monica McDermott lived in working-class neighborhoods in Boston and Atlanta and reported, "Claims by blacks that they had been discriminated against in some way were met with almost universal rage on the part of whites."[26]

Although the new legal environment originated in civil rights legislation that was passed in the 1960s, much of the actual change in race-related work practices began to occur in the 1970s, as was the case at Sparrows Point. By that time, the American economy was beginning its long decline from the postwar peak. Suddenly, it was harder for *anyone* to get a job for his son at the Point and at factories around the country. Black and white workers were all faced with diminishing work opportunities, and a job taken by a black applicant seemed like a job taken away from a white applicant. The simultaneous onset of legally enforced labor market changes and the globalization and automation of production quite probably amplified the reactions of whites. The co-occurrence of the easy-to-see increase in the hiring of black workers and the hard-to-understand deterioration of the economy encouraged white workers to blame the former for the latter.

Among blacks, the changes led to a relative improvement in their labor market position, even as the absolute level of industrial employment has declined for all workers since the 1970s. Although racial discrimination surely has not been eliminated over the ensuing decades, black workers are aware that conditions have improved. In fact, blacks have become more positive about their economic progress compared to their parents' generation while whites have become more negative. Since 1994, the GSS has asked respondents, "Compared to your parents when they were the age you are now, do you think your own standard of living now is much better, somewhat better, about the same, somewhat worse, or much worse than theirs was?" I examined the responses of adults who had completed less than four years of college. Between 1994 and 2012, the percentage of whites giving the negative responses "somewhat worse" or "much worse" increased from 13 percent to 21 percent. In contrast, the percentage of blacks giving the negative responses decreased from 19 percent to 11 percent. The racial difference extends to people's optimism or pessimism about the next generation. The GSS also asks, "When your children are at the age you are now, do you think their standard of living will be much better, somewhat better, about the same, somewhat worse, or much worse than yours is now?" Among whites, the negative responses increased from 12 percent to 15 percent between 1994 and 2012, whereas among blacks the negative responses decreased from 17 percent to 14 percent. In the 1990s, blacks were more negative than whites in their assessments of intergenerational progress, but now they are more positive.[27]

The more positive attitude of blacks was also apparent in our interviews. We asked the men how they thought their opportunities compared to the opportunities of the men in their fathers' generation. Black respondents were positive or at worst neutral. A black Boston man said: "I think there are better opportunities now because first of all, the economy's changing. The color barrier is not as harsh as it was back then. I mean, you know, yeah, I think things are changing and getting better." A black Chicago man pointed to the election of an African American president as symbolizing an increase in opportunities. However, it was not as though these men thought that racial inequities had disappeared—the Boston man went on to complain, "You look downtown across, and they got these high-rises that they're building, construction sites—you don't see any black workers, okay?" But our black interviewees recognized that an improvement had occurred.

White men, on the other hand, were negative or at best neutral. Keith, a thirty-five-year-old white Chicago man who did truck driving and construction jobs, had this conversation with the interviewer:

KEITH: So things have definitely changed. It's much harder for me as a grown man than it was for my father. Although my dad, when he was thirty-five, he tells me, "I had a house and I had five kids or four kids." You know, "Look where I was at." And I'm like, "Well Dad, things have changed."

INTERVIEWER: So he doesn't understand.

KEITH: He does not understand that at all. You know, he still can make a decent living, so he looks at it as that's his thing, you know.

INTERVIEWER: Right, well, that's interesting because some of the guys I've talked to had fathers that worked for AT&T for twenty-two years and that kind of thing.

KEITH: Yeah, see, if I could get into a job like that, see, you don't have job opportunities like that. If you don't know somebody, like my dad was a corporate America–type guy. So I didn't have that opportunity to get into that without a college degree and all that, you know. I'm sure if I had a college degree, life would have went different for me, but so I end up being a truck driver. I'm happy.

A white Chicago man noted how quickly the men and women in his father's generation started families:

> It's really weird. They all got married right away. They were all married by the time they were twenty. So yeah, I mean, they started families quickly, and at that time I believe there was more opportunities to get a job where you made more money. If I was going to be a forklift operator, I wouldn't make as much money as what the dollar's worth now compared to what the dollar was worth then and how much money he was making.

The white men we interviewed saw the deterioration in their labor market prospects compared to the previous generation, and they were right. In an environment in which overall opportunities for blue-collar labor are constricting, white workers perceive black progress as an unfair usurpation of opportunities rather than as a weakening of the privileged racial position they held.[28]

THE CASUALIZATION OF WORKING-CLASS LIFE

One way of thinking about the effects of the great changes in the economy and in culture since the postwar peak is to note that they have caused a casualization of the daily lives of the would-be working class. The work that non-college-educated young adults do is often casual—not in the sense of being easygoing or laid-back, but in the sense of being informal and unstructured. The sociologist Saskia Sassen and others define the casualization of employment relations in these terms: First, work is undertaken for a limited term rather than a longer, indefinite term. For young adults, work may have the character of what the sociologist Valerie Oppenheimer calls "stopgap jobs" rather than "career jobs." Second, work may not be contractual but rather based on informal understandings; there may not be an agreed-upon scope of work or a union contract. Third, work may be lightly regulated by law. Occupational standards of safety and health may not be enforced; eligibility for unemployment compensation may not be accrued. In this sense, we have seen the casualization of much of the work that young adults without bachelor's degrees can find: it is increasingly part-time or limited-term, there are no union protections, fringe benefits are limited, and the earnings may not even be reported to the government. Examples would include part-time work at restaurants or fast-food outlets or being hired off the books for a limited time by a general contractor renovating a home.[29]

In the realm of family formation, we have seen a parallel casualization of partnering and childbirth among the less-educated as they have shifted from marriage to cohabitation as the context for having children. Cohabitation has the same set of characteristics as casual labor. It is typically of limited duration: as I have noted, the United States has perhaps the briefest cohabiting unions of any Western nation. Within a few years, most Americans either end their cohabiting relationship or marry, and the proportion of those who break up rather than marry has been increasing. Cohabitation is also not a contractual relationship but rather one based on informal agreements: no ceremony marks the beginning of the arrangement, and many young couples gradually slide into cohabitation without much conscious planning. Moreover, cohabitation is largely unregulated by law: few laws protect the interests of the partners should the relationship end in a disruption. For example, there is no legal obligation for the partners to equally divide their property, unlike divorcing couples, who often are ordered by courts to do so. Although we cannot unambiguously assign cause and effect, it is likely that the changes in the labor market that underlie the casualization of work and the changes in values that have contributed to the casualization of family life have influenced and reinforced each other.[30]

More speculatively, one could argue that we have seen a related casualization of religious belief and behavior, as evidenced by the greater decline in religious attendance among the less-educated than among the highly educated, particularly among whites. White churches in the United States often function as strongholds of respectability and promote a family-centered spirituality that places a high value on marriage and parenting. When moderately educated white men could attain the disciplined sense of self through steady employment and marriage, they could find reinforcement from their churches for the lives they led. In other words, white married couples attend church with their children partly as a way of displaying to their fellow congregants, who are often their neighbors and friends, their work ethic and sense of responsibility—and also to gain reinforcement for their moral view of the world. But when the disciplined self is harder to attain—when employment difficulties prevent steady earnings and marriage—less-educated men, as well as the women who in a better economy might have married them, may be less likely to attend religious services. That is to say, changes in the labor market and the family appear to have undercut some of the resources that had until recently enabled many working-class adults to claim the respectability and ideals of success that are typically upheld by mainstream religious institutions. Instead, they may substitute informal religious activities for formal activities. They may retain a belief in God and engage in spiritual behaviors, such as praying or meditating, at much the same level as they did in the 1970s, but they may not attend church as often.[31]

The casualization of the labor market may be associated with the parallel casualization of family and religion not through a mechanical, imitative transfer but rather—at least in part—through the effects of casualization on one's sense of self. Self-identities cannot easily be attained on a symbolic level alone; rather, they must be grounded in the actual doing of social tasks. For whites, the newer, more casual work life supports a more expressive self that is more compatible with short-term cohabitation and a search across religious traditions for spiritual meaning. In contrast, one might expect continuity in the caring self that Lamont found among black working-class men. At a time of diminished employment opportunities, this ethic of sharing and mutual responsibility might even gain importance among them. Black churches, moreover, emphasize marriage less than white churches do, relative to qualities such as shared struggle and perseverance. For instance, when it comes to family life, they speak of parent and child, of broader networks of kin, and of the fictive kinship to be found among one's brothers and sisters in church. Thus, black men and their families may be able to maintain the caring sense of self even in an unfavorable economy and find support at church in ways that white men and their families cannot.[32]

Casualization, disengagement, rootlessness: these are the descriptors that seem apt when examining what has happened to the lives of less-educated young adults. Many of them lack strong connections to mainstream institutions such as marriage, the labor market, and organized religion. There is reason to think that men have become more disengaged than women. The average time that men spend in a job has decreased, whereas the opposite is true for women, who now spend more time in a job on average. Employment opportunities in the service sector, in which many occupations have been gender-typed as women's work, have not declined as much as opportunities in manufacturing. Women—especially women who are raising children—tend to be more enmeshed in kinship and friendship networks that provide support than are men, and women attend religious services more than men. But these are differences of degree rather than kind. Moderately educated women also face a labor market in which part-time, limited-term jobs are common. Their ratings of the most important aspects of jobs have changed nearly as much as men's ratings, and religious attendance has declined for both women and men.[33]

Overall, then, many less-educated men *and* women experience little that is lasting in their lives—not intimate relationships, not jobs, not religious beliefs. The lack of permanence is so broad that it has come to be seen as normal to young adults who cannot imagine anything lasting for life. This situation stands in sharp contrast to the greater stability of the lives of the highly educated. Their work lives are more continuous, their marriages are more likely to remain intact, and they are more likely to attend religious services. They are still firmly anchored to social institutions, whereas the less-educated have become unmoored and are drifting away. If this class divergence in lifestyle were freely chosen, one might be less concerned. But it is not. The decisions made by less-educated men and women in recent years have been constrained by the enormous changes in the economy that have occurred during the same period. The hollowing-out of the labor market—the loss of industrial jobs to offshoring and computerization—has removed the economic foundation of the kind of working-class lives that their mothers and fathers led. In the domain of the family, we have seen the descendants of the industrial working class struggle to construct what little satisfaction and stability they can find.

Chapter 7 | What Is to Be Done?

SHOULD ANYTHING BE done about the fall of the working-class family? Should our sense of social concern extend to the young adults who are trying to form families while dealing with the shrinking middle of the hourglass economy? Should we as a society take action to assist them in forming stable families? In any such effort, we need not hold the 1950s family as our model: its midcentury reign was sustained by the high-water mark of American capitalism, and its rigid distinction between the gender roles of men and women is out of step with the twenty-first century. Historically speaking, it was the exception rather than the rule.

The strongest case for action, I would claim, is to lessen the effects of the fall of the working-class family on children, because our entire society has an interest in the rearing of the next generation. These effects emanate from the unstable and complex family lives that many children are experiencing. We need to find ways to support stable partnerships without returning to the gender imbalances of the past. Stable partnerships do not necessarily involve marriage, but in the United States, unlike some European nations, cohabitation remains largely a short-term arrangement. So while supporting stable, long-term cohabiting relationships should be part of any effort to stabilize working-class families, in practice much of what we may choose to do will consist of strengthening marriage among those who want it—a constituency that still includes the vast majority of Americans. Moreover, in addition to our concern about children, we may be troubled by the disengagement of a generation of young adults from social institutions such as work, family, and religion and the implications for civil society of allowing this alienation to continue.

CULTURAL ABSOLUTISM

If we were to provide assistance to working-class families, what form should it take? There are still some observers who claim that the decline of stable marriage is almost entirely the result of an erosion of moral values. What we have seen, according to this view, is the demise of character: a growing failure of young adults to recognize the moral importance of the lasting bonds of marriage, a misguided impatience that leads them to have children prior to marriage, a reluctance of young men to work hard, and a self-centeredness that weakens their resolve to remain at a job or in a marriage even when problems arise. These cultural issues, it is said, are beyond the reach of government social policy. The political scientist James Q. Wilson, in a book about the consequences of the decline in marriage, argues that more women need to emphasize marriage over career, even though this may limit their autonomy. He offers sympathy, but little more, for the difficulty of this choice. Charles Murray takes a similar line in his analysis of the decline of marriage among the white working class: the independence of women, based on their earnings and government benefits, reduced the social status of working-class men who supported a family, and the sexual revolution made it easier for men to have sexual relations without getting married. "In such circumstances," he writes, "it is not surprising that male fecklessness bloomed, especially in the working class." Murray advocates less dependence on government social welfare programs and urges moral suasion by the upper class to promote the values that, in his opinion, have made America distinctive: industriousness, honesty, marriage, and religiosity. He and others have noted the puzzling fact that college-educated Americans are still following the education-then-marriage-then-childbearing life trajectory but are loath to recommend it to the less-educated for fear of being judgmental.[1]

The solution to the decline in marriage, according to these thinkers, is to strengthen traditional social norms. Public policies that may undermine these norms should be redesigned—or scrapped. This logic underlay the successful push in the mid-1990s for an overhaul of the Aid to Families with Dependent Children (AFDC) program that set a lifetime limit of five years of federal support. The same logic also suggests that the government should reduce the unintended income penalties that some low-income parents face if they marry. For instance, some single mothers would lose government benefits if they married because their household's joint income would move them above the threshold for eligibility. Other than changing the incentives of government programs, however, the cultural absolutists believe that little or nothing can be expected of changes in public policy. In particular, efforts to influence supply and demand in the labor market by, say, increasing the minimum wage would be ineffectual, if not harmful.[2]

While this cultural-absolutist line still has a constituency, a number of conservative thinkers are moving beyond it. Although they still believe in the importance of cultural change, they acknowledge the importance of changes in the labor market as well. For instance, a group of conservative writers and researchers who constitute a nascent "reform conservatism" movement issued a set of essays in 2014 that included attention to family policy. In the introductory essay, the author and commentator Peter Whener writes that the economy "has gone through some massive transformations in recent decades," such as favoring skilled labor and outsourcing production. "All of this," he concludes, "has caused painful dislocation." The sociologist W. Bradford Wilcox, in a chapter on strengthening marriage, concludes: "In seeking to explain why marriage is in retreat, conservatives have stressed the importance of changes in culture and public policy while liberals have stressed the importance of changes in the economy. And both are right." It is too soon to know how influential this new direction will be in wider conservative policy circles. And substantial differences still exist between reform conservatives and liberals. Nevertheless, this emerging viewpoint may make it easier for conservatives and liberals to find common ground in the family policy debates.[3]

My view of cultural influences, which I have presented throughout this book, is not focused on character or industriousness, which I do not think are important explanatory factors, but rather on the sweeping changes in attitudes toward marriage, intimate partnerships, and childbearing that have occurred throughout American society—not just among the less-educated—since the post–World War II peak. The acceptability of sexual relations outside of marriage and of cohabitation is much greater among nearly all young and middle-aged Americans than it was a half-century ago. The acceptability of having and rearing children outside of marriage is also much greater, except perhaps among the college-educated middle class. Marriage remains highly valued across all social classes and racial-ethnic groups, yet its place in the life course has changed. Whereas marriage was the first step into adulthood during the postwar peak, today it is often the last step. Young adults are reluctant to marry unless they are confident that they can succeed at maintaining it. These cultural changes in the meaning of marriage constitute the background to the equally important—if not more important—developments in the labor market. The altered cultural milieu influences what young adults do when they do not foresee entering a successful marriage—which is the case for more and more of the less-educated because of their vulnerable position in today's economy. In particular, unmarried young adults are much more likely to have a child outside of marriage today than fifty or one hundred years ago.

In the early 2000s, a group of conservative and centrist intellectuals, theologians, and academics proposed direct government interventions to encourage people to marry and to stay married. Their proposals engendered much debate about whether the government should support programs that favor marriage over other kinds of family life, such as single-parent families and cohabiting couples. Partisans on the liberal side objected to any programs that privileged marriage, and some viewed the push for marriage programs as an attempt to reassert male authority over women and children. Let's leave these debatable points aside for the moment and ask a more pragmatic question: is it likely that government programs could effectively encourage and support marriage? In 2002 a bill reauthorizing the Temporary Assistance for Needy Families program (the successor to AFDC, the program commonly known as "welfare") included funds for developing and testing highly structured programs to encourage and support marriage among low- and moderate-income young adults. Much of the money went to two large demonstration projects. One of them, "Building Strong Families," enrolled young, unmarried couples in eight sites around the country who had recently had a child. The program provided some family support services but mainly consisted of classes to teach relationship skills such as how to communicate, resolve conflicts, and build trust. These classes were based on marriage enhancement curricula that had been developed for middle-class couples and had been shown to be effective in small studies. Half of the couples, chosen at random, were offered the program and some additional services. The other half were not offered the program and served as a control group. Both sets of couples were followed for three years.[4]

The results, unfortunately, showed that three years later couples who were offered the program were no more likely to have remained together or to have married than were those who were not offered it. Nor was there a difference in relationship quality. Across all sites, only 57 percent of couples in the program were still romantically involved after three years. Attendance was poor: just 55 percent of couples in the program ever showed up for a relationship skills session. Advocates for the program argued that attendance was so low that the curriculum was never really tried. However, should such programs ever be implemented nationwide, no one could compel couples to attend; all that could be done would be to offer the curriculum, as Building Strong Families did. The sociologist Jennifer

Randles observed couples for eighteen months in a program that was similar in design but not affiliated with Building Strong Families. A staff member explained the program's chronic attendance problem:

> If we have a list of 20 couples who have enrolled in the class, five of those phone numbers are now disconnected because they can no longer pay the bill, four of the couples have broken up in the last five days, but half of those couples will probably be back together next week in the class, and they love each other. And some people can't come because of the health care situation. There are a lot of sick babies, and people have problems with their pregnancies. . . . We've had people in the classroom who are homeless.

Attendance increased only after the staff instituted a $100 "graduation stipend" for couples who attended the set of classes regularly—money the families needed for utility bills and gasoline.[5]

Building Strong Families and similar programs may have proven ineffective in supporting marriage because they focused on the *process* of relating to one's partner—developing listening skills, taking turns talking—on the assumption that marital issues can be overcome if better communication skills are developed. This assumption may hold for middle-class married couples, who can take the basics of day-to-day life for granted. But the constraints on the daily lives of low-income couples may be so limiting as to make process-oriented programs ineffective. For instance, the program that Randles studied encouraged couples to spend fifteen minutes per night actively listening to each other's feelings before going to sleep. But because many couples were living with parents or friends in crowded apartments, that assignment proved difficult. One participant told the class why he couldn't fulfill it:

> Cody answered that they had wanted to, but since they lived in a small studio apartment with his father, their daughter, and occasionally another friend who stayed at their place because he was homeless, they had no privacy and thus no opportunity to talk with the baby, the dad, and the friend sleeping on the floor right next to their bed. . . . Finally, he said, though he really wanted to know more about Mindy's day at home with the baby, he was simply too tired to keep his eyes open after working two full shifts during the day.

Couples found most valuable not the relationship skills training but rather the revelation that the issues they faced were common to other couples in their situation—knowledge that reduced their feelings of self-blame and loneliness. What seemed to work for the program, Randles observed, was not teaching general skills that ignored the social context of the parents' lives but confronting the specific everyday problems they faced.[6]

A second large-scale study, "Supporting Healthy Marriage," focused on already married low-income couples who wanted to strengthen their relationship. The enrollees were slightly older than those in Building Strong Families, and their daily lives were not quite as chaotic. Once again, half of the couples were randomly selected for the program, which centered on relationship and marriage education workshops but also included some support services. Final results after three years showed that the group enrolled in the program made small gains in marital happiness, warmth and support, communication, marital fidelity, and other similar characteristics, compared to the control group. There was no difference, however, in the proportion who stayed married and no difference in their children's well-being. Perhaps with further work some programs along these lines could be developed that would have stronger effects. Yet the picture painted by the random-assignment demonstrations is disappointing. The results suggest that it is very difficult to design interventions that strengthen relationships and increase marriage among low- and moderate-income couples.[7]

Character-flaw critics might take this failure as confirmation that public policy is ineffective; liberals might take it as confirmation that the reasons for the decline of marriage have little to do with relationship skills. But before abandoning behavioral approaches altogether, it's worth considering whether other messages could be useful in addressing the key problem of early, nonmarital childbearing, which is perhaps the major driver of family instability among non-college-educated young adults. One possibility is to focus public efforts on a message that is distinct from encouraging marriage per se: urging young adults to wait to have their first children until they are confident that they are in a committed, lasting partnership—either marital or cohabiting. This is a general message that would be relevant to all sexually active young adults. Moreover, it would directly address the problem of sexual partners conceiving children soon after they begin their relationship and ending it by the time the child is born. In their study of low-income mothers, the sociologists Kathryn Edin and Maria Kefalas note that

> once a young pair begins casually flirting, or "kicking it," the relationship
> often moves at lightning speed along a trajectory that culminates in the de-
> livery of a shared child. Kimberly, a twenty-seven-year-old Puerto Rican
> mother of two children, ages six and three, provides an excellent example:

"There's this bridge in Puerto Rico that he took me to [on our first date]. That's where he asked me to be his girlfriend. That's where we had our first kiss. . . . It was really nice. I got pregnant *quick* though. We started [dating] April 1, and by May I was pregnant.

Slowing down this trajectory would be beneficial to young adults and to the children they eventually have.[8]

Supporters of urging a delay in pregnancy point to the apparent success of efforts to reduce the adolescent birth rate (the likelihood that a teenager will give birth or father a child in a given year), which fell to an all-time low in early 2010. (Among teenagers who do give birth, the non-marital birth *ratio*—the share who are unmarried—has increased, but that is a different issue.) They maintain that similar efforts could be targeted at unmarried young adults in their early to mid twenties, the ages at which births to non-college-educated adults peak. For instance, the psychologist Ron Haskins and the economist Isabel Sawhill recommend that the government support the development of programs at community colleges to encourage pregnancy reduction. They note that it is common for community college students to become pregnant or get someone pregnant and that women who have children after enrolling in community college are less likely to complete their degree program. Haskins and Sawhill further remark that no other set of institutions except possibly churches reaches so many low- and moderate-income adults in their late teens and early to mid twenties. Whether the effort targets community colleges or not, the general point is to shift the emphasis of the message from getting married to postponing a first pregnancy.[9]

There are reasons, however, to think that successfully spreading this message of postponement to young adults would be more challenging than spreading the same message to adolescents proved to be. The fall in births among adolescents since about 1990 was due to both better use of contraception and a decrease—which no one predicted—in sexual activity. But the message of abstinence, which appeared to play a role in reducing the rate of sexual activity among adolescents, would be much less applicable to young adults, who may not marry until their late twenties or thirties. It is hard to imagine that a campaign urging twenty-one-year-olds in contemporary America to abstain from sex would have any success. Instead, a campaign would need to take a more nuanced approach that relies heavily on consistent use of contraception among sexually active young adults. Moreover, one likely reason for the success of efforts to lower the teenage birth rate is that it was seen as a way to combat the HIV epidemic. This public health crisis caused adults to speak more frankly to teenagers about the risks of unprotected sex than they otherwise would have. In particular, sex education courses in high school stressed the risks of HIV. Increases at first sex in condom usage, the most effective form of contraception against HIV transmission, constituted a substantial part of the overall increase in contraception, which suggests that the health-risk message had been received by students. It would be difficult to rely on this motivation to reduce births among unmarried young adults in the years ahead. Whether justifiably or not, public fear of HIV has abated with the introduction of effective drug therapy.[10]

Despite these limitations, disseminating the message of pregnancy postponement may be worth trying as part of a larger strategy to reduce the family instability and complexity that often follow early nonmarital childbearing. To have a chance of being successful, this message would need to be combined with labor market interventions. Young adults are unlikely to respond positively to pleas that they wait to have children until they are in committed, lasting relationships unless they are confident that they eventually *will* be in such relationships. Those who are on their way through college or who have recently graduated are generally convinced that when the time is right they will find a partner with whom to pool incomes in a lasting marriage. They know that they are on a path toward the more vibrant sector of the job market; indeed, many of them are postponing marriage while they invest in careers. Young adults who end their schooling after high school or who attend college but do not obtain a bachelor's degree are much less certain about their futures—and with good reason given the hollowing-out of the labor market. I would argue, then, that economic conditions are an important driver of marriage patterns and that any successful policies must have a labor-market component. There are three themes in the American discussions about what steps to take to improve the employment and income of the less-advantaged: economic growth, education, and institutions. Beyond them are European intellectual currents that are more radical and utopian. Let us examine these paths.[11]

ECONOMIC GROWTH

Some defenders of the unrestricted market economy argue that we need only focus on improving overall economic growth because its rising tide will lift all boats. They assert that employment prospects will improve, and incomes will rise, throughout the labor market if growth is sufficiently fast. They advocate government actions that remove restrictions on capital, such as lowering tax rates on investment income and pursuing international agreements to further reduce trade barriers. For instance, in one of a series of short books on values and capitalism published by the American Enterprise Institute, the economists Edd S. Noell and his colleagues argue that proponents of aid to low- and moderate-income families should support pro-growth policies because economic growth "raises the poor out of absolute poverty because their income rises along with everyone else's." This can happen, they add, even if the share of income going to the bottom layer of earners declines. Noell and his colleagues never mention *relative* poverty—how much income people like me have, compared to how much income people like you have. Inequality of income is not harmful per se, they argue, and could indeed result in increased gains for all. This view implies that a rising tide should be welcomed even if it raises yachts several feet and dinghies several inches. Yet after several decades of unequally rising tides, this vision has become increasingly unattractive, even to some proponents of pro-growth policies. For instance, the economist Glenn Hubbard, who was the chairman of the Council of Economic Advisers during the George W. Bush administration, wrote in a 2014 op-ed article, "The economic-growth-lifts-all-boats camp needs to confront the question of what happens when growth alone fails to generate inclusion."[12]

The position of the growth-only camp seems to be less and less tenable with the ever-increasing reach of globalization and computerization. Hubbard argues for considering additional steps beyond encouraging growth, specifically, creating vouchers that low-income individuals can use for education, training, tuition, or their children's education and expanding the eligibility for the Earned Income Tax Credit (EITC)—which at the time he wrote the article was largely restricted to workers who were raising children—to include childless workers. These suggestions are representative of two kinds of labor-market interventions that have been widely discussed of late: improving the stock of human capital—the level of education and training of workers—and directly subsidizing the wages or family incomes of less-educated workers. Most proponents of these types of policies have a more liberal political bent than Hubbard and would extend them further than most conservatives would, but his article shows that conservatives are willing to consider moving in this direction, even if they are more skeptical of the chances of success than are liberals.

EDUCATION

The most widely discussed policy for increasing employment and income, and the one with the broadest political support, is improving the education and training of children and young adults. The economists Claudia Goldin and Lawrence Katz provide the fullest account of this perspective in their 2008 book *The Race Between Education and Technology.* They warn that the United States has lost its edge in education and risks falling behind in producing the highly educated and skilled workers that the economy requires. "That the twentieth century was both the American Century *and* the Human Capital Century," they write, "is no historical accident."

> Economic growth in the more modern period requires educated workers, managers, entrepreneurs, and citizens. Modern technologies must be invented, innovated, put in place, and maintained. They must have capable workers at the helm. Rapid technological advance, measured in various ways, has characterized the twentieth century. Because the American people were the most educated in the world, they were in the best position to invent, be entrepreneurial, and produce goods and services using advanced technologies.

Until the 1970s, the average years of schooling had increased from generation to generation in the United States, with the result that Americans were the best-educated populace in the world. But since then, the supply of educated young adults has grown more slowly: the high school graduation rate leveled off until the 2000s, when it began to rise again, and postsecondary education increased for young women but not for young men. Other countries have caught up with and passed the United States in the education of their citizens. Unless the United States once again increases the educational level of its workforce, Goldin and Katz argue, it risks losing the "race" between education and technology. The result will be slower economic growth and a diminished position for the United States in the world economy as other nations catch up and then move ahead.[13]

In the meantime, computer-assisted technologies have raised the demand for highly educated and trained workers. Employers have increased the wages they will pay for workers with advanced skills that typically require a college education much more than they have increased the wages they will pay for less-educated workers. As a result, Goldin and Katz note, income inequality has risen markedly in the United States since the 1970s, with the college-educated top soaring above the high school–educated middle and the least-educated bottom. If inequality is due to a greater demand for highly educated workers, then the best way to move toward greater equality, according to these authors, is to increase the educational attainment of the segment of the American population that is now falling short.

Families at the top of the income distribution seem to need no help in achieving this goal. The gap between what parents with family incomes in the top 20 percent and the bottom 20 percent spent on enriching activities for their children nearly tripled between the early 1970s and the mid-2000s. High-income parents can use their greater expenditures to give their children cognitive advantages, such as those that accrue from attending the best preschool programs, and they can fund the cultural capital (for example, mastering a musical instrument or playing on a traveling soccer team) that college admissions officers look for in applications. Low-income children, in contrast, are more likely to be raised by single parents who may not have the time or resources to support their children's schooling. Low-income children are also more likely to live in neighborhoods where most other children are also from low- and moderate-income families and schools are resource-poor and suffer from high teacher turnover. The sociologist Sean Reardon has shown that the social class gap in children's educational test scores is now greater than the racial gap; the crossover happened among children who were born in the 1970s and attended school in the 1970s and 1980s. These were the years immediately following the postwar peak, when income inequality widened and family patterns began to diverge sharply across class lines.[14]

How might we intervene in the lives of low-income families in order to improve educational outcomes for their children? In recent years, preschool programs have received a great deal of attention from educational researchers. Social scientists such as the economist James Heckman have argued that, dollar for dollar, interventions during the preschool years are more efficient at producing long-term gains in areas such as adult literacy skills, attainment, and employability and reduced law enforcement expenditures than interventions with school-age children. Neuroscientific studies have shown that the brain is more responsive to many stimuli during the first few years of life as the circuitry that will remain throughout the rest of life develops. Once this period of plasticity is over, it can be more difficult to influence basic brain functions. In early childhood, the brain seems to be particularly receptive to information about fundamental linguistic and numerical concepts and behavioral attributes such as focusing attention and ignoring distractions—characteristics that can affect job performance in adulthood. These neuroscientific and economic arguments have increased support for universal preschool programs and for highly structured child care centers that emphasize school readiness. Between 2002 and 2012, the proportion of four-year-old children in the United States who were enrolled in state-supported preschool programs doubled to 28 percent. In 2013 the successful candidate for mayor of New York City, Bill de Blasio, ran on a platform that included universal pre-kindergarten for four-year-olds. Supporters of such programs have urged interventions at even younger ages for children in low-income families.[15]

There is no shortage of ideas for improving kindergarten through grade twelve schooling for disadvantaged students, but no clear blueprint as yet. Reformers urge a mixture of accountability, high standards, and support. The emphasis on high-stakes testing in the 2000s and on a common core of learning in the 2010s reflects the focus on accountability and on assessing individual students' performances. Yet there is also a realization that accountability and testing will not result in better outcomes for schools in disadvantaged neighborhoods without building blocks such as strong school leadership, lower teacher turnover, and assistance with curriculum development. Some schoolwide or systemwide reforms show promise. For example, career academies, which typically operate as small schools within larger high schools, are devoted to educating students for a particular set of careers (health sciences, business and finance). They have been shown to have long-term positive effects on earnings when the students enroll in them voluntarily and when they can provide work-based learning opportunities with local firms. On the other hand, the charter school movement, introduced with great fanfare as a publicly funded alternative to conventional schools, has had mixed results. Despite widely reported individual successes, the most reliable evaluations suggest that, on average, charter schools do not produce better student outcomes.[16]

How could we improve access to higher education? High school graduates from low- and moderate-income neighborhoods face several barriers: Some are inadequately prepared academically and need to take remedial courses in college in order to master material they should have learned before entering. Others are discouraged by the high and growing cost of college: tuition has greatly exceeded the growth of family incomes since 1980, and many students are forced to borrow large sums that they have difficulty paying back. In addition, some low-income parents cannot manage the increasingly complex undertaking of applying to college and obtaining financial aid. Applying to college is now a multi-year process that involves identifying appropriate colleges, completing a complex financial aid form, and interacting with high school guidance counselors and college admissions officers; all of these tasks are often difficult for low-income parents who have not attended college themselves. Surely, efforts to subsidize the cost of college and assist parents in navigating the admissions process would be valuable.[17]

The underlying assumption of initiatives to encourage more young adults to complete college, however, is that if a much higher proportion of the population earned a bachelor's degree, the American economy could absorb them into the labor force in jobs commensurate with their skills. This optimistic view is based on technological progress continuing, though in ways we cannot always anticipate. For example, a few decades ago, when desktop personal computers were first introduced into the workplace, the secretarial staff of my department at Johns Hopkins felt threatened by the machines. They feared that the faculty would no longer need secretaries once they could type their own manuscripts and send out their own correspondence. What no one anticipated was that decades later the department would employ a larger support staff than in the past, but that they would need a higher level of skills: today's staff members must be able to manage the department's web pages and enter information into complex computerized accounting systems. Consequently, they need more education than in the past. No one anticipated the development of these new tasks, which increased our need for a highly educated support staff. Similarly, the education advocates would say, we cannot today fully anticipate the uses to which highly educated workers will be put in the future. The claim is that the American economy has always been innovative and entrepreneurial in ways that lead to further growth and there is no reason to think that capacity has ended. If you educate them, the jobs will come.[18]

A more skeptical view is that if the nation greatly increased the production of college graduates, their wages would not grow as fast as in the recent past. Some of the occupations that require college degrees are routine enough that they can now be done by workers overseas and may someday be automated. Large firms already outsource tasks such as payroll accounting or accounts receivable to countries with lower wages, such as India: the day's financial data can be sent overseas electronically, processed by workers during the Western night, and then sent back by the start of the next day at a fraction of the cost of an on-site backroom operation. More complex tasks, such as reading the results of radiology examinations, can be accomplished overseas by physicians and technicians who earn less than their Western counterparts. In short, the fear is that the demand for well-paid college graduates will not keep up with the supply.[19]

In fact, the earnings of college graduates with a bachelor's degree but no master's or PhD degree have been stagnant since about 2000. Moreover, an increasing share of recent college graduates have already been unable to find work that requires their skills. Some analysts are calling this phenomenon "mal-employment": workers with bachelor's degrees accepting employment in occupations in which the knowledge they gained in college is underutilized. Think of college graduates working as office clerks or customer service representatives. The share of mal-employed recent graduates has increased since 2000: according to one study, this kind of underemployment rose from 34 percent in 2001 to 44 percent in 2012. It is possible that the decades-long increase in the demand for workers with high cognitive skills may be slowing as high-tech industries mature and their need for ever-larger numbers of high-skilled employees abates.[20]

These developments raise the question of whether a bachelor's degree should be the goal for all young adults. Some researchers and policy analysts say that we should support educational alternatives. They note that good middle-of-the-labor-market occupations that do not require a bachelor's degree still exist and may even be growing in some fields, such as medical technicians and operators of computer numerically controlled machines. These occupations require specialized training after completing high school. Would it not be preferable, supporters ask, to channel some adolescents into training programs, perhaps beginning in career academy–type programs and continuing at community colleges, coupled with internships and apprenticeships at organizations that hire such workers? The economist Robert Lerman has argued that apprenticeship programs can be effective in high school and after high school in increasing the employment of youth who might prefer—or be better suited to—middle-skilled careers. Endorsing this path requires abandoning the goal of a bachelor's degree for all, which is hard to part with because it embodies the American ideal of equal opportunity. Yet apprenticeships and internships are likely to be valuable paths to steady employment for high school graduates who may not aspire to college or who may succeed better at skilled midlevel work.[21]

INSTITUTIONS

Although improving the access of young adults to higher education, whether in pursuit of a bachelor's degree or training at a community college, would undoubtedly be helpful, it might not be sufficient to lower economic inequality. To accomplish that goal, many observers argue, we also need to focus on an important set of social institutions that shape the labor market: labor unions, which bargain on behalf of workers; Congress and state legislatures, which enact legislation on wage levels and taxes; and government agencies, which issue financial regulations. According to this view, the relatively equal distribution of wages and incomes of the postwar peak reflected not just rising levels of education and the dominant postwar position of the United States but also the influence of institutions such as these. Since then, it is argued, the influence of institutions has weakened significantly. The economists Frank Levy and Peter Temin write:

> In our interpretation, the recent impacts of technology and trade have been amplified by a collapse of these institutions that occurred as economic forces reshaped the political environment in the 1970s and 1980s. If our argument

is correct, no rebalancing of the labor force–educational mix can restore a more equal distribution of productivity gains without government intervention and changes in private-sector behavior.

The institutionalists, as I call them, also point to the importance of social norms of fairness, such as what constitutes a fair distribution of income or an appropriate level of compensation for CEOs.[22]

The institutionalists do not deny the importance of skill-biased technological change and the need to better educate the labor force; they do think, however, that such efforts will be insufficient to bring income inequality anywhere near what it was during the postwar peak. Indeed, there is considerable overlap between the educationist and institutionalist perspectives. For instance, Goldin and Katz, at the end of their book advocating better education and training policies, state that the erosion of labor market institutions such as unions and minimum wage levels has contributed to growing inequality and that some enhancement of these institutions could be included in future policies without serious consequences for employment levels. The French economist Thomas Piketty, in his influential critique of twenty-first-century capitalism, argues that although investing in education and skills training is the best way to reduce wage inequalities, the rules and regulations of the labor market play an important role and should be scrutinized.[23]

The institutionalists argue that the way the American economy has evolved reflects not just the invisible hand of the capitalist market but also factors such as political decisions and the bargaining power of labor. They highlight the cooperative agreements between management and labor during the 1950s and 1960s that resulted in large gains in wages and productivity and the demise of such agreements afterward. The economic dominance of the United States in the 1950s and the resultant high profit levels of the era allowed owners and managers of firms to agree to higher wages and benefits and to accede to the widespread norm that the wealthy should pay substantially higher taxes. The institutionalists point out that the federal minimum wage was worth 24 percent more in purchasing power during the 1970s than during the 2000s. They note that in the mid-1950s the marginal federal income tax rate for income over $1,000,000 (in today's dollars) for a married couple filing jointly was about 80 percent, whereas in 2013 it was about 40 percent. They remind us that starting in the 1970s, as the postwar prosperity began to wane, Democratic and Republican administrations pushed for deregulation of the financial industry—including the progressive weakening and then repeal of the Depression-era legislation that had prohibited commercial banks from investing in and trading securities—and lower trade barriers. They note that President Ronald Reagan changed the tone of government support for the unfettered market through actions such as firing air traffic controllers after their union began an illegal strike, reducing the top tax rate on nonlabor income from 70 to 50 percent, and appointing a management consultant who specialized in defeating union campaigns to the National Labor Relations Board. They would argue, finally, that actions such as these have resulted in a distribution of income that is more unequal than in any other wealthy country. High inequality is in part a political choice, according to this view, and also a reflection of changed attitudes toward the rights of workers and the accumulation of wealth. Until those decisions and norms are altered, say the institutionalists, high levels of inequality will remain.[24]

Would there be costs to strengthening the institutions and norms that regulate capitalism? In Europe, social institutions and regulations concerning capital and labor are stronger; more workers are in unions, and the laws in many countries make firing a worker more difficult. Venture capital and securities markets are more regulated, which, according to some observers, can make investment in start-up companies more difficult. Economic growth has been somewhat slower and unemployment higher than in the United States since about 1995. Critics of the European model argue that the greater flexibility of capital and labor in the United States has produced higher growth and that strengthening institutions would lower that growth. They could be right, but the distribution of the rewards of economic growth in the United States has become so unequal that many people would choose to rein in capital and strengthen labor anyway. In 2010 the ratio of corporate profits to the gross domestic product reached 12.4 percent, the highest percentage ever recorded since the government began gathering this information in the 1940s. I would agree that we should strengthen the institutions that influence the workings of the market.[25]

BEYOND LABOR MARKET INTERVENTION

A number of European intellectuals have moved beyond the loyal opposition of the American institutionalists, who still envision working within the same framework as the advocates for growth and for education. Piketty argues that substantial inequality in income and wealth has been the normal condition of capitalist economies, with the post–World War II era being the sole exception. In the United States, economic inequality has returned to levels not seen since the early twentieth century. Much of the recent increase, according to Piketty and Emmanuel Saez, has been driven by unprecedented increases in incomes among the top 1 percent—and even more so, among the top one-tenth of 1 percent—of the American population. Piketty argues for high marginal tax rates on large incomes to discourage corporate executives from seeking huge salaries, and he advocates a global taxation on capital.[26]

Some writers even predict that the technological transformations of the economy may soon lead our society to run out of work. A growing proportion of the labor force, according to the British economist Guy Standing, has become a class-in-the-making he calls the "precariat"—a term that combines the connotations of "precarious" work and "proletariat." These workers have no formal employment agreements and no trust in their employers. Instead, they have anger, anxiety, and alienation. Standing's solution is not to go back to the agreements between capital and labor of the postwar peak, given the drudgery and loss of autonomy that industrial work entailed, but rather to include in the definition of work alternatives activities, such as volunteer work and care work, that are currently unpaid. In addition, like Piketty, he calls for redistributing the financial returns to capital and for taxing speculative investment both within countries and globally. The German sociologist Ulrich Beck suggests that wealthy countries may be moving toward a "post-full-employment" society in which individuals can alternate between conventional work and substitutes such as parental labor and work in the arts and culture—and be paid for it, presumably by the government.[27]

One need not agree with Standing's and Beck's policy recommendations to be intrigued by the idea that we have (or soon will) run out of work as we conventionally define it. New computer-based technologies have resulted in the automation of tasks ranging from building automobiles to answering telephone calls, and this process will undoubtedly continue. Even the demand for workers with bachelor's degrees may be cooling off. Yet we have seen arguments that work is disappearing before. Think of the Luddites, the artisans who smashed machinery in early-nineteenth-century textile mills in Britain because the new technology threatened their livelihoods. They, too, thought that the world of work was shrinking. To be sure, industrialization reduced the demand for craft labor, but it increased the demand for the newer, factory-based labor and for white-collar clerical and managerial workers. It may not have been good for the average worker. Master craftsmen and journeymen endured painful changes in the conditions of their employment. But in the long run, the overall demand for labor, while transformed, did not decrease. How can we be sure that the current transformations of the labor market will reduce the demand for paid labor rather than opening up new opportunities and increasing the demand? We cannot yet determine whether

Standing, Beck, and others are prescient predictors of the future of work or whether they are the new Luddites.

Charles Dickens ends the first paragraph of *A Tale of Two Cities*, which begins with the famous phrase "It was the best of times, it was the worst of times," with a less frequently quoted line: "In short, the period was so far like the present period, that some of its noisiest authorities insisted on its being received, for good or for evil, in the superlative degree of comparison only." In other words, our fascination with our own times, and our preoccupation with both its perils and its promise, can lead us to believe that we're experiencing something entirely new in human history, which is unlikely to be true. I used the best-and-worst metaphor to describe the 1950s family in the opening pages of this book and again in chapter 4. Chastened by Dickens's observation, I hesitate to use it again to describe families in the current era. Perhaps these are not the best and worst of times, but nevertheless, family life does seem decidedly better for some groups and worse for others. We see stable, prosperous, married-couple families among the college-educated middle class and unstable, struggling families among the less-educated. Yet in presenting this contrast, have I engaged in the overstatement of problems and exaggeration of differences to which social observers are vulnerable? What is truly new about the current situation?

That great social class differences exist is not new. The marriage gap we see in the New Gilded Age today is similar to the gap during the Old Gilded Age of the late 1800s. Sharp inequalities in income and in marriage characterize both eras. During the Old Gilded Age, journeymen and apprentices were transformed into low-paid factory workers. At the same time, an expanding middle class solidified its position, and a small elite grew fabulously wealthy. In the New Gilded Age, the wages of skilled and semi-skilled industrial workers have stagnated or declined as outsourcing and automation erode the demand for their labor. Meanwhile, a college-educated middle class has benefited from the rising wages and salaries paid to people with higher education. And once again an elite has grown fabulously wealthy. In both eras, men in professional, managerial, or technical positions were the most likely to marry, and the probability of marriage dropped substantially toward the bottom of the occupational hierarchy. In that sense, there is nothing new about a large marriage gap. Rather, it was the midtwentieth century, with its compressed wage differential and marriage differential, that was the outlier.

But the cultural contexts of the two Gilded Ages were vastly different. In the late 1800s, living together while unmarried was scandalous, as was having children outside of marriage. Divorce rates were far lower than today. Unmarried young adults lived either with their parents or as boarders in other people's homes. Few had children prior to marrying (although premarital pregnancies were common). Women's options for independent lives outside of marriage were limited, and once married, few worked outside of the home, at least among whites. By the turn of the twenty-first century, however, cohabitation was broadly acceptable across all classes, and having a child outside of marriage carried much less stigma. Cohabiting relationships had short life spans: most couples either broke up or married within a few years. Divorce rates were much higher than in the late 1800s, even after the recent decrease in rates among the college-educated. Overall, parenthood was less centered on marriage, and intimate partnerships were less stable.

When the labor market polarized after about 1985, resulting in the highest levels of economic inequality since the Old Gilded Age, the marriage gap also returned to levels not seen since then. But because of the cultural shift, the personal and family lives of *unmarried* young adults in the more recent period were vastly different from the lives of their counterparts in the earlier period. Unmarried young adults commonly live apart from their parents (although there has been some movement back home in recent decades); they are sexually active and have modern contraceptive methods available to them (yet the usage of these methods is far from consistent and universal); and the majority of them live with at least one partner prior to marrying. Young adults with bachelor's degrees—the dividing line between a college-educated middle class that has prospered in the transformed economy and less-educated groups that have not fared as well—still wait to have children until they are married. Among young adults without bachelor's degrees, however, having children before marrying is common: at current rates, a majority of all births to non-college-educated young adults are likely to be nonmarital.[28]

Some ascribe the increase in nonmarital births *entirely* to the cultural changes that have weakened the place of marriage. This logic falters, however, on the following fact: members of the college-educated middle class have been exposed to the same cultural bent, yet their childbearing still centers on marriage. They are culturally liberal enough that a majority of them live with a partner prior to marrying, and a majority of wives work outside of the home. Still, they are far less likely to have children outside of marriage than are the less-educated today, and they divorce much less often. I have heard it said that the reason college-educated young adults are hesitant to divorce is that they are determined not to repeat the mistakes that their divorce-prone parents' generation made, but surely non-college-educated young adults whose parents divorced have the same desire. Why have the college-educated been much more successful in avoiding their parents' marital fate? Because, unlike the less-educated and the poor, they have not just the desire to avoid divorce but the economic resources to do so.

It is the conjunction of the polarized job market and the acceptance of partnering and parenting outside of marriage that makes the current state of American family life historically unique. There has never been such a large, class-linked divergence in nonmarital childbearing. There has never been such a split between marriage-based families on the top rungs of the social ladder and cohabitation- and single-parent-based families on the middle and bottom rungs. The segment of the population that has been most affected by these recent developments are the sons and daughters of the industrial working class. They have been hit the hardest by the lack of opportunities in the middle of the labor market, and in response they have turned to new patterns of family formation. These patterns have significant social costs: children face instability and complexity in their home lives, and adults drift away from the institutions that historically have anchored civic life. We could do more to reverse these developments. We could attempt to promulgate a message of waiting longer before having a first child. We could try to improve the education and training of young adults and strengthen institutions and policies that might lead to higher incomes for those in the vast middle of the labor market. These efforts, as difficult as they might be, could help to provide a firmer basis for long-term relationships among adults and secure home environments for their children as they cope with the chaos of postmodern culture and the constraints of the hourglass economy.

Notes

CHAPTER 1: INTRODUCTION

1. I use the term "boarder" to refer to someone who paid to live with a host family or in a commercial boardinghouse and also to eat meals there. I use the term "lodger" in the more restricted sense of someone who paid for housing accommodations but did not eat meals there.

2. More generally, this period constituted the peak years for nearly all of the developed capitalist nations, but among this group, the United States was in the dominant position (see Hobsbawm 1994; on long-term trends in income inequality in the United States, see Piketty and Saez 2003). Here I often refer to the 1945–1975 period as the "postwar peak" or as the "peak years."

3. These are my tabulations from *Historical Statistics of the United States: Millennial Edition Online* (Carter et al. 2006), a source I refer to throughout this book. The figures are based on series Ae230, Ae231, Ba453, and Ba462.

4. The male breadwinner was well-suited to industrial society. See Parsons (1943).

5. Parsons (1942), 612. On the idea that the required tasks of the housewife were diminishing, see Thistle (2006).

6. Change in the gender composition of jobs, my calculations from the Integrated Public Use Microdata Series (IPUMS); see Ruggles et al. (2010). The problem that has no name, Betty Friedan, *The Feminine Mystique* (1963).

7. Prisoners of prosperity, see Milkman (1997).

8. By a bachelor's degree I mean a degree such as a bachelor of arts or bachelor of science given by a college or university for a course of study that is designed to be completed optimally in four years but sometimes takes longer. Unusual for non-college-graduates to have all their children within marriage: Among mothers age twenty-six to thirty-one who have no bachelor's degree, 74 percent of them have had at least one child outside of marriage (see Cherlin, Talbert, and Yasutake 2014).

9. Other factors in Britain's leading role in the industrial revolution included the establishment of secure property rights and the emergence of a politically powerful merchant class in the 1600s (see Hillman 2013); on dating the first use of the term "working class," see Hobsbawn (1962), 209.

10. On the IPUMS data, see Ruggles et al. (2010). When I refer to "middle-class" families from the 1800s through the post–World War II peak years, I mean married couples with children and in which the husband held a professional, technical, or managerial occupation or worked in a white-collar clerical or sales job. I use a family-based definition of "working-class" rather than an individual one because this is a study of family history and sociology, not labor history and sociology. See chapter 5 for my reconsideration of social class after 1975.

11. I chose the age limits of twenty to forty-nine because few men were married before age twenty and because by age forty-nine men were growing too old to manage the often physically arduous task of factory work; S. J. Kleinberg (1989) argues that men tended to withdraw from industrial labor by age fifty. I only counted men who were employed in the three industrial sectors (manufacturing, construction, and transportation) and who were not in professional, technical, or managerial positions, because I did not want to include men in high-level occupations such as factory managers, construction supervisors, or transportation planners. The data points for 1890 were interpolated linearly because the 1890 census records were destroyed.

12. Manufacturing output, see Carter et al. (2006), series Dd309. I use the terms "black" and "African American" interchangeably.

13. On employment at the Sparrows Point steelwords, see Hanah Cho, "Sparrows Point Steel Mill Will Close in June," *Baltimore Sun*, May 24; see also Rudacille (2010).

14. On union membership, see U.S. Department of Labor (2014).

15. On polarization and "hollowing-out," see Autor, Katz, and Kearney (2006); on the hourglass economy, see Massey and Hirst (1998).

16. Some jobs left in the middle, see Holzer (2010); the wages of men without bachelor's degrees have fallen, see Autor (2010); on number of steel workers, see Cowie (2010).

17. Two scholars who argue for a distinctive working-class family life are Jefferson Cowie (2010) and Lillian Rubin (1976).

18. Karen Olson (2005) reports that women were not allowed to enter most of the Sparrows Point steelworks.

19. Based on my calculations from IPUMS data (Ruggles et al. 2010) of the percentage of men who were married, had a spouse present and children younger than age eighteen living in the household, were employed as craftsmen, operatives, service workers, or laborers, and had been born outside of the United States.

20. On high school graduation rates in the 1920s, see Carter et al. (2006), series Af274–94.
21. On the prevalence of clocks and watches, see O'Malley (1992). E. P. Thompson developed these terms (1967).
22. On the disciplined self, see Lamont (2000).
23. Olson (2005).
24. Only 33 percent of girls and 47 percent of boys agreed, see Thornton and Young-DeMarco (2001); 67 percent of girls and 72 percent of boys agreed, see Johnston, Bachman, and O'Malley (2013).
25. For statistics for 1960 on the percentage of children born to married women, see Ventura and Bachrach (2000). For current statistics, see Martin et al. (2012).
26. Only 6 percent in the mid-2000s were unmarried when they had a child, see Kennedy and Bumpass (2008); most of the growth has been to women in cohabiting relationships, see Bumpass and Lu (2000) and Kennedy and Bumpass (2008). Between the early 1990s and the mid-2000s, the percentage of women who were cohabiting at birth (as opposed to being married or not living with a partner) rose from 12 percent to 33 percent among those with a high school degree (my calculations from Kennedy and Bumpass [2008] and from the 2006–2008 round of the National Survey of Family Growth [NSFG]). A substantial share of the cohabiting unions doesn't begin until after the woman gets pregnant, according to my calculations from the National Longitudinal Survey of Youth, 1997 Cohort (NLSY-97), followed through 2010.
27. Murray (2012). In 1996 AFDC was renamed Temporary Assistance for Needy Families (TANF).
28. The high-school educated man earned more than his father did: Levy (1998). To construct figure 1.2, I used the IPUMS data files for the decennial censuses available online (Ruggles et al. 2010). By "married" I mean the census category "married, spouse present," which excludes a small number of men whose wives may have been institutionalized or otherwise absent for reasons other than marital discord. The decennial census did not ask individuals whether they were married until 1880. Data points for 1890 have been interpolated linearly because the 1890 census records were destroyed. My occupational classification was derived directly from the major categories of the IPUMS variable OCC1950. The top category combined "professional and technical" with "managers, officials, and proprietors." Clerical work, sales work, and skilled blue-collar work are the key middle-skill categories in the economic history literature (see Katz and Margo 2013); consequently, I constructed categories for "clerical and kindred," "sales workers," and a category that combines "craftsmen" and "operatives." The lowest categories were "service workers" and "laborers." For clarity, I have graphed only three categories in figure 1.2: (1) professional, technical, and managerial workers; (2) craftsmen and operatives; and (3) service workers. These three categories

illustrate the top, approximate middle, and bottom of the marriage gap in nearly all census years. In an appendix available at this book's web page (https://www.russellsage.org/publications/labors-love-lost), I present graphs that include all of the categories I constructed. The results are very similar.

I excluded men whose occupations were in the categories "farmers" or "farm laborers" because of my focus on the industrial working class. I also excluded immigrants (men who had been born outside of the United States) because of their imbalanced sex ratio: it was difficult for immigrant men to find spouses because of a shortage of women. Moreover, immigrants may have married prior to entering the United States, and they may have maintained values about marriage that were specific to their countries of origin. Nevertheless, I have included in the appendix on the web page a chart that includes immigrants, and the results show a similar pattern. As mentioned, I also restricted the charts to men ages twenty to forty-nine, for the reasons noted in note 11.

Another potential confound is that assignment to the category "married, spouse present" at the time of the census was influenced not only by rates of marriage but also by rates of mortality and divorce, which could vary by occupational category. I therefore compiled parallel tables in which the outcome was percentage ever married, which includes individuals classified as currently married, married but with spouse absent, separated, divorced, or widowed. Once again, these results were very similar, and the charts are available in the appendix on the web page.

By "percentage-point difference" I mean the actual number that results when one subtracts the percentage of service workers who are married from the percentage of professional, technical, and managerial workers who are married.

Charts that include other occupational categories in intermediate positions, such as clerical and sales workers, are available in the web-page appendix. I have omitted these groups for clarity, but their inclusion would not change the story.

29. On income inequality since 1900, see Goldin and Katz (2008); on the polarization of the labor market since 1987, see Autor et al. (2006); on the nineteenth century, see Katz and Margo (2013). It is possible, of course, that there was a *third* marriage gap sometime prior to 1880, when the Census Bureau first began to ask about marriage. But that hypothetical third gap would have occurred before the era of rapid industrialization.

30. Newspaper circulation quadrupled: Carter et al. (2006), series Dg256. The Gilded Age: Twain and Warner (1873). On the increasing income share of the top 1 percent of earners in recent decades, see Piketty and Saez (2003).

31. Murray's response: "Why Economics Can't Explain Our Cultural Divide," *Wall Street Journal*, March 16, 2012.

32. I have written about the likely economic and cultural influences on the decline of marriage among African Americans in Cherlin (1992).
33. The United States has the shortest average duration of cohabiting unions: Cherlin (2009); Half are no longer living together after five years: Bendheim-Thoman Center for Child Wellbeing (2007); Twice the rate for children born to married parents: Heuveline, Timberlake, and Furstenberg (2003).
34. See Putnam (2002).
35. Their numbers are large: see U.S. Department of Commerce (2013b).

CHAPTER 2: THE EMERGENCE OF THE WORKING-CLASS FAMILY: 1800–1899

1. The editor's testimony is from Hareven and Langenbach (1978), 19. Mintz (2004) describes the typical ages at which boys entered the mills. On the Lowell mill girls, see Kennedy (1979), chapter 2. Mothers in cities with heavy industry rarely worked outside the home, see S. J. Kleinberg (1989). On the typical ages at which boys entered the mills, see Mintz (2004).
2. Hareven and Langenbach (1978), 255.
3. The quotation is from Glenna Matthews (1989), 98. On the growth of ready-to-wear, see Arnesen (2007).
4. On the decline of boarding, see Harris (1994). My analyses using the IPUMS database (Ruggles et al. 2010) showed that immigrant families were more likely to take in boarders, many of whom, presumably, were immigrants themselves: in 1910—when, according to my calculations, boarding and lodging reached its peak in households headed by craftsmen, operatives, service workers, and common laborers—8.2 percent of all households with native-born heads included boarders, compared to 12.9 of all households with foreign-born heads. (All of my calculations exclude household heads in farm occupations.) In addition, families were more likely to take in boarders when their children were older: in the 1880–1950 censuses combined, 5.6 percent of households with children under age six contained boarders, compared to 6.8 percent of households with children between the ages of six and seventeen and 7.8 percent of households with children who were eighteen or older.
5. The quotation is from Olson (2005), 65–66. Taking advantage of shiftwork: Rudacille (2010).
6. For a description of the survival strategies of these working-class wives, see DeVault (2013).
7. Hareven and Langenbach (1978), 264.
8. Ibid., 275.
9. The quotation is from Hopkins (1994), 80.
10. On the Rhode Island mill, see Mintz (2004). On the ten-hour movement, see

Creighton (2012). Mintz (2004) describes the typical ages at which boys entered the mills and the decline of child labor.

11. On the history of American family law with respect to domestic violence, see Pleck (1987), Siegel (1996), and Hartog (2000). Data showing that women working in comparable industries were paid far less than men can be found in Lebergott (1960), table 2. Women gained some property rights, see Hartog (2000).

12. On masculinity being precarious: Gilmore (1990), 1. On masculinity being defined more by relations with other men than by relations with women, see Michael Kimmel (2012, 5), in which the author calls masculinity a "homosocial accomplishment." R. W. Connell (1995) uses the term "hegemonic masculinity" for a form that's similar to what I am calling conventional masculinity. Alfredo's story is told in Gilmore (1990), 52–55.

13. Proving manhood in three ways: Gilmore (1990), 222–23. Hareven and Langenbach (1978), 274–75 relate the story of the family whose father was laid off after an injury.

14. Reva Siegel (1996) argues that by the 1870s nearly all judges rejected the idea that husbands were entitled to correct wives' behavior by hitting them. Nevertheless, judges remained reluctant to intervene in what they saw as domestic matters.

15. On the typical number of children: The total fertility rate in 1880 was 4.2 for white women and 7.3 for black women; see Carter et al. (2006), series Ab63 and Ab85.

16. The quotation from *Ladies' Magazine* is taken from Cott (1977), 64.

17. Gilmore (1990) argues that femininity was largely seen as a biological and cultural given. Chodorow's argument is presented in *The Reproduction of Mothering* (1978).

18. Lionel Tiger and Robin Fox provide a classic statement of the evolutionary view in *The Imperial Animal* (1971), which we would now label as sociobiological. Gilmore provides a largely social-constructionist view in *Manhood in the Making* (1990). The most important statement about multiple kinds of masculinity, including the currently dominant or "hegemonic" kind, is Connell (1995).

19. Jerome Chauncey, *History of the American Clock Business for the Past Sixty Years* (New Haven, 1860), quoted in Murphy (1966), 173.

20. Murphy (1966).

21. E. P. Thompson's thesis of a shift in time sense can be found in "Time, Work-Discipline, and Industrial Capitalism" (1967). On the waves of immigrants who needed to learn to do timed-disciplined work, see Gutman (1973).

22. See Roger Ekirch, (2005), and Craig Koslofsky, (2011). Both quotations are from Ekirch (2005), 302.

23. On both ways of experiencing time existing in women's lives, see Leccardi and Rampazi (1993).

24. Immigration between 1840 and 1860: see Kessler-Harris (1982). David Montgomery (1976) provides statistics on the number of immigrants who arrived between 1865 and 1900 and their ethnic composition. On immigrants replacing mill girls, see Kennedy (1979), 46–47. There were other factors: wages for schoolteachers, an alternative occupation open to young women, were rising, making that occupation more attractive; and working conditions in the mills had deteriorated. I calculated the percent of operatives who were foreign born from two series in the *Historical Statistics of the United States: Millennial Edition Online*, Ba1041 and Ba1153 (Carter et al. 2006).

25. Irish and French-Canadian women have the highest rates of employment: Kessler-Harris (1982). Young Irish women commonly worked as domestic servants, see Mintz (2004). The figure of 25 percent of Irish women working as domestics is from Kessler-Harris (1982), 55.

26. The quote from Amelia Gazaille is from Hareven (1982), 204. The 1900 figures are from the 1900 census records from Manchester, New Hampshire, as reported in Haveven (1982).

27. Virginia Yans-McLaughlin (1977), is the most widely cited source on the reluctance of Italian immigrants to include women's work in their family strategies. For a detailed examination of schooling laws and Italian Immigrants in New Haven, Connectcut, aee also Lassonde. The quotation from the school superintendent is from Lassonde (2005), 34.

28. School attendance laws in Connecticut and the Northeast: Lassonde (2005). The adulting of the labor force: Cunningham (2000). Viviana Zelizer (1985) describes the rise of the sentimentalized child.

29. As with the marriage gap, see figure 1.2 in chapter 1.

30. Gender differences in children's employment: My calculations from the IPUMS data, (Ruggles et al. 2010).

31. See Caldwell (1980) on the effects of mass schooling. The Italian barber is quoted in Lassonde (2005), 1.

32. Schools emphasized obedience and discipline: Mintz (2004); the quotation about the New York City schools is on p. 92. On parents providing more schooling for boys than for girls, see Lassonde (2005), 75–79.

33. The Utica study: Ryan (1981). When "white collar" entered into common usage: Author's calculations from the online "Google Books (American)" corpus compiled by Mark Davies (2011). The percentage of native-born in occupations in 1880: Author's calculations from the IPUMS database, Ruggles et al. (2010).

34. On middle-class childhood, see Clement (1997). The drop in boarders among professional and managerial households: Author's calculations from the IPUMS database, Ruggles et al. (2010).

35. See Rotundo (1993), 168. On the disciplined self of the working-class man and his distrust of ambition, which I discuss further in later chapters, see Lamont (2000).

36. On fraternal orders and the reaction to them, see Rotundo (1993), 168.
37. The decline in fertility in Utica: Ryan (1981), 155. On middle-class childrearing, see Mintz, (2004), ch. 4.
38. On the evolution of child-rearing values during this period: see Clement (1997); Illick (2002); Mintz (2004); Ryan (1981). The Ryan quote is from *Cradle of the Middle Class* (1981), 161.
39. On reflexivity, see Giddens (1991). On the history of sexual identities, see Robb (2003).
40. On expressive and utilitarian individualism, see Bellah et al. (1985). "Cautious, prudent, small-business man": Ryan (1981), 161. On Benjamin Franklin, see Bigelow, ed. (1872). The differences have been visible ever since: I will return to this topic in subsequent chapters and demonstrate the continuity.
41. Hareven and Langenbach (1978), 44.
42. The quotation is from Cott (1977), 64. For a review of scholarship on the separate spheres ideal, see Kerber (1988).
43. Cott (1977). The best-known article on women's rituals is Carroll Smith-Rosenberg, "The Female World of Love and Ritual: Relations Between Women in Nineteenth-Century America" (1975).
44. Sonya O. Rose (1992), 138, comes to the conclusion that, for the British case, wives earning money through work in the home was acceptable. Jane Addams is quoted in May (1984), 355. Married women would make up 50 percent of the labor force: DeVault (2013), 13.
45. Rose (1992), 132–33; see also Creighton (1996) and Janssens (1997). Two early articles in the historical debate, which took the position that the movement for the family wage was mainly about men maintaining power over women (Hartmann 1979) or that it was mainly about working-class resistance to exploitation by employers (Humphries 1977). More recent scholarships suggests that both interests were involved but that, early on, class politics seemed to dominate; see May (1985), 147.
46. The figures on cotton imports and cloth production are from Hobsbawm (1962), 38.
47. The figure on the rural-urban distribution of African Americans at this time is from Carter et al. (2006), series Aa722 and Aa746. On black iron workers and railroad firemen, see Zieger (2007) and Jones (1999). The quotation on firemen's wages can be found on Jones (1999), 131.
48. Fifty percent of black women in New York City worked as domestics: Kessler-Harris (1982), 55. The percentages showing that more married black women reported paid jobs compared to white married immigrant and native-born women in 1880 are from DeVault (2013), table 3. On marketing among West African women, see Bledsoe (1980). The central work on the issue of possible African cultural survivals is Herskovits (1990).
49. The Dred Scott case: Dred Scott v. Sandford, 60 U.S. 393 (1856).

50. A genre of "whiteness studies" has emerged over the past few decades to study this phenomenon. See McDermott and Samson (2005). On the Irish, see Ignatiev (1995). Fisher is quoted on p. 191. The Jews "desecrated" the Sabbath, of course, by celebrating it on Saturday rather than Sunday. The best-known work on the consequences of white racial ethnicity for the black working class is David R. Roediger, *The Wages of Whiteness: Race and the Making of the American Working Class* (1999); Du Bois is quoted in Du Bois (1935), 700.

51. One British traveler in America wrote in 1819: "Servants, let me here observe, are called 'helps:' [sic] if you call them servants they leave you without notice. Englishmen often incur their displeasure by negligence in continuing to use this prohibited word. . . . The term 'boss,' as I have observed, is substituted for that of master" Fearon (1819), 80–81. The 1898 and 1905 quotations are from Zieger (2007), 62 and 63–64.

52. Lodges would not admit black workers: Zieger (2007), 2. Local chapters often segregated: Jones (1999), 129. The American Federation of Labor and black membership: Zieger (2007), 27–29.

53. Six out of ten employed black women were domestics in 1940: Cherlin (1992), 99.

54. The Gompers quotation can be found in Zieger (2007), 29.

55. See Saxton (1971), 271. The Gompers quotation is from p. 271. On Mexican workers, see Gómez-Quiñones (1982).

56. See Roediger (1999).

57. Advocating for the family wage may have been a good short-term strategy: Sse Creighton (1996), who cites Goldin (1990).Why the family wage was so widely liked, see May (1985), 16–17.

58. Unions advocated for the family wage, see Folbre (2009).

CHAPTER 3: GOOD TIMES AND HARD TIMES: 1900–1945

1. Komarovsky (1940), 99–101.

2. All percentages are based on the civilian labor force, except the 32 percent rate for the nonfarm civilian labor force in 1932. The 1930s figures are for workers ages fourteen and older, whereas the 2000s figures are for workers ages sixteen and older, there being few full-time workers under age sixteen in the later period. For the 1930s, see Carter et al. (2006), series Ba475 (entire civilian labor force) and Ba476 (private nonfarm civilian labor force). For the 2000s, see U.S. Department of Labor (2013), series LNU04000000.

3. The earnings increases were calculated in constant 1928 dollars, see Carter et al. (2006), Series Ba4336, Ba4341, Ba4342, and Ba4346 for annual earnings; and series Cc1 for the consumer price index. Average number of children per woman: Data on the total fertility rate (the mean number of children that a

woman would be expected to have during her lifetime if age-specific fertility rates were to remain unchanged) is also from Carter et al. (2006), Series Ab63 for whites and Series Ab85 for blacks.

4. Only the most skilled and unionized workers achieved it, see May (1982).The AFL spokesman is quoted in May (1985), 147.

5. See May (1982) and Loizides (2011). The information on the $5 wage comes from these two articles unless otherwise indicated.

6. "There is no injustice there": quoted in Loizides (2011), 28. Eighty-two women were fired: May (1982), 413–14.

7. "A man shall provide generously": quoted in Loizides (2011), 20. "Roomers and boarders must go": Loizides (2011), 21. "We encourage better housing": Loizides (2011), 20.

8. The historian Sonya O. Rose (1992), 138–39. Lodging remained common: As late as 1930, 11 percent of households in the urban United States had one or more boarders; see Harris (1994).

9. Eleven mentions of the word housewife, see any concordance of the words in Shakespeare's plays, such as http://www.opensourceshakespeare.org/concordance/. The quotation is from *Cymbeline*, Act IV, Scene 2. The perfect lady, see Eisenstein (2012). Prevalence of domestic servants, see Folbre (1991). The Protestant, native-born middle-class family, see Ryan (1981).

10. The database and some results are described in Davies (2011), and Michel et al. (2011).

11. The source of the quote on homemaking versus housekeeping is "Home-Making and House-Keeping," *The Home-Maker* 1 (1, October 1888): 4. The other quotations are from of "The Home Club," *The Outlook* 61 (14, April 8, 1899): 850.

12. A housekeeper can be hired: Gillis (1996), 122. Official report of the Eighth Biennial Convention of the General Federation of Women's Clubs, (1906), 367.

13. This paragraph draws upon Gillis (1996). Previously associated with holy places: Gillis (1996), 116. Most powerful source of identity, Gillis (1996), 114.

14. See Nancy Folbre (1993).

15. The construction of new housing and restaurants: Folbre (1993). The automat: see Wingfield (2010). Forty of them in New York City: James T. Farrell, "The Last Automat," *New York*, May 14, 1979.

16. On the timing of the introduction of refrigerators and washing machines, see Carter et al. (2006), Series Dd419 and Dd420. Lamenting the lack of capable, reliable service: Elizabeth Inman, "Household Service," *The Home-Maker*, 1(4, January 1889), 284–85.

17. Forty-one states had passed limits on work hours, see Skocpol (1992). Brandeis's brief was submitted for the case Muller v. Oregon, 208 U.S. 412 (1908).

18. As Brandeis wrote: Louis D. Brandeis, "Brief for Defendant in Error," Muller v. Oregon, 208 U.S. 412 (1908), 18. The British physician is quoted on p. 93.
19. The Pennsylvania judge is quoted in Skocpol (1992), 369. Agricultural and domestic workers excluded from the Social Security Act: see Katznelson (2005). Agricultural and domestic workers excluded from the Fair Labor Standard Act of 1938, see Mutari, Power, and Figart (2002).
20. The number of states with age and hours restrictions increased, see Zelizer (1985), 76. By 1930, nearly all children were in school through age 14: Zelier (1985), 97. Fair Labor Standards Act: Felt (1970).
21. It isn't clear that parents would have obeyed them: The economist Claudia Goldin (2006) argues that compulsory education laws were generally not binding; students who had obtained a work permit and had a minimum level of schooling, or who could claim family hardship, could be excused from remaining in school until the compulsory age. See Goldin (2006). A major change in how children were viewed, see Zelizer (1985). On Utica: Ryan (1981).
22. Zelizer (1985), 138–39.
23. On adolescence: Hall (1904). On Hall's view of adolescence as a biological stage, see Mintz (2004).
24. The percentage who graduated from high school from 1900 to 1930: see Carter et al. (2006), series Bc264. Secondary School enrollment in 1930: Carter et al. (2006), series Bc492-Bc500. One high school opened each day, see Mintz (2004), 175.
25. Caldwell's wealth flows theory: Caldwell (1982). You just can't have so many children: quoted in Lynd and Lynd (1929), 131.
26. The quotations on the definition of the business class and the working class are from Lynd and Lynd (1929), 22 (emphasis in the original). About 70 percent: Lynd and Lynd (1929), 22. "While an effort will be made": Lynd and Lynd (1929), 23–24.
27. Percentages selecting particular child-rearing values: as summarized in Alwin (1988), 523, table 14. "I am afraid" and "Obedience may be all right": quoted in Lynd and Lynd (1929), 144.
28. Parents are becoming puzzled and unsure: Lynd and Lynd (1929), 143. The patterns were about 100 years old: see the discussion in chapter 2; see also Ryan (1981).
29. "In the past the man has been first": Taylor (1914), 7. Ford's first assembly line: see May (1982).
30. The transition from an institution to a companionship, see Burgess and Locke (1945), 162.
31. "Scores of studies have established": McWilliams (2006), 162. "Highly likely": Fischer (2010), 118.

32. Greater leisure time and increased contraceptive usage signaled rising romance and affection in marriage, see Weiss (2000).

33. Lack of companionship and working-class marital tensions: Lynd and Lynd (1929), 118, 119, respectively. Burgess's concentric zone theory: His original diagram illustrating the concentric zone theory was published in his paper, "The Growth of the City: An Introduction to a Research Project" (1925); Burgess and Locke included a version of it, annotated with dominant family types, in *The Family* (1945, 117). Boarders: Carter et al (2006), series Ba5083–Ba5085. Women's Bureau report, Pidgeon (1937).

34. On the Temporary Emergency Relief Administration in New York State, see Eisenstadt and Moss, (2005). Komarovsky's study (1940).

35. One family took in boarders: Komarovsky (1940), 30. Occupations with a high percentage of women workers were relatively protected, see Kessler-Harris (1982). Employed wife who shows tact: Komarovsky (1940), 56.

36. He used to be so good and kind: Komarovsky (1940), 94. The Johnsons' apartment: Komarovsky (1940), 9.

37. Jessie Bernard, "The Good-Provider Role: Its Rise and Fall" (1981), 4. Mr. Brady, it's only natural: Komarovsky (1940), 98.

38. A majority had two earners: By 1980, 50.1 percent of all married women were in the labor force—that is, they were either working outside the home or looking for work); see Carter et al. (2006), Series Ba579.

39. Decreasing frequency of sexual relations: Komarovsky (1940), 130. It's a crime: Komarovsky (1940), 131. Declining total fertility rate between 1930 and 1936: Carter et al. (2006), Series Ab63 (comparable figures for blacks are unavailable).

40. Komarovsky (1940), 54–56; quotations from p. 56. See, for example, Cavan and Ranck (1938) and Angell (1936).

41. Glen H. Elder, Jr., *Children of the Great Depression: Social Change in Life Experience* (1974).

42. Henry taking his place at the dinner table: Komarovsky (1940), 101.

43. Quote from Mr. Adams: Komarovsky (1940), 118. Depression is just a handy phrase: Komarovsky (1940), 118. I'll vote Republican: Komarovsky (1940), 122. Just look at the street cars: Komarovsky (1940), 119. The colored people have more food: Komaovsky (1940), 121.

44. Employment increased 60 percent: U.S. Department of Labor (1946), 3n2.

45. On Rosie the Riveter, see U.S. Library of Congress (2010). The majority of former housewives were in the manufacturing sector: U.S. Department of Labor (1946), 10. I calculated the percentages who were working during the war by combining information from U.S. Department of Labor (1946, 29, table I-2; 45, table IV-1) and using some algebra. Table IV-1 shows that 44 percent of women employed during the war were married. Table I-2 shows that 26 percent had been housewives. By subtraction (44 − 26), I calculated

that 18 percent were married women who had not been housewives, that is, they had been employed before the war. That left the other, nonmarried 56 percent, whom I divided into those who had been working before the war and those who had not. Table I-2 says that 53 percent of all women workers (regardless of marital status) had been employed before the war. But I calculated that 18 percent of all women workers were married women who had been employed before the war. Therefore, women workers who were unmarried and who had been employed before the war constituted 35 percent (53 − 18) of all women workers. In sum, by my calculations, the distribution of women who were employed during the war, according to this survey of over 13,000 women conducted by the Women's Bureau in 1944 and 1945, was as follows:

Married, not employed before the war (housewives)	26%
Married, employed before the war	18%
Nonmarried, not employed beforehand	21%
Nonmarried, employed beforehand	35%
Total	100%

Three-fourths wanted to keep working after the war: Table I-5, p. 31. But only 20 percent of former housewives: Table I-7, p. 32.

46. Older married women were less likely to leave their jobs; black women benefited: see Kessler-Harris (1982). Married women with preschool-aged children moved into the labor force in the 1950s, see Cherlin (1992). Public opinion was less hostile to mothers who sought employment after all of their children were in school: Starting as early as 1970, survey researchers have repeatedly asked national samples whether they think a preschool-age child would suffer if his or her mother works; the fact that none have chosen to even ask about mothers with only school-age children suggests that the public was less concerned about the mothering of older children. See Mason and Bumpass (1975). Percentage of employed black women who were private household workers: My calculations from the IPUMS data (Ruggles et al. 2010).

47. The median age at marriage dropped: see Carter et al. (2006), series Ae481 and Ae482.

48. This section reprises ideas and facts presented earlier. I will provide citations only to new material.

49. Labor market polarization from 1850 to1910: see Katz and Margo (2013).

50. Among white, nonfarm, married-couple households headed by a manual worker, the percentage that took in boarders declined after 1910. For instance, in 1910, 12 percent of the households that were headed by a service worker or laborer had boarders, compared to 10 percent of households that were headed by a professional, technical, or managerial worker. But by 1940, only 5 per-

cent of each group had boarders (my calculations from the IPUMS data; Ruggles et al., 2010).

51. Eddie Bartee and his family: see Joe Nawrozki, "The Rise And Fall of Life and Steel at 'The Point,'" *Baltimore Sun*, December 22, 2002. Blacks entered the industrial working-class in substantial numbers, see figure 1.1, which shows a sharp rise after 1900 in the percentage of black husbands who were working in manufacturing.

52. A public and psychological wage: Du Bois (1935), 700.

CHAPTER 4: THE PEAK YEARS, 1945–1975

1. The interviews were done as part of the research for Timothy Nelson's 2013 book with Kathryn Edin, *Doing the Best I Can: Fathering in the Inner City*. The men had to be earning less than $8 per hour, to have at least one noncustodial child living elsewhere, and to be U.S. citizens. I thank him for sharing his field notes with me. *Leave It to Beaver*, see Brooks and Marsh (2003).

2. On historical nostalgia, see Stern (1992).

3. No women have mentioned June Cleaver: personal communication from Kathryn Edin.

4. Wartime deaths: although there are no official statistics, the estimates of the relative numbers of deaths are consistent across a number of unofficial sources. American manufacturing and exports as a share of the world total: French (1997).

5. This paragraph, including the statistics on median wages and benefits, draws upon Levy and Temin (2010). The quote from Reuther is from a review of a biography of him; see Brinkley (1995). On trends in income inequality, see Goldin and Katz (2008).

6. Changes in the occupational distribution of black women and men ages eighteen to forty-nine between 1940 and 1970: author's calculations from the IPUMS data (Ruggles et al. 2010) . The woman whose father worked at Sparrows Point: interview, April 13, 2013.

7. "Estimated Median Age at Marriage, by Sex: 1890 to the Present": U.S. Department of Commerce (2012). As far back as 1850: Carter et al. (2006), Series Ae481-Ae488. A girl who hasn't a man in sight: Sidonie M. Gruenberg. "Why They Are Marrying Younger" (1955). Percent ever-marrying: Davis (1972). The intervals between birth shortened: Ryder (1980).

8. The total fertility rate is the mean number of children that a woman would be expected to have during her lifetime if age-specific fertility rates were to remain unchanged; the date are from Carter et al. (2006), series AB52.

9. Quoted in Weiss (2000), 115. Richard A. Easterlin first described this small cohort, high-demand phenomenon in *Birth and Fortune: The Impact of Numbers on Personal Welfare* (1980).

10. See Hernandez (1993), especially fig. 4.8 on p. 123.

11. Scholars claiming the breadwinner-homemaker family was a myth: For instance, historian Robert Self (2012, 275) as written, "For all the challenges to the breadwinner ideal—the white, patriotic, heterosexual male at the head of the nuclear family with which the book began—it remained a powerful myth."

12. The figures on the 1950s and 1960s, as well as the suggestion of a slower, sexual evolution, are from England, Wu, and Fitzgibbons (2013). By women in their prime childbearing age in the 1950s I mean women born in 1930 to 1934; similarly, women in their prime childbearing years in the 1960s were born in 1940 to 1944. Percent of births in 2010 that were outside of marriage: U.S. National Center for Health Statistics, "Births: Final Data for 2010" (2012). Black unmarried mother families in 1910: Morgan et al. (1993).

13. Stephanie Coontz (1992, 36) notes that tranquilizers were developed in the mid-1950s as a response to the perceived mental health problems of women and were widely prescribed by 1960.

14. On the relatively high proportion of children who lived with two parents, see Ellwood and Jencks, (2004). Children face sharply higher rates of family instability today, see my book, *The Marriage-Go-Round: The State of Marriage and the Family in America Today* (2009). I will have more to say about family instability in chapter 6. Rising college enrollment: Carter et al. (2006), series Bc524.

15. See May (1988, 201, 202).

16. Komarovsky (1962).

17. On the companionate marriage, see Burgess and Locke (1945). The classic studies referred to are Herbert J. Gans's, *The Urban Villagers: Group and Class in the Lives of Italian-Americans* (1962) and *Blue-Collar Aristocrats: Life-Styles at a Working-Class Tavern* by E. E. LeMasters (1975).

18. Even among the middle-class it may have remained an ideal: Weiss (2000), 228. Komarovsky's findings: Komarovsky (1962).

19. The quotation is from Rubin (1976), 12.

20. Rubin (1976). The quotation beginning "Despite the Yearning," is from p. 123. The quotation beginning "I guess in order to live" is from p. 133. Wives' labor force participation: Author's calculations from the IPUMS data archive (Ruggles et al. 2010). Being in the labor force means being either employed or actively looking for work.

21. The quotation beginning "I've never given a dinner party" is from Rubin (1976), 195.

22. Olson's oral histories were the basis for her book, *Wives of Steel: Voices of Women from the Sparrows Point Steelmaking Communities*. The quotation "I came from a block where most of the mothers stayed home" is from pp. 73–74. The quotation "we had it made" is from p. 73. The quotation "Most of the women I knew worked" is from pp. 72–73. Some had college degrees, see Rudacille (2010), 116.

23. On home ownership rates and the "unit security system", see Rudicille (2010). The quotation is from Rudicille (2010), 120.

24. "We never had any financial problems": Olson (2005), 83. "I'm as independent as I am": Olson (2005), 87. "It was hard and it was pleasant": Olson (2005), 86–87.

25. Gans's book on Boston was *The Urban Villagers: Group and Class in the Lives of Italian-Americans* (1962). The best-selling books on conformity were David Riesman, *The Lonely Crowd: A Study of the Changing American Character* (1953) and William H. Whyte, Jr.'s *The Organization Man* (1956).

26. Gans (1967), xxvi.

27. Gans on the lower middle class: see pp. 27–29.

28. The quotation is from Gans, p. xvi.

29. Female malaise: Gans, p. 225. "Urban safety valve" and quote: Gans, p. 230.

30. On the desegregation of Levittown, New Jersey, see Gans, 371–84.

31. The database and some results are described in Davies (2011) and Michel et al. (2011).

32. On the emergence of the middle class, see Ryan (1981).

33. Lamont (2000). "Family is very important to my life": Lamont (2000), 29.

34. Richard Sennett and Jonathan Cobb, *The Hidden Injuries of Class* (1972). "They care more": Lamont (2000), 99.

35. Ibid., 61.

36. Ibid., 169.

37. "Help people if I could": Lamont (2000), 47. "Blacks have a strong sense of family": Lamont (2000), 79. "Black people are sensitive": Lamont (2000), 79.

38. "Better Living Through TV," *The Honeymooners*, 1955.

39. "Could not control their wives": Coontz (1992).

40. Coontz's famous phrase: see Coontz (1992).

41. Black occupational gains, see figures presented earlier in this chapter. Percentage of black men who were married: Author's calculations from the IPUMS data (Ruggles et al. 2010). Births outside of marriage: U.S. National Center for Health Statistics (2009). Total fertility rates: Carter et al., (2006), series Ab74. These figures are for *all* births to African American women, whereas the figures earlier in the chapter were for first births.

42. Spread of household appliances by the early 1960s, see Thistle (2006). Wives not working outside the home cleaned as frequently as women in the 1920s: Vanek (1974). Merchandisers added steps to recipes: Coontz (1992), 165. "They can make some impression" and "just a housewife like myself": Weiss (2000), 206.

43. Author's calculations from the IPUMS data (Ruggles et al. 2010). The rise of the "pink collar" metaphor can be tracked using the Google books corpus (Davies 2011).

44. Percentage of married women with children of various ages in labor force:

U.S. Department of Commerce (1970), table 331. Rises were led by working-class and lower-middle-class women: see Coontz (1992), 163.

45. For the *Ladies Home Journal* article, see Meyerowitz (1994), 238.

CHAPTER 5: THE FALL OF THE WORKING-CLASS FAMILY: 1975–2010

1. I derived the number of steelworkers from the IPUMS data (Ruggles et al. 2010) using the 1990 industry codes for persons employed in blast furnaces, steelworks, rolling and finishing mills, and iron and steel foundries.

2. In one set of concessions to General Motors, see Milkman (1997). The quotation is from p. 3.

3. My estimates from the IPUMS data (Ruggles et al. 2010), using the 1990 occupation codes.

4. I tabulated the figures on operators of machinery using the IPUMS data (Ruggles et al. 2010). The 1970 source is the census of 1970; the 2010 source is the American Community Survey (ACS) conducted by the Census Bureau. To estimate the number of operators, I used the IPUMS 1990 occupational codes of 700 to 799. Lathe, milling, and turning operatives were given the specific code 703.

5. Author's estimates from the IPUMS data (Ruggles et al. 2010). I tabulated the figures on designers of numerically controlled machine tools using the 1990 occupational code of 233. Recall that by a bachelor's degree I mean a degree such as a bachelor of arts or bachelor of science given by a college or university for a course of study that usually takes four years but can take longer.

6. Service jobs have increased: Author's calculations from the IPUMS data (Ruggles et al. 2010). Nonroutine manual tasks, see Autor, Levy, and Murnane (2003).

7. On polarization, see Autor, Katz, and Kearney (2006); on the hourglass economy, see Massey and Hirst (1998). The number of health technicians of various types: Author's calculation from the IPUMS data (Ruggles et al. 2010). On opportunities in the middle, see Holzer (2010). Increasing demand for delivery drivers and protective service workers: Wyatt and Hecker (2006).

8. On trends in women's occupations, see Autor (2010). On gender differences in college graduates, see U.S. Department of Commerce (1996, 2014).

9. The sociological literature on marital formation and dissolution refers to the income and independence effects of women's earnings; see Hannan, Tuma, and Groeneveld (1978) and Oppenheimer (1997). Economists write more generally about the income and substitution effects of an increase in earnings on the purchase of alternative goods (such as "marriage" and "singlehood"). In 1996, when the main welfare program, now called Temporary Assistance for

Needy Families (TANF), put a five-year limit on benefits, enrollments dropped sharply; it may have played a larger role in encouraging independence prior to then. I discuss the decline in marriage among the less-educated and the increase in cohabiting couples and single parents later in this chapter and in the next chapter. Between 1980 and 2010, the percentage of women with less than four years of college who ever married decreased from 96 percent to 85 percent for those ages forty to forty-nine. Among women with four or more years of college, the comparable decline was more modest: 91 percent to 87 percent. Thus, by 2010, women ages forty to forty-nine with four or more years of college were more likely to have ever married than similar-aged women with less education. Author's calculations from the IPUMS database (see Ruggles et al. 2010).

10. By the time they are in their forties, highly educated women are more likely to marry: see my calculations in note 9, and Martin (2004). A half-century ago, women with good economic prospects were *less* likely to ever marry, see Sweeney (2002). Earnings increase their attractiveness to potential spouses: In searching for a spouse, men now place greater importance on a spouse's earning potential than they did a half-century ago. This is shown by a series of surveys of desirable characteristics for a spouse conducted between 1939 and 1996; see Buss et al. (2001).

11. John Meyer (1994) argues for the growing importance of education in stratification systems, in part due to credentialism.

12. Wage trends prior to and after 2000: see Autor (2014). Downward displacement of workers with less education, see Beaudry, Green, and Sand (2013).

13. College graduates are increasingly marrying each other, see Schwartz and Mare (2005). College-educated parents are increasingly emphasizing autonomy and self-development, see Lareau (2011).

14. Sixty-five percent were professional, managerial, or technical workers: author's calculation from the IPUMS data (Ruggles et al. 2010). The reference to Vice-President Biden's working-class background is in the 2011 State of the Union address. The White House's statement on Pell grants is "Helping Middle Class Families Pay for College" (2013). Americans don't say they are in the working class unless they are prompted with the term, see Hout (2008).

15. 41 percent were service workers or laborers: author's calculations from the IPUMS database. By common laborers, I mean workers with occupational codes (1990 revision) of 860-899, comprising workers such as construction laborers, other laborers, garage attendants, and car wash workers. On the income gap between the middle and the bottom of the labor market, see Autor et al. (2006).

16. The lower the husband's income, the more likely is the wife to out-earn him, see Winkler (1998). On how wives and husbands decide on their class identity, see Davis and Robinson (1998) and Zipp and Plutzer (2000).

17. On the "motherood penalty," see Waldfogel (1997), Budig and England (2001), and Budig and Hodges (2010).
18. On birth rates: I am speaking of trends in the total fertility rate. See Carter et al. (2006), series Ab52. Margaret Sanger was quoted in Seidman (1991), 76.
19. Premarital sex had been slowly increasing: see England et al. (2013). Premarital sex was "always wrong": Thornton (1989). Percentage of mothers who had a premarital first birth: England, Shafer, and Wu (2012), tables 3a (whites) and 3b (blacks).
20. Staying together for the sake of the children, see Thornton (1989). Divorce rates and the new view of marriage: see Cherlin (1992). On no-fault divorce laws, see Glendon (1987).
21. Increase in mothers in the labor force: As noted in the previous chapter, by 1969, 29 percent of married women with preschool-age children and 49 percent of married women with school-age children were in the labor force, many of them working part-time, see U.S. Department of Commerce (1970), table 331. For the liberal side of the debate, see Wilson (1987) and Auletta (1982). For the conservative side, see Murray (1984) and Mead (1986).
22. The statistics on the growth of the Hispanic population are from Carter et al, 2006, series Aa2189 and Aa185 and author's calculations from the IPUMS database (Ruggles et al. 2010). On the effects of immigration laws on Hispanic immigration, see Durand, Telles, and Flashman (2006). For a demographic history of Hispanic immigration, see Rumbaut (2006).
23. Nancy Landale, Salvador Oropesa, and Cristina Bradatan (2006) report that levels of nonmarital childbearing among Puerto Ricans and Dominicans are comparable to levels for African Americans, whereas levels among Cubans are comparable to those of non-Hispanic whites. On consensual unions, see Landale and Fennelly (1992). I have been unable to find a good recent study on the current prevalence of consensual unions; this tradition may not as strong now as it had been historically.
24. On the Hispanic labor force, see Brian Duncan, V. Joseph Hotz, and Stephen J. Trejo, "Hispanics in the U.S. Labor Market" (2006). Educational attainment of Hispanics and African Americans: U.S. Department of Commerce (2013a) tables show that among twenty-five- to twenty-nine-year-olds, 76 percent of Hispanics had graduated from high school compared to 89 percent of African Americans; and 16 percent had graduated from college, compared to 20 percent of African Americans.
25. On birth rates, see Durand, Telles, and Flashman (2006). Levels of nonmarital childbearing that sit between African Americans and non-Hispanic whites, see Landale, Oropesa, and Bradatan (2006).
26. Cuban marriage and fertility rates: Rumbaut (2006). On Cuban entrepreneurship, see Portes and Jensen (1989). Cuban, non-Hispanic white, and overall Hispanic total fertility rates: Martin et al. (2012).

27. Increases in age at marriage: U.S. Department of Commerce (2012). Substituting cohabitation for early marriage: Smock (2000) and Bumpass, Sweet, and Cherlin (1991). More than doubled from 1987 to 2009–2010: Manning (2013). Nearly 40 percent didn't start cohabiting until the woman was pregnant: Rackin and Gibson-Davis (2012).

28. Low-income single women: Edin and Kefalas (2005).

29. The composition of the nonwhite group shifted between 1980 and 2010 owing to immigration. In 1980, 69 percent of nonwhites were African American; in 2010, 51 percent were African American. The percentage of nonwhites who were Asian or Pacific Islander increased from 9 to 20 percent over the same period. Most of the remainder of the nonwhite population was Hispanic. The Census Bureau asks Hispanics to select a race, which seems to confuse many respondents, some of whom choose "white" or "black," while others choose "other nonwhite."

30. Toledo study: Smock, Manning, and Porter (2005), 687.

31. The couple pays for the wedding themselves: According to the American Wedding Study, commissioned by *Brides* magazine, 36 percent of couples paid the entire cost of their wedding receptions in 2012, up from 29 percent in 2009, and another 26 percent contributed to the cost. "I don't want to go downtown" and "he wants a big wedding"; Smock et al. (2005), 688.

32. See Sassler, Miller, and Favinger (2009), 223; see also Sassler and Miller (2011). The quotation beginning , "I want this to be because you are marrying me," is from Sassler, Miller, and Favinger (2009), 223; and the quotation beginning, "you need to have way better reasons" is from the same article, p. 225.

33. Survey of adults around age fifty: see the analysis of the 2010 waves of the National Longitudinal Survey of Youth, 1979 Cohort (NLSY-79) (not to be confused with its sister study of a 1997 cohort, in Aughinbaugh, Robles, and Sun (2013); see also Isen and Stevenson (2011). General Social Survey: author's tabulations from GSS data (Smith, Marsden, et al. 2013). College educated" means having completed and received credit for at least sixteen years of schooling. On divorce: In almost every survey round, the GSS asked, "Should divorce in this country be easier or more difficult to obtain than it is now?" Between the 1970s and the 1980s, the percentage of college-educated respondents under age thirty-five who replied "more difficult" increased from 30 percent to 49 percent. Among comparable respondents with twelve to fifteen years of schooling, the percentage who replied "more difficult" rose from 39 percent to 50 percent. Among those with less than twelve years of schooling, the percentage who replied "more difficult" rose from 39 to 43 percent.

34. College graduates have separated themselves from the rest of the marriage market: Kalmijn (1991). The data on increases in median incomes (which are corrected for increases in the cost of living) are from U.S. Department of Com-

merce" (2013c). The economists Betsey Stevenson and Justin Wolfers (2007, 49) call the income-pooling style of marriage among the highly educated the "consumption-oriented marriage."

35. The consent decree pertaining to blue-collar jobs at the plants was affirmed by an appeals court in 1975: U.S. v. Allegheny-Ludlum Industries, Inc., 517 F.2D 826 (5th Cir. 1975).

36. Rudacille (2010), 162.

37. "The men are out to impress each other": Olson (2005), 105–6. "Prior to working at Bethlehem Steel": Olson (2005), 100. Rise in the percentage of separated, divorced, or never-married mothers: Author's calculations using the IPUMS database.

38. On the busing controversy in Boston, see Lukas (1985). Nan Robertson, "A Wallace Backer Stirred by Busing," *New York Times*, May 14, 1972. The interview was unearthed by Jefferson Cowie and reprinted in in *Stayin' Alive: The 1970s and the Last Days of the Working Class* (2010). On aggrieved entitlement, see Kimmel (2013).

39. The study of teenagers followed to their late twenties is the National Longitudinal Survey of Youth, 1997 Cohort (not to be confused with its sister study of the 1979 cohort), which selected a national sample of twelve- to sixteen-year-olds in 1997 and has interviewed them annually. We used information from the interviews through 2011, when rewspondents were ages twenty-six to thirty-one. See Cherlin et al. (2014). Forty-eight percent had ended their relationships: Bendheim-Thoman Center for Child Wellbeing (2007).

40. A report based on the the NLSY-79 shows that by age forty-six, 89 percent of those with a bachelor's degree or higher had ever married, compared to 87 percent of those with a high school education but not a bachelor's degree and 81 percent of those without a high school diploma. As for age at marriage, those with bachelor's degrees had the highest mean age, 26.5 years, compared to 24.2 for those with some college, 23.6 for those with a high school degree, and 22.7 for those without high school degrees. Thus, the highly educated are more likely to have ever been married, but they take longer to get around to it. See Aughinbaugh, Robles, and Sun (2013).

CHAPTER 6: THE WOULD-BE WORKING CLASS TODAY

1. Nelson is the co-author, with Kathryn Edin, of *Doing the Best I Can: Fathering in the Inner City* (2013). Between June 2012 and February 2013, Nelson recruited men in neighborhoods with a relatively high concentration of moderately educated adults through several means: He contacted local organizations within the target neighborhoods, such as temporary labor agencies and Head Start centers, that were likely to have working-class men and families

as clients. He left flyers in strategic locations such as corner stores, barber shops, and coin laundry facilities. He placed advertisements in community papers. He also used a limited snowball sampling technique in which respondents could refer no more than two acquaintances. The interviews lasted approximately two hours, and the subjects were paid $40. I have changed the names and some of the identifying information of the men to preserve confidentiality.

2. Statistics on women's labor force participation and marital status: author's calculations from the IPUMS (Ruggles et al. 2010). The statistics on wives' labor force participation and earnings are from (Winkler 1998). By" husbands with average incomes," I mean husbands whose earnings place them in the middle quintile of the earnings distribution for all married men. By "working mothers," I mean women who are in the labor force and who have children under age eighteen living in their households. The statistics on marital status of working mothers are from calculations by the author using the IPUMS (Ruggles et al. 2010). Some are cohabiting: According to author's calculations from the March 2010 Current Population Survey, 16 percent of unmarried women in the labor force who had a moderate education and a child less than age eighteen living in the household were cohability at the time of the survey.

3. The high school–educated young adult who has all his children within marriage is the outlier: see Cherlin et al. (2014). Figure 5.2 demonstrated that the prevalence of nonmarital childbearing has increased greatly since 1980.

4. Merton (1938), 679.

5. Murray (2012), 135. On the two studies, see Johnston, Bachman, and O'Malley (2013).

6. Author's calculations from GSS data. The questions were asked in fifteen surveys between 1973 and 1994, and then in 2006 and in 2012. I grouped together the responses in the first seven years (1973–1984), the next eight years (1985–1994), and the more recent two years (2006 and 2012). I chose age twenty-five as the lower bound because many young adults under twenty-five are still completing their education, and I chose age forty-four as the upper bound to focus on recent cohorts. Another item was "no danger of being fired." There was a broad-based increase in the percentage of twenty-five- to forty-four-year-old adults who rated it as most important or second most important (from 19 to 36 percent among men, and from 16 to 31 percent among women), but this rise may have been due less to changes in motivation than to the sharp increase in insecure and unstable employment. There was little change in the proportion of men and women rating the item "high income" as most important or second most important. Finally, there was a decline from 52 to 45 percent for men and from 52 to 50 percent for women in the ranking of "chances for advancement." On the trends for women: Among women ages

twenty-five to forty-four, the percentage who ranked "working hours are short, lots of free time" as most or second most important increased from 12 percent in the 1973–1994 period to 24 percent in 2006 and 2012. Among the same group of women, the percentage who ranked "work important and gives a feeling of accomplishment" as most or second most important decreased from 73 to 49 percent.

7. Author's calculations from the IPUMS data (Ruggles et al. 2010). Work hours for men with college degrees and for dual-earner countries, see Jacobs and Gerson (2004), table 1.2.

8. Marlis Buchmann and Manuel Eisner (1997) suggested these terms. Their work, as well as mine, draws on the distinction between utilitarian individualism and expressive individualism in Bellah et al. (1985). On the disciplined self among white working-class men, see Lamont (2000).

9. On reflexivity, see Giddens (1991) and Beck, Giddens, and Lash (1994).

10. On postmodern values, see Inglehart (1997).

11. I based the timing of the transition in Europe on Buchmann and Eisner (1997).

12. The quotation is from Silva (2013), 21. Silva defines "working class" as having a father without a college degree.

13. In a report by the Pew Research Center (2012), 19.6 percent of respondents said that they were atheists, agnostics, "something else," or "nothing in particular." Of this group, 37 percent said that they were "spiritual but not religious." Thus, $(19.6 \times 0.37) = 7.3$ percent of all respondents in the survey could be classified as spiritual but not religious. On the spiritual of seeking, see Wuthnow (1998), 2.

14. On the questing style of religiosity, see Roof (1999). On trends in religious attendance, see Wilcox et al. (2012). The decline in attendance among the non-college-educated was very similar for men and women. Religious participation has dropped more than spirituality, see Roof (1999).

15. "I keep talking to him about communication": Rubin (1976), 120. On the companionate and individualistic styles of marriage, see Amato (2009) and Cherlin (2004).

16. On changes in men's abilities to conceptualize and communicate the emotions, see Illouz (2008).

17. On hegemonic masculinity see Connell (1995).

18. Child-rearing of the nascent middle-class, see the discussion in Ryan (1981), ch. 2. On Middletown, see Lynd and Lynd (1929), chs. 3 and 4. In his well-known study based on a 1964 survey of fathers, Melvin Kohn (1969) found similar class differences.

19. Duane Alwin (1988) reports on the replication of the Muncie study. 1983 data: author's tabulations from the GSS. Other studies have found similar results, see, for example, Wright and Wright (1976). On the long-term historical shift, see Alwin (2001).

20. See Kornrich and Furstenberg (2013). These authors also note that whereas parents spent more on boys than girls, on average, in the 1970s, they now spend slightly more on girls than on boys. This turnaround could be one factor in the rising educational attainment of young women relative to young men.

21. Half break up within five years, see Bendheim-Thoman Center for Child Wellbeing (2007).

22. Unless otherwise noted, the information in this paragraph comes from Cherlin (2009). Eighteen percent of children had parents who were cohabiting at birth, see Kennedy and Bumpass (2008). On family instability and child outcomes, see for example, Cavanagh and Huston (2006), Fomby and Cherlin (2007), and Cooper et al. (2011).

23. More multi-partner fertility than in Austalia, Norway, or Sweden: Thomson et al. (2014). Worse outcomes when living with half-sib than full-sib: Dorius and Guzzo (2013).

24. Over half of all prisoners are parents: see U.S. Department of Justice (2008). On the percentage of children who will experience parental incarceration before age eighteen, see Pettit (2012). On increases in the risk of divorce with incarceration, see Lopoo and Western (2005).

25. Family complexity in non-Western societies: Furstenberg (2014).

26. McDermott (2006), 68.

27. Author's tabulations from the GSS; see Smith, Hout, and Marsden (2013).

28. Young men without college degree earning less than their fathers did, see Levy (1998).

29. On stopgap jobs, see Oppenheimer et al. (1997). On the casualization of employment relations, see Sassen (2000) and Sassen (2006).

30. Patrick Heuveline and Jeffrey M. Timberlake (2004) show that the United States has the shortest average duration of cohabiting unions in twelve Western nations. The proportion that break-up has been increasing, see Seltzer (2004). Sliding into cohabitation, see Manning and Smock (2005). On the lack of any obligation of cohabiting partners to divide assets equally: see Carbone and Cahn (2014).

31. I thank W. Bradford Wilcox for his insights on religion and social class. See Wilcox et al. (2012). On white churches and respectability, see Wilcox and Wolfinger (2008). On their family-centeredness, see Edgell (2006). On retaining a belief in God but not attending religious services more often, see Wuthnow (1998).

32. On the need for identities to be grounded in the associated social tasks, see Jenkins (2004). On black churches emphasizing marriage less than white churches, see Ellison and Sherkat (1995) and Lincoln and Mamiya (1990).

33. On time spent in the same job (known as" job tenure" in the literature) among men and women, see Kalleberg (2011), 92–93. There is a long literature on what might be called women-centered kinship networks and on women's key roles in intergenerational exchanges within low- and moderate-income families, although more recent studies have suggested that assistance among the poor and near-poor may be more variable than was once thought; see Harknett and Hartnett (2011) and Swartz (2009). On women's ratings of job characteristics changing nearly as much as men's: see the discussion earlier in this chapter. On women attending religious services more than men, see Wilcox et al. (2012).

CHAPTER 7: WHAT IS TO BE DONE?

1. On the view that the problem is a lack of necessary character, see Schulz (2013). James Q. Wilson's book on marriage: *The Marriage Problem: How Our Culture Has Weakened Families* (2002). Charles Murray's explanation can be found in a *Wall Street Journal* article, "Why Economics Can't Explain Our Cultural Divide" (March 16, 2012), which was written shortly after his book, *Coming Apart: The State of White America* (2012) was published. He defended his decision to ignore the role of the labor market in his book, writing that "the purported causes don't explain the effects." He added, "If changes in the labor market don't explain the development of the new lower class, what does? My own explanation is no secret. In my 1984 book 'Losing Ground,' I put the blame on our growing welfare state and the perverse incentives that it created. I also have argued that the increasing economic independence of women, who flooded into the labor market in the 1970s and 1980s, played an important role."

2. In 1996, Congress passed the Personal Responsibility and Work Opportunity Act, which overhauled AFDC and renamed it Temporary Assistance for Needy Families (TANF); see Haskins (2006).

3. The "reform conservatism" movement, see YG Network (2014). Whener's essay is quoted from p. 12. See also Tanenhaus (2014).

4. In full disclosure, I wrote an article ("Should the Government Promote Marriage?") expressing skepticism about government programs to support marriage; see Cherlin (2003). But I believe that the random-assignment marriage support programs that I consider in this chapter were worth trying. My article discusses the liberal and conservative views on this issue. On the Building Strong Families randomized-controlled trial, see Wood et al. (2012).

5. Supporters of behavioral interventions noted that in Oklahoma City, one of the eight sites, couples in the treatment group were more likely to have lived with their children since birth. Even in Oklahoma City, however, the results

were weaker than the supporters had originally expected. Perhaps the Oklahoma model deserves further testing to see if it can be replicated. But overall, the results of the Building Strong Families program must be viewed as weak and disappointing, The program that Randles studied had the same funding source as Building Strong Families but was unaffiliated with it; see Randles (2014), 396.

6. Randles (2014), 399.

7. For an evaluation of the Supporting Healthy Marriage program, see Lundquist et al. (2014).

8. See Edin and Kefalas (2005), 30.

9. The adolescent birth rates fell to an all-time low, see Martin et al. (2012). On postponing pregnancies, see Haskins and Sawhill (2009). Haskins and Sawhill wish to urge young adults to wait until *marriage* to have a first pregnancy, but I think this is unrealistic, given the rise of cohabitation and the postponement of marriage. I would favor a message that urges young adults to wait until they are confident that they are in a committed, lasting relationship.

10. On the more or less equal contributions of reduced sexual activity and increased contraception to the decline in the adolescent birth rate, see Kearney and Levine (2012). On the increase in adolescent use of condoms at first sex, see U.S. National Center for Health Statistics (2011).

11. The economists Melissa Kearney and Phillip Levine (2014) have found that it is more common for a low-socioeconomic-status woman to have an early nonmarital birth if she lives in a state with a greater degree of income inequality—perhaps, they speculate, because she sees less chance of economic success.

12. Economic growth and absolute poverty, see Noell, Smith, and Webb (2013), 35. Glenn Hubbard's op-ed article, "Tax Reform is the Best Way to Tackle Income Inequality," *Washington Post*, January 10, 2014.

13. Goldin and Katz (2008), 2. On the recent rise in high school graduation rates, see U.S. National Center for Education Statistics (2013), table 124.

14. The gap in spending on children nearly tripled, see Duncan and Murnane (2014). On the widening class gap, see Reardon (2011).

15. Heckman's research, see Heckman (2008). On neuroscientific research on developmental plasticity, see Nelson and Sheridan (2011). Preschool enrollment of four-year-olds, see Barnett et al. (2012).

16. Reformers urge a mixture of factors, see Duncan and Murnane (2014). A long-term evaluation of career academies by MDRC showed positive effects: see Kemple (2008). On charter school effectiveness, see Betts and Tang (2011).

17. Growing cost of college tuition, see Goldin and Katz (2008), figure 7.10. The complex process of applying to college, see Lareau (2011).

18. For instance, Goldin and Katz (2008) reject the position that "we have reached some natural limit to educational attainment; see pp. 336–37.

19. Outsourcing accounting functions, see Nicholson et al. (2006). Outsourcing

radiology readings, see Andrew Pollack, "Who's Reading Your X-Ray?" *New York Times*, November 16, 2003.

20. Earnings of college graduates stagnant since 2000, see Autor (2014) and Mishel (2011). Mal-employment, see Fogg and Harrington (2011). Underemployment rose from 2001 to 2012, see Abel, Deitz, and Su (2014). The maturing of high-tech industry and the slowing of demand for cognitive skills: see Beaudry et al. (2013).

21. On apprenticeships and other types of career-focused training, see Lerman (2007).

22. On the importance of institutions and norms in shaping economic action, see Guillén et al. (2002), 19. On support for minimum wage increases, see Reich (2010).

23. The overlap between educationalists and institutionalists, see Goldin and Katz (2008): 351–52. See also Piketty (2014).

24. The cooperative agreements between management and labor constitute a style of corporate governance that Sanford Jacoby (2010) calls "producerism." The value of the minimum wage, see Economic Policy Institute (2012), table 4.39. Marginal tax rates, see Tax Foundation (2013). On Reagan's actions, see Levy and Temin (2010).

25. On the European model of economic growth, see Eichengreen (2007). On corporate profits, see Haskel et al. (2012).

26. On Piketty and Saez's work, see Piketty (2014) and Piketty and Saez (2003).

27. The precariat: see Standing (2011). The post-full-employment society, see Beck (2000). For a review of the work of Beck, Standing, and others along these lines, see Kalleberg (2013).

28. In an analysis of data from the National Longitudinal Survey of Youth, 1997 Cohort, which had followed a national sample of twelve- to sixteen-year-olds until they were ages twenty-six to thirty-one in 2011, 56 percent of births to women who had not obtained a bachelor's degree by 2011 had occurred outside of marriage. Although a greater percentage of this cohort's future births will have occurred within marriage, the non-college-educated group was approaching the end of its active years of childbearing by 2011. Therefore, at the end of their childbearing years, a majority of all births to the non-college-educated are likely to have occurred outside of marriage. See Cherlin et al. (2014).

References

Abel, Jaison R., Richard Deitz, and Yaqin Su. 2014. "Are Recent College Graduates Finding Good Jobs?" *Current Issues* (Federal Bank of New York) 20(1): 1–8.

Alwin, Duane F. 1988. "From Obedience to Autonomy: Changes in Traits Desired in Children, 1924–1978." *Public Opinion Quarterly* 52(1): 33–52.

———. 2001. "Parental Values, Beliefs, and Behavior: A Review and Promulga for Research into the New Century." *Advances in Life Course Research* 6: 97–139.

Amato, Paul R. 2009. "Institutional, Companionate, and Individualistic Marriage: A Social Psychological Perspective on Marital Change." In *Marriage and Family: Perspectives and Complexities*, ed. H. Elizabeth Peters and Claire M. Kamp Dush. New York: Columbia University Press.

Angell, Robert Cooley. 1936. *The Family Encounters the Depression.* New York: Charles Scribner's Sons.

Arnesen, Eric, ed. 2007. *Encyclopedia of U.S. Labor and Working-Class History.* Vol. 1. New York: Taylor and Francis.

Aughinbaugh, Alison, Omar Robles, and Hugette Sun. 2013. "Marriage and Divorce: Patterns by Gender, Race, and Educational Attainment." *Monthly Labor Review* (October): 1–18.

Auletta, Ken. 1982. *The Underclass.* New York: Random House.

Autor, David. 2010. "The Polarization of Job Opportunities in the U.S. Labor Market: Implications for Employment and Earnings." Washington, D.C.: Center for American Progress (April). Available at: http://www.brookings.edu/~/media /Files/rc/papers/2010/04_jobs_autor/04_jobs_autor.pdf (accessed May 23, 2014).

———. 2014. "Skills, Education, and the Rise of Earnings Inequality Among the 'Other 99 Percent.'" *Science* 344(6186): 843–51.

Autor, David H., Lawrence F. Katz, and Melissa Kearney. 2006. "The Polarization of the U.S. Labor Market." *American Economic Review* 96(2): 189–94.

Autor, David H., Frank Levy, and Richard J. Murnane. 2003. "The Skill Content of

Recent Technological Change: An Empirical Exploration." *Quarterly Journal of Economics* 118(4): 1279–1333.

Barnett, W. Steven, Megan E. Carolan, Jen Fitzgerald, and James H. Squires. 2012. *The State of Preschool, 2012.* Available at: http://nieer.org/publications/state -preschool-2012 (accessed August 27, 2014).

Beaudry, Paul, David A. Green, and Benjamin M. Sand. 2013. "The Great Reversal in the Demand for Skill and Cognitive Tasks." Working Paper 18901. Cambridge, Mass.: National Bureau of Economic Research.

Beck, Ulrich. 2000. *Brave New World of Work.* Cambridge: Polity Press.

Beck, Ulrich, Anthony Giddens, and Scott Lash. 1994. *Reflexive Modernization: Politics, Tradition, and Aesthetics in the Modern Social Order.* Cambridge: Polity Press.

Bellah, Robert, Richard Madsen, William M. Sullivan, Ann Swidler, and Steven M. Tipton. 1985. *Habits of the Heart: Individualism and Commitment in America.* Berkeley: University of California Press.

Bendheim-Thoman Center for Child Wellbeing. 2007. Fragile Families Research Brief. *Parents' Relationship Status Five Years After a Nonmarital Birth.* Available at: http://www.fragilefamilies.princeton.edu/briefs/ResearchBrief39.pdf (accessed July 30, 2014).

Bernard, Jessie. 1981. "The Good-Provider Role: Its Rise and Fall." *American Psychologist* 36(1): 1–12.

Betts, Julian R., and Y. Emily Tang. 2011. "The Effects of Charter Schools on Student Achievement: A Meta-Analysis of the Literature." Seattle: University of Washington Bothell, National Charter School Research Project (October). Available at: http://files.eric.ed.gov/fulltext/ED526353.pdf (accessed March 2, 2014).

Bigelow, John, ed. 1872. *The Autobiography of Benjamin Frankin.* Philadelphia: J. P. Lippincott.

Bledsoe, Caroline H. 1980. *Women and Marriage in Kpelle Society.* Palo Alto, Calif.: Stanford University Press.

Brinkley, Alan. 1995. "Last of His Kind." *New York Times Book Review,* December 17.

Brooks, Tim, and Earle Marsh. 2003. *The Complete Directory to Prime Time Network and Cable TV Shows, 1946–Present.* 8th ed. New York: Ballantine Books.

Buchmann, Marlis, and Manuel Eisner. 1997. "The Transition from the Utilitarian to the Expressive Self: 1900–1992." *Poetics* 25(2): 157–75.

Budig, Michelle, and Paula England. 2001. "The Wage Penalty for Motherhood." *American Sociological Review* 66(2): 204–25.

Budig, Michelle J., and Melissa J. Hodges. 2010. "Differences in Disadvantage: Variation in the Motherhood Penalty Across White Women's Earnings Distribution." *American Sociological Review* 75(5): 705–28.

Bumpass, Larry L., and Hsien-hen Lu. 2000. "Trends in Cohabitation and Implications for Children's Family Contexts in the United States." *Population Studies* 54(1): 19–41.

Bumpass, Larry L., James A. Sweet, and Andrew J. Cherlin. 1991. "The Role of Cohabitation in Declining Rates of Marriage." *Journal of Marriage and Family* 53(4): 338–55.

Burgess, Ernest W. 1925. "The Growth of the City: An Introduction to a Research Project." In *The City*, ed. Robert E. Park, Ernest W. Burgess, and Robert D. McKenzie. Chicago: University of Chicago Press.

Burgess, Ernest W., and Harvey J. Locke. 1945. *The Family: From Institution to Companionship*. New York: American Book Co.

Buss, David M., Todd K. Shackelford, Lee A. Kirkpatrick, and Randy J. Larsen. 2001. "A Half-Century of Mate Preferences: The Cultural Evolution of Values." *Journal of Marriage and Family* 63(2): 491–503.

Caldwell, John C. 1980. "Mass Education as Determinant of the Timing of Fertility Decline." *Population and Development Review* 6(2): 225–55.

———. 1982. *Theory of Fertility Decline*. New York: Academic Press.

Carbone, June, and Naomi Cahn. 2014. *Marriage Markets: How Inequality Is Remaking the American Family*. New York: Oxford University Press.

Carter, Susan B., Scott Sigmund Gartner, Michael R. Haines, Alan L. Olmstead, Richard Sutch, and Gavin Wright. 2006. *Historical Statistics of the United States: Millennial Edition Online*. Cambridge: Cambridge University Press. Available at: http://hsus.cambridge.org/.

Cavan, Ruth Shonle, and Katherine Howland Ranck. 1938. *The Family and the Depression: A Study of 100 Chicago Families*. Chicago: University of Chicago Press.

Cavanagh, Shannon E., and Aletha C. Huston. 2006. "Family Instability and Children's Early Problem Behavior." *Social Forces* 85(1): 551–81.

Cherlin, Andrew J. 1992. *Marriage, Divorce, Remarriage*. Revised and expanded edition. Cambridge, Mass.: Harvard University Press.

———. 2003. "Should the Government Promote Marriage?" *Contexts* 2(4): 22–29.

———. 2004. "The Deinstitutionalization of American Marriage." *Journal of Marriage and Family* 66(4): 848–61.

———. 2009. *The Marriage-Go-Round: The State of Marriage and the Family in America Today*. New York: Alfred A. Knopf.

Cherlin, Andrew J., Elizabeth Talbert, and Suzumi Yasutake. 2014. "Changing Fertility Regimes and Transitions to Adulthood: Evidence from a Recent Cohort." Paper presented to the annual meeting of the Population Association of America. Boston (May 3).

Chodorow, Nancy. 1978. *The Reproduction of Mothering: Psychoanalysis and the Sociology of Gender*. Berkeley: University of California Press.

Clement, Patricia Ferguson. 1997. *Growing Pains: Children in the Industrial Age, 1850–1890*. New York: Twayne.

Connell, R. W. 1995. *Masculinities*. Cambridge: Polity Press.

Coontz, Stephanie. 1992. *The Way We Never Were: American Families and the Nostalgia Trap*. New York: Basic Books.

Cooper, Carey E., Cynthia A. Osborne, Audrey N. Beck, and Sara S. McLanahan. 2011. "Partnership Instability, School Readiness, and Gender Disparities." *Sociology of Education* 84(3): 246–59.

Cott, Nancy F. 1977. *The Bonds of Womanhood: "Women's Sphere" in New England, 1780–1835.* New Haven, Conn.: Yale University Press.

Cowie, Jefferson. 2010. *Stayin' Alive: The 1970s and the Last Days of the Working Class.* New York: New Press.

Creighton, Colin. 1996. "The Rise of the Male Breadwinner Family: A Reappraisal." *Comparative Studies in Society and History* 38(2): 310–37.

———. 2012. "The Ten-Hour Movement and the Rights of Childhood." *International Journal of Children's Rights* 20(4): 457–85.

Cunningham, Hugh. 2000. "The Decline of Child Labour: Labour Markets and Family Economies in Europe and North America Since 1830." *Economic History Review* 53(3): 409–28.

Davies, Mark. 2011. "Google Books (American)—155 Billion Words (N-Grams)" [1810–2009]. Available at: http://googlebooks.byu.edu/ (accessed March 14, 2014).

Davis, Kingsley. 1972. "The American Family in Relation to Demographic Change." In *Demographic and Social Aspects of Population Growth,* ed. Charles F. Westoff and Robert Parke Jr. Washington: U.S. Government Printing Office.

Davis, Nancy J., and Robert V. Robinson. 1998. "Do Wives Matter? Class Identification of Wives and Husbands in the United States." *Social Forces* 76(3): 1063–86.

DeVault, Ileen A. 2013. "Family Wages: The Roles of Wives and Mothers in U.S. Working-Class Survival Strategies." *Labor History* 54(1): 1–20.

Dorius, Cassandra, and Karen Benjamin Guzzo. 2013. "The Long Arm of Maternal Multipartnered Fertility and Adolescent Well-being." Paper presented at the annual meeting of the American Sociological Association, New York, August 9.

Du Bois, W. E. B. 1935. *Black Reconstruction: An Essay Toward a History of the Part Which Black Folk Played in the Attempt to Reconstruct Democracy in America, 1860–1880.* New York: Harcourt, Brace and Co.

Duncan, Brian, V. Joseph Hotz, and Stephen J. Trejo. 2006. "Hispanics in the U.S. Labor Market." In *Hispanics and the Future of America,* ed. Marta Tienda and Faith Mitchell. Washington, D.C.: National Academy of Sciences Press.

Duncan, Greg J., and Richard J. Murnane. 2014. *Restoring Opportunity: The Crisis of Opportunity and the Challenge for American Education.* Cambridge, Mass., and New York: Harvard University Press and Russell Sage Foundation.

Durand, Jorge, Edward Telles, and Jennifer Flashman. 2006. "The Demographic Foundations of the Latino Population." In *Hispanics and the Future of America,* ed. Marta Tienda and Faith Mitchell. Washington, D.C.: National Academy of Sciences Press.

Easterlin, Richard A. 1980. *Birth and Fortune: The Impact of Numbers on Personal Welfare.* New York: Basic Books.

Economic Policy Institute. 2012. *The State of Working America*. 12th ed. Available at: http://www.stateofworkingamerica.org/ (accessed March 5, 2014).

Edgell, Penny. 2006. *Religion and Family in a Changing Society*. Princeton, N.J.: Princeton University Press.

Edin, Kathryn, and Maria J. Kefalas. 2005. *Promises I Can Keep: Why Poor Women Put Motherhood Before Marriage*. Berkeley: University of California Press.

Edin, Kathryn, and Timothy J. Nelson. 2013. *Doing the Best I Can: Fathering in the Inner City*. Berkeley: University of California Press.

Eichengreen, Barry. 2007. *The European Economy Since 1945: Coordinated Capitalism and Beyond*. Princeton, N.J.: Princeton University Press.

Eisenstadt, Peter R., and Laura-Eve Moss. 2005. *The Encyclopedia of New York State*. Syracuse, N.Y.: Syracuse University Press.

Eisenstein, Sarah. 2012. *Give Us Bread but Give Us Roses: Working Women's Consciousness in the United States, 1890 to the First World War*. Routledge Library Editions: Women's History, vol. 15. New York: Routledge.

Ekirch, A. Roger. 2005. *At Day's Close: Night in Times Past*. New York: W. W. Norton.

Elder, Glen H., Jr. 1974. *Children of the Great Depression: Social Change in Life Experience*. Chicago: University of Chicago Press.

Ellison, Christoper G., and Darren L. Sherkat. 1995. "The 'Semi-Involuntary Institution' Revisited: Regional Variations in Church Participation Among Black Americans." *Social Forces* 73(4): 1415–37.

Ellwood, David T., and Christopher Jencks. 2004. "The Uneven Spread of Single-Parent Families: What Do We Know? Where Do We Look for Answers?" In *Social Inequality*, ed. Kathryn M. Neckerman. New York: Russell Sage Foundation.

England, Paula, Emily Fitzgibbons Shafer, and Lawrence L. Wu. 2012. "Premarital Conceptions, Postconception ('Shotgun') Marriages, and Premarital First Births: Education Gradients in U.S. Cohorts of White and Black Women Born 1925–1959." *Demographic Research* 27(6): 153–66.

England, Paula, Lawrence L. Wu, and Emily Fitzgibbons Shafer. 2013. "Cohort Trends in Premarital First Births: What Role for the Retreat from Marriage?" *Demography* 50(6): 2075–2104.

Fearon, Henry Bradshaw. 1819. *Sketches of America: A Narrative of a Journey of Five Thousand Miles Through the Eastern and Western States of America*. 3rd ed. London: Strahan and Spottiswoode.

Felt, Jeremy P. 1970. "The Child Labor Provisions of the Fair Labor Standards Act." *Labor History* 11(4): 467–81.

Fischer, Claude S. 2010. *Made in America: A Social History of American Culture and Character*. Chicago: University of Chicago Press.

Fogg, Neeta P., and Paul E. Harrington. 2011. "Rising Mal-Employment and the Great Recession: The Growing Disconnection Between Recent College Graduates and the College Labor Market." *Continuing Higher Education Review* 75(Fall): 51–65.

Folbre, Nancy. 1991. "The Unproductive Housewife: Her Evolution in Nineteenth Century Economic Thought." *Signs* 16(3): 463–84.
———. 1993. "Women's Informal Market Work in Massachusetts, 1875–1920." *Social Science History* 17(1): 135–60.
———. 2009. *Greed, Lust, and Gender: A History of Economic Ideas.* New York: Oxford University Press.
Fomby, Paula, and Andrew J. Cherlin. 2007. "Family Instability and Child Well-being." *American Sociological Review* 72(2): 181–204.
French, Michael. 1997. *United States Economic History Since 1945.* Manchester: Manchester University Press.
Friedan, Betty. 1963. *The Feminine Mystique.* New York: W. W. Norton.
Furstenberg, Frank F. 2014. "Fifty Years of Family Change: From Consensus to Complexity." *Annals of the American Academy of Political and Social Science* 655(1): 12–30.
Gans, Herbert J. 1962. *The Urban Villagers: Group and Class in the Lives of Italian-Americans.* New York: Free Press.
———. 1967. *The Levittowners: Ways of Life and Politics in a New Suburban Community.* New York: Alfred A. Knopf.
General Federation of Women's Clubs, "Eighth Biennial Convention, Official Report" (1906).
Giddens, Anthony. 1991. *Modernity and Self-Identity.* Stanford, Calif.: Stanford University Press.
Gillis, John R. 1996. *A World of Their Own Making: Myth, Ritual, and the Quest for Family Values.* New York: Basic Books.
Gilmore, David D. 1990. *Manhood in the Making: Cultural Concepts of Masculinity.* New Haven, Conn.: Yale University Press.
Glendon, Mary Ann. 1987. *Abortion and Divorce in Western Law.* Cambridge, Mass.: Harvard University Press.
Goldin, Claudia. 1990. *Understanding the Gender Gap: An Economic History of American Women.* New York: Oxford University Press.
———. 2006. "Education." In *Historical Statistics of the United States: Millennial Edition Online,* ed. Susan B. Carter et al. Cambridge: Cambridge University Press.
Goldin, Claudia, and Lawrence F. Katz. 2008. *The Race Between Education and Technology.* Cambridge, Mass.: Harvard University Press.
Gómez-Quiñones, Juan. 1982. *Development of the Mexican Working Class North of the Rio Bravo: Work and Culture Among Laborers and Artisans, 1600–1900.* Los Angeles: University of California, Chicano Studies Research Center.
Guillén, Mauro F., Randall Collins, Paula England, and Marshall Meyer. 2002. *The Revival of Economic Sociology: Developments in an Emerging Field.* New York: Russell Sage Foundation.
Gruenberg, Sidonie M. 1955. "Why They Are Marrying Younger." *New York Times Magazine,* January 30.

Gutman, Herbert G. 1973. "Work, Culture, and Society in Industrializing America, 1815–1919." *American Historical Review* 78(3): 531–88.

Hall, G. Stanley. 1904. *Adolescence: Its Psychology and Its Relations to Anthropology, Sociology, Sex, Crime, Religion, and Education.* New York: Appleton.

Hannan, Michael T., Nancy Brandon Tuma, and Lyle P. Groeneveld. 1978. "Income and Independence Effects on Marital Dissolution: Results from the Seattle and Denver Income-Maintenance Experiments." *American Journal of Sociology* 84(3): 611–33.

Hareven, Tamara K. 1982. *Family Time and Industrial Time.* Cambridge: Cambridge University Press.

Hareven, Tamara K., and Randolph Langenbach. 1978. *Amoskeag: Life and Work in an American Factory-City.* Hanover, N.H.: University Press of New England.

Harknett, Kristen S., and Caroline Sten Hartnett. 2011. "Who Lacks Support and Why? An Examination of Mothers' Personal Safety Nets." *Journal of Marriage and Family* 73(4): 861–75.

Harris, Richard. 1994. "The Flexible House: The Housing Backlog and the Persistence of Lodging, 1891–1951." *Social Science History* 18(1): 31–53.

Hartmann, Heidi. 1979. "The Unhappy Marriage of Marxism and Feminism: Towards a More Progressive Union." *Capital and Class* 8(Summer): 1–32.

Hartog, Hendrik. 2000. *Man and Wife in America: A History.* Cambridge, Mass.: Harvard University Press.

Haskel, Jonathan, Robert Z. Lawrence, Edward E. Leamer, and Matthew J. Slaughter. 2012. "Globalization and U.S. Wages: Modifying Classic Theory to Explain Recent Effects." *Journal of Economic Perspectives* 26(2): 119–40.

Haskins, Ron. 2006. *Work over Welfare: The Inside Story of the 1996 Welfare Reform Law.* Washington, D.C.: Brookings Institution Press.

Haskins, Ron, and Isabel Sawhill. 2009. *Creating an Opportunity Society.* Washington, D.C.: Brookings Institution Press.

Heckman, James J. 2008. "The Case for Investing in Disadvantaged Young Children." In *Big Ideas: Investing in Our Nation's Future.* First Focus Campaign for Children. Available at: http://www.firstfocus.net/library/reports/big-ideas-investing-our-nations-future.

Hernandez, Donald J. 1993. *America's Children: Resources from Family, Government, and the Economy.* New York: Russell Sage Foundation.

Herskovits, Melville J. 1990. *The Myth of the Negro Past.* Reissued with an introduction by Sidney W. Mintz. Boston: Beacon Press.

Heuveline, Patrick, and Jeffrey M. Timberlake. 2004. "The Role of Cohabitation in Family Formation: The United States in Comparative Perspective." *Journal of Marriage and Family* 66(5): 1214–30.

Heuveline, Patrick, Jeffrey M. Timberlake, and Frank F. Furstenberg Jr. 2003. "Shifting Childrearing to Single Mothers: Results from 17 Western Countries." *Population and Development Review* 29(1): 47–71.

Hillmann, Henning. 2013. "Economic Institutions and the State: Insights from Economic History." *Annual Review of Sociology* 39: 251–73.

Hobsbawm, Eric. 1962. *The Age of Revolution: 1789–1848*. London: Weidenfeld and Nicolson.

———. 1994. *The Age of Extremes: A History of the World, 1914–1991*. New York: Vintage.

Holzer, Harry J. 2010. *Is the Middle of the U.S. Job Market Really Disappearing?* Washington, D.C.: Center for American Progress (May 13). Available at: http://www.americanprogress.org/issues/labor/report/2010/05/13/7843/is-the-middle-of-the-u-s-job-market-really-disappearing/.

Hopkins, Eric. 1994. *Childhood Transformed: Working-Class Children in Nineteenth-Century England*. Manchester, U.K.: Manchester University Press.

Hout, Michael. 2008. "How Class Works in Popular Conception: Most Americans Identify with the Class Their Income, Occupation, and Education Implies for Them." In *Social Class: How Does It Work?* ed. Annette Lareau and Dalton Conley. New York: Russell Sage Foundation.

Humphries, Jane. 1977. "The Working-Class Family, Women's Liberation, and Class Struggle: The Case of Nineteenth-Century British History." *Review of Radical Political Economics* 9(Fall): 25–42.

Ignatiev, Noel. 1995. *How the Irish Became White*. New York: Routledge.

Illick, Joseph E. 2002. *American Childhoods*. Philadelphia: University of Pennsylvania Press.

Illouz, Eva. 2008. *Saving the Modern Soul: Therapy, Emotions, and the Culture of Self-Help*. Berkeley: University of California Press.

Inglehart, Ronald. 1997. *Modernization and Postmodernization: Cultural, Economic, and Political Change in 43 Societies*. Princeton, N.J.: Princeton University Press.

Isen, Adam, and Betsey Stevenson. 2011. "Women's Education and Family Behavior: Trends in Marriage, Divorce, and Fertility." In *Demography and the Economy*, ed. John B. Shoven. Chicago: University of Chicago Press.

Jacobs, Jerry A., and Kathleen Gerson. 2004. *The Time Divide: Work, Family, and Social Policy in the 21st Century*. Cambridge, Mass.: Harvard University Press.

Jacoby, Sanford M. 2010. "Finance and Labor: Perspectives on Risk, Inequality, and Democracy." In *Labor in the Era of Globalization*, ed. Clair Brown, Barry Eichengreen, and Michael Reich. Cambridge: Cambridge University Press.

Janssens, Angélique. 1997. "The Rise and Decline of the Male Breadwinner Family? An Overview of the Debate." *International Review of Social History* 42(supplement): 1–23.

Jenkins, Richard. 2004. *Social Identity*. 2nd ed. London: Routledge.

Johnston, Lloyd D., Jerald G. Bachman, and Patrick M. O'Malley. 2013. *Monitoring the Future: Questionnaire Responses from the Nation's High School Seniors, 2011*. Ann Arbor: University of Michigan, Institute for Social Research, Survey Research Center. Available at: http://monitoringthefuture.org/datavolumes/2011/2011dv.pdf (accessed July 4, 2013).

Jones, Jacqueline. 1999. *A Social History of the Laboring Classes: From Colonial Times to the Present.* Malden, Mass.: Blackwell.

Kalleberg, Arne L. 2011. *Good Jobs, Bad Jobs: The Rise of Polarized and Precarious Employment Systems in the United States, 1970s to 2000s.* New York: Russell Sage Foundation.

———. 2013. "Globalization and Precarious Work." *Contemporary Sociology* 42(5): 700–706.

Kalmijn, Matthijs. 1991. "Shifting Boundaries: Trends in Religious and Educational Homogamy." *American Sociological Review* 56(6): 786–800.

Katz, Lawrence F., and Robert A. Margo. 2013. "Technical Change and the Relative Demand for Skilled Labor: The United States in Historical Perspective." Working Paper 18752. Cambridge, Mass.: National Bureau of Economic Research.

Katznelson, Ira. 2005. *When Affirmative Action Was White: An Untold History of Racial Inequality in Twentieth-Century America.* New York: W. W. Norton.

Kearney, Melissa Schettini, and Phillip B. Levine. 2012. "Explaining Recent Trends in the U.S. Teen Birth Rate." Working Paper 17964. Cambridge, Mass.: National Bureau of Economic Research.

———. 2014. "Income Inequality and Early Nonmarital Childbearing." *Journal of Human Resources* 49(1): 1–31.

Kemple, James J. 2008. "Career Academies: Long-Term Impacts on Labor Market Outcomes, Educational Attainment, and Transitions to Adulthood." MDRC (June). Available at: http://www.mdrc.org/sites/default/files/full_50.pdf (accessed March 2, 2014).

Kennedy, Sheela, and Larry Bumpass. 2008. "Cohabitation and Children's Living Arrangements: New Estimates from the United States." *Demographic Research* 19(47): 1663–92.

Kennedy, Susan Estabrook. 1979. *If All We Did Was to Weep at Home: A History of White Working-Class Women in America.* Bloomington: Indiana University Press.

Kerber, Linda K. 1988. "Separate Spheres, Female Worlds, Woman's Place: The Rhetoric of Women's History." *Journal of American History* 75(1): 9–39.

Kessler-Harris, Alice. 1982. *Out to Work: A History of Wage-Earning Women in the United States.* New York: Oxford University Press.

Kimmel, Michael. 2012. *Manhood in America: A Cultural History.* 3rd ed. New York: Oxford University Press.

———. 2013. *Angry White Men: American Masculinity at the End of an Era.* New York: Nation Books.

Kleinberg, S. J. 1989. *In the Shadow of the Mills: Working-Class Families in Pittsburgh, 1870–1907.* Pittsburgh: University of Pittsburgh Press.

Kohn, Melvin L. 1969. *Class and Conformity: A Study in Values.* Homewood, Ill.: Dorsey Press.

Komarovsky, Mirra. 1940. *The Unemployed Man and His Family.* New York: Octagon Books.

———. 1962. *Blue-Collar Marriage.* New York: Random House.

Kornrich, Sabino, and Frank Furstenberg. 2013. "Investing in Children: Changes in Parental Spending on Children, 1972–2007." *Demography* 50(1): 1–23.

Koslofsky, Craig. 2011. *Evening's Empire: A History of the Night in Early Modern Europe.* Cambridge: Cambridge University Press.

Lamont, Michèle. 2000. *The Dignity of Working Men: Morality and the Boundaries of Race, Class, and Immigration.* Cambridge, Mass.: Harvard University Press.

Landale, Nancy S., and Katherine Fennelly. 1992. "Informal Unions Among Mainland Puerto Ricans: Cohabitation or an Alternative to Legal Marriage?" *Journal of Marriage and Family* 54(2): 269–80.

Landale, Nancy S., R. Salvador Oropesa, and Cristina Bradatan. 2006. "Hispanic Families in the United States: Family Structure and Process in an Era of Family Change." In *Hispanics and the Future of America,* ed. Marta Tienda and Faith Mitchell. Washington, D.C.: National Academy of Sciences Press.

Lareau, Annette. 2011. *Unequal Childhoods: Class, Race, and Family Life.* 2nd ed. Berkeley: University of California Press.

Lassonde, Stephen. 2005. *Learning to Forget: Schooling and Family Life in New Haven's Working Class.* New Haven, Conn.: Yale University Press.

Lebergott, Stanley. 1960. "Wage Trends, 1800–1900." In *Trends in the American Economy in the Nineteenth Century,* ed. Conference on Research in Income and Wealth. Princeton, N.J.: Princeton University Press.

Leccardi, Carmen, and Marita Rampazi. 1993. "Past and Future in Young Women's Experience of Time." *Time and Society* 2(3): 353–79.

LeMasters, E. E. 1975. *Blue-Collar Aristocrats: Life-Styles at a Working-Class Tavern.* Madison: University of Wisconsin Press.

Lerman, Robert. 2007. "Career-Focused Education and Training for Youth." In *Reshaping the American Workforce in a Changing Economy,* ed. Harry J. Holzer and Demetra S. Nightingale. Washington, D.C.: Urban Institute Press.

Levy, Frank. 1998. *The New Dollars and Dreams: American Incomes and Economic Change.* New York: Russell Sage Foundation.

Levy, Frank, and Peter Temin. 2010. "Institutions and Wages in Post–World War II America." In *Labor in the Era of Globalization,* ed. Clair Brown, Barry J. Eichengreen and Michael Reich. Cambridge: Cambridge University Press.

Lincoln, C. Eric, and Lawrence H. Mamiya. 1990. *The Black Church in the African American Experience.* Durham, N.C.: Duke University Press.

Loizides, Georgios Paris. 2011. "Families and Gender Relations at Ford." *Michigan Sociological Review* 25(Fall): 19–32.

Lopoo, Leonard M., and Bruce Western. 2005. "Incarceration and the Formation and Stability of Marital Unions." *Journal of Marriage and Family* 67(3): 721–34.

Lukas, J. Anthony. 1985. *Common Ground: A Turbulent Decade in the Lives of Three American Families.* New York: Alfred A. Knopf.

Lundquist, Erika, JoAnn Hsueh, Amy E. Lowenstein, Kristen Faucetta, Daniel Gubits, Charles Michalopoulos, and Virginia Knox. 2014. "A Family-Strengthening Program for Low-Income Families: Final Impacts from the Supporting Healthy Marriage Evaluation." Report 2014-09A. Washington: U.S. Administration for Children and Families, Office of Planning, Research, and Evaluation.

Lynd, Robert S., and Helen Merrill Lynd. 1929. *Middletown: A Study in Modern American Culture.* New York: Harcourt, Brace, and World.

Manning, Wendy D. 2013. "Trends in Cohabitation: Over Twenty Years of Change, 1987–2010." Bowling Green, Ohio: Bowling Green State University, National Center for Family and Marriage Research. Available at: http://ncfmr.bgsu .edu/pdf/family_profiles/file130944.pdf (accessed August 14, 2013).

Manning, Wendy D., and Pamela J. Smock. 2005. "Measuring and Modeling Cohabitation: New Perspectives from Qualitative Data." *Journal of Marriage and Family* 67(4): 989–1002.

Martin, Joyce A., Brady E. Hamilton, Stephanie J. Ventura, Michelle J. K. Osterman, Elizabeth C. Wilson, and T. J. Mathews. 2012. "Births: Final Data for 2010." *National Vital Statistics Report* 61(1, August 28). Washington: U.S. National Center for Health Statistics. Available at: http://www.cdc.gov/nchs/data/nvsr /nvsr61/nvsr61_01.pdf (accessed September 1, 2014).

Martin, Steven P. 2004. "Women's Education and Family Timing: Outcomes and Trends Associated with Age at Marriage and First Birth." In *Social Inequality*, ed. Kathryn M. Neckerman. New York: Russell Sage Foundation.

Mason, Karen Oppenheim, and Larry L. Bumpass. 1975. "U.S. Women's Sex-Role Ideology, 1970." *American Journal of Sociology* 80(5): 1212–19.

Massey, Douglas S., and Deborah S. Hirst. 1998. "From Escalator to Hourglass: Changes in the U.S. Occupational Wage Structure 1949–1989." *Social Science Research* 27(1): 51–71.

Matthews, Glenna. 1989. *Just a Housewife: The Rise and Fall of Domesticity in America.* New York: Oxford University Press.

May, Elaine Tyler. 1988. *Homeward Bound: American Families in the Cold War Era.* New York: Basic Books.

May, Martha. 1982. "The Historical Problem of the Family Wage: The Ford Motor Company and the Five Dollar Day." *Feminist Studies* 8(2): 399–424.

———. 1984. "The 'Good Managers': Married Working Class Women and Family Budget Studies, 1895–1915." *Labor History* 25(3): 351–72.

———. 1985. "Bread Before Roses: American Workingmen, Labor Unions, and the Family Wage." In *Women, Work, and Protest: A Century of U.S. Women's Labor History*, ed. Ruth Milkman. New York: Routledge.

McDermott, Monica. 2006. *Working-Class White: The Making and Unmaking of Race Relations.* Berkeley: University of California Press.

McDermott, Monica, and Frank L. Samson. 2005. "White Racial and Ethnic Identity in the United States." *Annual Review of Sociology* 31: 245–61.

McWilliams, James E. 2006. "Marketing Middle-Class Morality." *Reviews in American History* 34(2): 162–68.

Mead, Lawrence M. 1986. *Beyond Entitlement: The Social Obligations of Citizenship.* New York: Free Press.

Merton, Robert K. 1938. "Social Structure and Anomie." *American Sociological Review* 3(5): 672–82.

Meyer, John W. 1994. "The Evolution of Modern Stratification Systems." In *Social Stratification: Class, Race, and Gender in Sociological Perspective,* ed. David B. Grusky. Boulder, Colo.: Westview Press.

Meyerowitz, Joanne. 1994. "Beyond the Feminine Mystique: A Reassessment of Postwar Mass Culture, 1946–1958." In *Not June Cleaver: Women and Gender in Postwar America, 1945–1960,* ed. Joanne Meyerowitz. Philadelphia: Temple University Press.

Michel, Jean-Baptiste, Yuan Kui Shen, Aviva Presser Aiden, Adrian Veres, Matthew K. Gray, Joseph P. Pickett, Dale Hoiberg, Dan Clancy, Peter Norvig, Jon Orwant, Steven Pinker, Martin Nowak, and Erez Lieberman Aiden. 2011. "Quantitative Analysis of Culture Using Millions of Digitized Books." *Science* 331(6014): 176–82.

Milkman, Ruth. 1997. *Farewell to the Factory: Auto Workers in the Late Twentieth Century.* Berkeley: University of California Press.

Mintz, Steven. 2004. *Huck's Raft: A History of American Childhood.* Cambridge, Mass.: Belknap Press of Harvard University Press.

Mishel, Lawrence. 2011. "Education Is Not the Cure for High Unemployment or for Income Inequality." Briefing Paper 286. Washington, D.C.: Economic Policy Institute.

Montgomery, David. 1976. "American Labor, 1865–1902: The Early Industrial Era." *Monthly Labor Review* 99(7): 10–17.

Morgan, S. Philip, Antonio McDaniel, Andrew T. Miller, and Samuel H. Preston. 1993. "Racial Differences in Household and Family Structure at the Turn of the Century." *American Journal of Sociology* 98(4): 799–828.

Murphy, John Joseph. 1966. "Entrepreneurship in the Establishment of the American Clock Industry." *Journal of Economic History* 26(2): 169–86.

Murray, Charles. 1984. *Losing Ground: American Social Policy, 1950–1980.* New York: Basic Books.

———. 2012. *Coming Apart: The State of White America, 1960–2010.* New York: Crown Forum.

Mutari, Ellen, Marilyn Power, and Deborah M. Figart. 2002. "Neither Mothers nor

Breadwinners: African-American Women's Exclusion from U.S. Minimum Wage Policies, 1912–1938." *Feminist Economics* 8(2): 37–61.

Nelson, Charles A., III, and Margaret A. Sheridan. 2011. "Lessons from Neuroscience Research for Understanding Causal Links Between Family and Neighborhood Conditions and Educational Outcomes." In *Whither Opportunity? Rising Inequality, Schools, and Children's Life Chances*, ed. Greg J. Duncan and Richard J. Murnane. New York: Russell Sage Foundation.

Nicholson, Brian, Julian Jones, and Susanne Espenlaub. 2006. "Transaction Costs and Control of Outsourced Accounting: Case Evidence from India." *Management Accounting Research* 17(3): 238–58.

Noell, Edd S., Stephen L. S. Smith, and Bruce G. Webb. 2013. *Economic Growth: Unleashing the Potential of Human Flourishing*. Washington, D.C.: AEI Press.

Olson, Karen. 2005. *Wives of Steel: Voices of Women from the Sparrows Point Steelmaking Communities*. University Park: Pennsylvania State University Press.

O'Malley, Michael. 1992. "Time, Work, and Task Orientation: A Critique of American Historiography." *Time and Society* 1(3): 341–58.

Oppenheimer, Valerie Kincade. 1997. "Women's Employment and the Gain to Marriage: The Specialization and Trading Model." *Annual Review of Sociology* 23: 431–53.

Oppenheimer, Valerie Kincade, Matthjis Kalmijn, and Nelson Lim. 1997. "Men's Career Development and Marriage Timing During a Period of Rising Inequality." *Demography* 34(3): 311–30.

Parsons, Talcott. 1942. "Age and Sex in the Social Structure of the United States." *American Sociological Review* 7(5): 604–16.

———. 1943. "The Kinship System of the Contemporary United States." *American Anthropologist* 45(1SW): 22–38.

Pettit, Becky. 2012. *Invisible Men: Mass Incarceration and the Myth of Black Progress*. New York: Russell Sage Foundation.

Pew Research Center. 2012. "'Nones' on the Rise: One-in-Five Adults Have No Religious Affiliation." Available at: http://www.pewforum.org/files/2012/10/NonesOnTheRise-full.pdf (accessed February 3, 2014).

Pidgeon, Mary Elizabeth. 1937. *Women in the Economy of the United States of America*. Washington: U.S. Government Printing Office.

Piketty, Thomas. 2014. *Capital in the Twenty-First Century*. Cambridge, Mass.: Belknap Press of Harvard University Press.

Piketty, Thomas, and Emmanuel Saez. 2003. "Income Inequality in the United States, 1913–1998." *Quarterly Journal of Economics* 118(1): 1–41.

Pleck, Elizabeth. 1987. *Domestic Tyranny: The Making of American Social Policy Against Family Violence from Colonial Times to the Present*. New York: Oxford University Press.

Portes, Alejandro, and Leif Jensen. 1989. "The Enclave and the Entrants: Patterns of Ethnic Enterprise in Miami Before and After Mariel." *American Sociological Review* 54(6): 929–49.

Putnam, Robert D., ed. 2002. *Democracies in Flux: The Evolution of Social Capital in Contemporary Society*. Oxford: Oxford University Press.

Rackin, Heather, and Christina M. Gibson-Davis. 2012. "The Role of Pre- and Post-conception Relationships for First-Time Parents." *Journal of Marriage and Family* 74(3): 526–39.

Randles, Jennifer M. 2014. "Partnering and Parenting in Poverty: A Qualitative Analysis of a Relationship Skills Program for Low-Income Unmarried Families." *Journal of Policy Analysis and Management* 33(2): 385–412.

Reardon, Sean F. 2011. "The Widening Academic Achievement Gap Between the Rich and the Poor: New Evidence and Possible Explanations." In *Whither Opportunity: Rising Inequality, Schools, and Children's Life Chances*, ed. Greg J. Duncan and Richard J. Murnane. New York: Russell Sage Foundation.

Reich, Michael. 2010. "Minimum Wages in the United States: Politics, Economics, and Econometrics." In *Labor in the Era of Globalization*, ed. Clair Brown, Barry Eichengreen, and Michael Reich. Cambridge: Cambridge University Press.

Riesman, David. 1953. *The Lonely Crowd: A Study of the Changing American Character*. New York: Doubleday.

Robb, Graham. 2003. *Strangers: Homosexual Love in the Nineteenth Century*. New York: W. W. Norton.

Roediger, David R. 1999. *The Wages of Whiteness: Race and the Making of the American Working Class*. Rev. ed. London: Verso.

Roof, Wade Clark. 1999. *Spiritual Marketplace: Baby Boomers and the Remaking of American Religion*. Princeton, N.J.: Princeton University Press.

Rose, Sonya O. 1992. *Limited Livelihoods: Gender and Class in Nineteenth-Century England*. Berkeley: University of California Press.

Rotundo, E. Anthony. 1993. *American Manhood: Transformations in Masculinity from the Revolution to the Modern Era*. New York: Basic Books.

Rubin, Lillian B. 1976. *Worlds of Pain: Life in the Working-Class Family*. New York: Basic Books.

Rudacille, Deborah. 2010. *Roots of Steel: Boom and Bust in an American Mill Town*. New York: Random House.

Ruggles, Steven, J. Trent Alexander, Katie Genadek, Ronald Goeken, Matthew B. Schroeder, and Matthew Sobek. 2010. *Integrated Public Use Microdata Series: Version 5.0* (machine-readable database). Minneapolis: University of Minnesota, Minnesota Population Center.

Rumbaut, Rubén G. 2006. "The Making of a People." In *Hispanics and the Future of America*, ed. Marta Tienda and Faith Mitchell. Washington, D.C.: National Academy of Sciences Press.

Ryan, Mary P. 1981. *Cradle of the Middle Class: The Family in Oneida County, New York, 1790–1865*. Cambridge: Cambridge University Press.

Ryder, Norman B. 1980. "Components of Temporal Variations in American Fertility." In *Demographic Patterns in Developed Societies*, ed. R. W. Hiorns. London: Taylor and Francis.

Sassen, Saskia. 2000. "The Demise of Pax Americana and the Emergence of Informalization as a Systemic Trend." In *Informalization: Process and Structure*, ed. Faruk Tabak and Michaeline A. Crichlow. Baltimore: Johns Hopkins University Press.

———. 2006. *Cities in a World Economy*. 3rd ed. Thousand Oaks, Calif.: Pine Forge Press.

Sassler, Sharon, and Amanda J. Miller. 2011. "Class Differences in Cohabitation Processes." *Family Relations* 60(2): 173–77.

Sassler, Sharon, Amanda Miller, and Sarah M. Favinger. 2009. "Planned Parenthood? Fertility Intentions and Experiences Among Cohabiting Couples." *Journal of Family Issues* 30(2): 206–32.

Saxton, Alexander. 1971. *The Indispensable Enemy: Labor and the Anti-Chinese Movement in California*. Berkeley: University of California Press.

Schulz, Nick. 2013. *Home Economics: The Consequences of Changing Family Structure*. Washington, D.C.: AEI Press.

Schwartz, Christine R., and Robert D. Mare. 2005. "Trends in Educational Assortative Marriage from 1940 to 2003." *Demography* 42(4): 621–46.

Seidman, Steven. 1991. *Romantic Longings: Love in America*. New York: Routledge.

Self, Robert O. 2012. *All in the Family: The Realignment of American Democracy Since the 1960s*. New York: Hill and Wang.

Seltzer, Judith A. 2004. "Cohabitation in the United States and Britain: Demography, Kinship, and the Future." *Journal of Marriage and Family* 66(4): 921–28.

Sennett, Richard, and Jonathan Cobb. 1972. *The Hidden Injuries of Class*. New York: Alfred A. Knopf.

Siegel, Reva B. 1996. "'The Rule of Love': Wife Beating as Prerogative and Privacy." *Yale Law Journal* 105(8): 2117–2207.

Silva, Jennifer M. 2013. *Coming Up Short: Working-Class Adulthood in an Age of Uncertainty*. Oxford Oxford University Press.

Skocpol, Theda. 1992. *Protecting Soldiers and Mothers: The Political Origins of Social Policy in the United States*. Cambridge, Mass.: Belknap Press of Harvard University Press.

Smith, Tom W., Michael Hout, and Peter V. Marsden. 2013. General Social Surveys, 1972–2012: Cumulative Codebook. Chicago: National Opinion Research Center, University of Chicago.

Smith, Tom W., Peter Marsden, Michael Hout, and Jibum Kim. 2013. *General Social Surveys, 1972-2012* (machine-readable database). Edited by National Opinion Research Center. Chicago: Roper Center for Public Opinion Research.

Smith-Rosenberg, Carroll. 1975. "The Female World of Love and Ritual: Relations Between Women in Nineteenth-Century America." *Signs* 1(1): 1–29.

Smock, Pamela J. 2000. "Cohabitation in the United States: An Appraisal of Research Themes, Findings, and Implications." *Annual Review of Sociology* 26: 1–20.

Smock, Pamela J., Wendy D. Manning, and Meredith Porter. 2005. "'Everything's There Except Money': How Money Shapes Decisions to Marry Among Cohabitors." *Journal of Marriage and Family* 67(3): 680–96.

Standing, Guy. 2011. *The Precariat: The New Dangerous Class.* London: Bloomsbury Academic.

Stern, Barbara B. 1992. "Historical and Personal Nostalgia in Advertising Text: The *Fin de Siècle* Effect." *Journal of Advertising* 21(4): 11–22.

Stevenson, Betsey, and Justin Wolfers. 2007. "Marriage and Divorce: Changes and Their Driving Forces." *Journal of Economic Perspectives* 21(2): 27–52.

Stykes, Bart, and Seth Williams. 2013. *Diverging Destinies: Children's Family Structure Variation by Maternal Education.* Available at: http://ncfmr.bgsu.edu/pdf/family_profiles/file134877.pdf (accessed July 30, 2014).

Swartz, Teresa Toguchi. 2009. "Intergenerational Family Relations in Adulthood: Patterns, Variations, and Implications in the Contemporary United States." *Annual Review of Sociology* 35: 191–212.

Sweeney, Megan M. 2002. "Two Decades of Family Change: The Shift in Economic Foundations of Marriage." *American Sociological Review* 67(1): 132–47.

Tanenhaus, Sam. 2014. "Can the G.O.P. Be a Party of Ideas?" *New York Times Magazine,* July 6.

Tax Foundation. 2013. "U.S. Federal Individual Income Tax Rates History, 1862–2013 (Nominal and Inflation-Adjusted Brackets)." October 17. Available at: http://taxfoundation.org/article/us-federal-individual-income-tax-rates-history-1913-2013-nominal-and-inflation-adjusted-brackets (accessed March 5, 2014).

Taylor, Frederick Winslow. 1914. *The Principles of Scientific Management.* New York: Harper and Brothers.

Thistle, Susan. 2006. *From Marriage to the Market: The Transformation of Women's Lives and Work.* Berkeley: University of California Press.

Thompson, E. P. 1967. "Time, Work-Discipline, and Industrial Capitalism." *Past and Present* 38(December): 56–97.

Thomson, Elizabeth, Trude Lappegård, Marcia Carlson, Ann Evans, and Edith Gray. 2014. "Childbearing Across Partnerships in Australia, the United States, Norway, and Sweden." *Demography* 51(2): 485–508.

Thornton, Arland. 1989. "Changing Attitudes Toward Family Issues in the United States." *Journal of Marriage and Family* 51(4): 873–93.

Thornton, Arland, and Linda Young-DeMarco. 2001. "Four Decades of Trends in Attitudes Toward Family Issues in the United States: The 1960s Through the 1990s." *Journal of Marriage and Family* 63(4): 1009–37.

Tiger, Lionel, and Robin Fox. 1971. *The Imperial Animal.* New York: Holt, Rinehart, and Winston.

Twain, Mark, and Charles Dudley Warner. 1873. *The Gilded Age: A Tale of To-day.* Hartford: American Publishing Co.

U.S. Department of Commerce. U.S. Bureau of the Census. 1970. *Statistical Abstract of the United States: 1970.* Washington: U.S. Government Printing Office.

———. 1996. "Table 1. Educational Attainment of Persons 15 Years Old and Over, by Age, Sex, Race, and Hispanic Origin: March 1995." Available at: http://www.census.gov/prod/2/pop/p20/p20489ta.pdf (accessed May 24, 2014).

———. 2012. "Table MS-2. Estimated Median Age at First Marriage, by Sex: 1890 to the Present." Available at: http://www.census.gov/hhes/families/files/ms2.xls (accessed February 26, 2013).

———. 2013a. "Educational Attainment in the United States: 2013—Detailed Tables." Available at: http://www.census.gov/hhes/socdemo/education/data/cps/2013/tables.html (accessed May 31, 2014).

———. 2013b. "Table 1: Educational Attainment of the Population 18 Years and Over, by Age, Sex, Race, and Hispanic Origin: 2012." Available at: http://www.census.gov/hhes/socdemo/education/data/cps/2012/Table1-01.xls (accessed July 5, 2013).

———. 2013c. "Table F-7: Type of Family, All Races by Median and Mean Income: 1947 to 2012." Available at: http://www.census.gov/hhes/www/income/data/historical/families/2012/F07AR_2012.xls (accessed December 17, 2013).

———. 2014. "Table 1. Educational Attainment of the Population 18 Years and Over, by Age, Sex, Race, and Hispanic Origin: 2013." Available at: https://www.census.gov/hhes/socdemo/education/data/cps/2013/Table%201-01.xlsx (accessed May 24, 2014).

U.S. Department of Justice. Bureau of Justice Statistics. 2008. "Parents in Prison and Their Minor Children." Available at: http://www.bjs.gov/content/pub/pdf/pptmc.pdf (accessed February 7, 2014).

U.S. Department of Labor. 1946. "Women Workers in Ten War Production Areas and Their Postwar Employment Plans." *Bulletin of the Women's Bureau* 209. Washington: U.S. Government Printing Office.

U.S. Department of Labor. U.S. Bureau of Labor Statistics. 2013. "Labor Force Statistics from the Current Population Survey." Available at: http://data.bls.gov/timeseries/LNU04000000?years_option=all_years&periods_option=specific_periods&periods=Annual+Data (accessed October 6, 2013).

———. 2014. *Union Members 2013.* Available at: http://www.bls.gov/news/release/union2.nr0.htm (accessed August 28, 2014).

U.S. Library of Congress. 2010. "Rosie the Riveter: Real Women Workers in World War II." Journeys and Crossings (July 10). Available at: http://www.loc.gov/rr/program/journey/rosie-transcript.html (accessed October 21, 2013).

U.S. National Center for Education Statistics. 2013. *Digest of Educational Statistics: 2012.* Available at: http://nces.ed.gov/programs/digest/index.asp (accessed August 28, 2014).

U.S. National Center for Health Statistics. 2009. Changing Patterns of Nonmarital Childbearing in the United States. *Data Brief no. 18.* Available at: http://www.cdc.gov/nchs/data/databriefs/db18.pdf (accessed May 14, 2009).

———. 2011. *Teenagers in the United States: Sexual Activity, Contraceptive Use, and Childbearing, 2006–2010 National Survey of Family Growth.* Available at: http://www.cdc.gov/nchs/data/series/sr_23/sr23_031.pdf (accessed February 28, 2014).

———. 2012. "Births: Final Data for 2010." Available at: http://www.cdc.gov/nchs/data/nvsr/nvsr61/nvsr61_01.pdf (accessed September 1, 2014).

Vanek, Joann. 1974. "Time Spent in Housework." *Scientific American* 231(5): 116–20.

Ventura, Stephanie J., and Christine A. Bachrach. 2000. "Nonmarital Childbearing in the United States, 1940–1999." *National Vital Statistics Report* 48(16, October 18). Washington: U.S. National Center for Health Statistics. Available at: http://www.cdc.gov/nchs/data/nvsr/nvsr48/nvs48_16.pdf (accessed February 4, 2009).

Waldfogel, Jane. 1997. "The Effect of Children on Women's Wages." *American Sociological Review* 62(2): 209–17.

Weiss, Jessica. 2000. *To Have and to Hold: Marriage, the Baby Boom, and Social Change.* Chicago: University of Chicago Press.

White House. 2013. "Helping Middle-Class Families Pay for College." Available at: http://www.whitehouse.gov/economy/middle-class/helping-middle-class-families-pay-for-college (accessed January 2, 2014).

Whyte, William H., Jr. 1956. *The Organization Man.* New York: Simon & Schuster.

Wilcox, W. Bradford, Andrew J. Cherlin, Jeremy E. Uecker, and Matthew Messel. 2012. "No Money, No Honey, No Church: The Deinstitutionalization of Religious Life Among the White Working Class." *Research in the Sociology of Work* 23: 227–50.

Wilcox, W. Bradford, and Nicholas H. Wolfinger. 2008. "Living and Loving 'Decent': Religion and Relationship Quality Among Urban Parents." *Social Science Research* 37(3): 828–43.

Wilson, James Q. 2002. *The Marriage Problem: How Our Culture Has Weakened Families.* New York: HarperCollins.

Wilson, William Julius. 1987. *The Truly Disadvantaged: The Inner City, the Underclass, and Public Policy.* Chicago: University of Chicago Press.

Wingfield, Valerie. 2010. "Before the Big Mac: Horn & Hardart Automats." In *Food for Thought.* New York: New York Public Library.

Winkler, Anne E. 1998. "Earnings of Husbands and Wives in Dual-Earner Families." *Monthly Labor Review* 42(April): 42–48.

Wood, Robert G., Quinn Moore, Andrew Clarkwest, Alexandra Killewald, and

Shannon Monahan. 2012. *The Long-Term Effects of Building Strong Families: A Relationship Skills Education Program for Unmarried Parents: Executive Summary.* Available at: http://www.acf.hhs.gov/sites/default/files/opre/bsf_36_mo _impact_exec_summ.pdf (accessed February 25, 2014).

Wright, James D., and Sonia R. Wright. 1976. "Social Class and Parental Values for Children: A Partial Replication and Extension of the Kohn Thesis." *American Sociological Review* 41(3): 527–37.

Wuthnow, Robert. 1998. *After Heaven: Spirituality in America Since the 1950s.* Berkeley: University of California Press.

Wyatt, Ian D., and Daniel E. Hecker. 2006. "Occupational Changes During the Twentieth Century." *Monthly Labor Review* (March): 35–57.

Yans-McLaughlin, Virginia. 1977. *Italian Immigrants in Buffalo, 1880–1930.* Ithaca, N.Y.: Cornell University Press.

YG Network. 2014. *Room to Grow: Conservative Reforms for a Limited Government and a Thriving Middle Class.* Available at: http://ygnetwork.org/roomtogrow/ (accessed August 28, 2014).

Zelizer, Viviana. 1985. *Pricing the Priceless Child: The Changing Social Value of Children.* New York: Basic Books.

Zieger, Robert H. 2007. *For Jobs and Freedom: Race and Labor in America Since 1865.* Lexington: University Press of Kentucky.

Zipp, John F., and Eric Plutzer. 2000. "From Housework to Paid Work: The Implications of Women's Labor Force Experiences on Class Identity." *Social Science Quarterly* 81(2): 538–54.

Index

245